Security Breaches and Threat Prevention in the Internet of Things

N. Jeyanthi
VIT University, India

R. Thandeeswaran
VIT University, India

A volume in the
Advances in Information
Security, Privacy, and
Ethics (AISPE) Book Series

www.igi-global.com

Published in the United States of America by
IGI Global
Information Science Reference (an imprint of IGI Global)
701 E. Chocolate Avenue
Hershey PA 17033
Tel: 717-533-8845
Fax: 717-533-8661
E-mail: cust@igi-global.com
Web site: http://www.igi-global.com

Library of Congress Cataloging-in-Publication Data

Names: Jeyanthi, N., 1977- editor. | Thandeeswaran, R., 1971- editor.
Title: Security breaches and threat prevention in the internet of things / N.
  Jeyanthi and R. Thandeeswaran, editors.
Description: Hershey, PA : Information Science Reference, [2017] | Includes
  bibliographical references.
Identifiers: LCCN 2016058435| ISBN 9781522522966 (hardcover) | ISBN
  9781522522973 (ebook)
Subjects: LCSH: Internet of things--Security measures.
Classification: LCC TK5105.8857 .S43 2017 | DDC 005.8--dc23 LC record available at https://
lccn.loc.gov/2016058435

This book is published in the IGI Global book series Advances in Information Security, Privacy,
and Ethics (AISPE) (ISSN: 1948-9730; eISSN: 1948-9749)

British Cataloguing in Publication Data
A Cataloguing in Publication record for this book is available from the British Library.

Advances in Information Security, Privacy, and Ethics (AISPE) Book Series

ISSN:1948-9730
EISSN:1948-9749

MISSION

As digital technologies become more pervasive in everyday life and the Internet is utilized in ever increasing ways by both private and public entities, concern over digital threats becomes more prevalent.

The **Advances in Information Security, Privacy, & Ethics (AISPE) Book Series** provides cutting-edge research on the protection and misuse of information and technology across various industries and settings. Comprised of scholarly research on topics such as identity management, cryptography, system security, authentication, and data protection, this book series is ideal for reference by IT professionals, academicians, and upper-level students.

COVERAGE

- Privacy Issues of Social Networking
- Telecommunications Regulations
- Electronic Mail Security
- Security Classifications
- CIA Triad of Information Security
- Cyberethics
- Information Security Standards
- Data Storage of Minors
- Device Fingerprinting
- Security Information Management

IGI Global is currently accepting manuscripts for publication within this series. To submit a proposal for a volume in this series, please contact our Acquisition Editors at Acquisitions@igi-global.com or visit: http://www.igi-global.com/publish/.

The Advances in Information Security, Privacy, and Ethics (AISPE) Book Series (ISSN 1948-9730) is published by IGI Global, 701 E. Chocolate Avenue, Hershey, PA 17033-1240, USA, www.igi-global.com. This series is composed of titles available for purchase individually; each title is edited to be contextually exclusive from any other title within the series. For pricing and ordering information please visit http://www.igi-global.com/book-series/advances-information-security-privacy-ethics/37157. Postmaster: Send all address changes to above address. Copyright © 2017 IGI Global. All rights, including translation in other languages reserved by the publisher. No part of this series may be reproduced or used in any form or by any means – graphics, electronic, or mechanical, including photocopying, recording, taping, or information and retrieval systems – without written permission from the publisher, except for non commercial, educational use, including classroom teaching purposes. The views expressed in this series are those of the authors, but not necessarily of IGI Global.

Titles in this Series

For a list of additional titles in this series, please visit: www.igi-global.com

IGI GLOBAL
DISSEMINATOR of KNOWLEDGE

www.igi-global.com

701 East Chocolate Avenue, Hershey, PA 17033, USA
Tel: 717-533-8845 x100 • Fax: 717-533-8661
E-Mail: cust@igi-global.com • www.igi-global.com

Table of Contents

Detailed Table of Contents

Chapter 1

H. Parveen Sultana, VIT University, India

Internet of Things (IoT) is an emerging area for the researchers. IoT with the combination of thing, gateway, and Internet perform any operation in a smart way. This chapter discusses the importance of Internet of Things in various application areas. It has been elucidated that how IoT can be used effectively in the smart wireless networks. Most of the devices used in the IoT system are of sensor and actuator devices. The architectural model and communication layout of IoT is explicated through appropriate diagrams. A 16 bit and 32 bit microcontroller based processors are used in the IoT devices to send and receive instructions from the machine to machine, people to people and people to machine. As and when changes or any variations occur in the smart environment suitable instructions are forwarded through gateway to execute corrective task.

Chapter 2

Kijpokin Kasemsap, Suan Sunandha Rajabhat University, Thailand

This chapter reveals the overview of the Internet of Things (IoT); the IoT, Wireless Sensor Networks (WSNs), and Radio Frequency Identification (RFID); the technology of the IoT; the IoT and security concerns; the information security aspects of the IoT; the applications of the IoT in modern health care; and the implications of the IoT in the digital age. Organizations can utilize the IoT to gain the considerable cost savings by improving asset utilization, enhancing process efficiency, and increasing productivity in global operations. However, the IoT has its own challenges, such as the privacy of personal data, the lack of compatibility, and security breach. The chapter argues that utilizing the IoT and security techniques has the potential to enhance organizational performance and meet security requirements toward threat prevention in global operations.

Chapter 3

The internet of things (IoT) is an imminent model in the field of wireless telecommunications. It is also considered as a third wave of information technology after the Internet and mobile communication. Basically, IoT is a wireless interconnected network of variety of objects such as radio frequency identification (RFID) tags, sensors, actuators, mobile phones and other types of wireless devices. It has extensible application in the areas such as public security, infrastructure development, modern agriculture, environment protection, urban management, healthcare, enhanced learning, and business service, among others. IoT is a self-configuring wireless network of sensors where the primary goal of establishing connection is to offer interconnectivity of various objects. The concept of IoT was coined by the Auto-Id center of the Massachusetts Institute of Technology (MIT) in 1999

Chapter 4

IoT is an acronym for Internet of Things. It is the revolutionary area that transforms the digital world into a device world. IoT helps in not only fulfilling human requirements, but also they act as a communication medium between humans and electronic devices. The birth of IoT started in early 2000s, but since then, it is an amazing fact that now at least 65% of devices are connected with IoT technology with the term "smart" in their prefix and it would be up by 30% at the end of 2016. Since then, many security issues were raised, and have been risen all these years due to the flaws in that devices. This made attackers to take advantage over that devices and started controlling them. This chapter studies IoT application layer protocols, services offered and gives an idea of existing cyber attacks and threat. In addition, the authors give the possible attacks on the IoT devices, in particular at application layer, and give the necessary precautions to overcome the cyber attacks both for consumers and vendors.

Chapter 5

N. Jeyanthi, VIT University, India
Shreyansh Banthia, VIT University, India
Akhil Sharma, VIT University, India

An attempt to do a comparison between the various DDoS attack types that exist by analysing them in various categories that can be formed, to provide a more comprehensive view of the problem that DDoS poses to the internet infrastructure today. Then DDoS and its relevance with respect to IoT (Internet of Things) devices are analysed where attack types have been explained and possible solutions available are analysed. This chapter does not propose any new solutions to mitigating the effects of DDoS attacks but just provides a general survey of the prevailing attack types along with analysis of the underlying structures that make these attacks possible, which would help researchers in understanding the DDoS problem better.

Chapter 6

R. Thandeeswaran, VIT University, India
Rajat Pawar, VIT University, India
Mallika Rai, VIT University, India

The automotive industry has reached a stage categorisation of the degree of the automation has become crucial. According to the levels of automation defined by SAE, the automotive industry is already past the first four and development is now being heavily concentrated on level 5, that is, driving independent of human control. This obviously requires an array of sensors, microcontrollers and visual feedback systems like cameras, LiDAR (Light Detection and Ranging) to be present in the vehicle. With security concerns omnipresent among these devices, they are now ported to the realm of vehicles and must be tackled so that unsafe driving conditions are never experienced. In this paper, Section 3 elaborates upon the technologies that have shaped autonomous cars into the form known today and Section 4 explains the network architecture and network security amongst these cars. Section 5 describes the rippling effect of this evolution in the automotive industry on other supportive industries, Section 6 talks about the challenges posed to the development of AVs and finally, Section 7 discusses the future of autonomous vehicles in India.

Chapter 7

The maturity of the IoT depends on the security of communications and the protection of end-user's privacy. However, technological and material heterogeneities, and the asymmetric nature of communications between sensor nodes and ordinary Internet hosts, make the security in this case more problematic. Major problem facing the large deployment of IoT is the absence of a unified architecture and a lack of common agreement in defining protocols and standards for IoT parts. Many solutions have been proposed for the standardization of security concepts and protocols in IoT at different layers. Even though many advances and proposals were made for IoT adaptation as IPv6 for Low Power Wireless Personal Area Network (6LoWPAN), and at application layer with protocols such as XMPP, MQTT, CoAP, etc., security of the IoT remains a very challenging task and an open research topic. This chapter focuses on existing protocols and different proposed mechanisms in literature to secure communications in the IoT.

Chapter 8

The fields of computer science and electronics have merged to result into one of the most notable technological advances in the form of realization of the Internet of Things. The market for healthcare services has increased exponentially at the same time security flaws could pose serious threats to the health and safety of patients using wearable technologies and RFID. The volume and sensitivity of data traversing the IoT environment makes dangerous to messages and data could be intercepted and manipulated while in transit. This scenario must absolutely respect the confidentiality and privacy of patient's medical information. Therefore, this chapter presents various security issues or vulnerabilities with respect to attacks and various situations how information will be attacked by the attacker in healthcare IoT. The working principle of healthcare IoT also discussed. The chapter concludes the performance of various attacks based on the past work. In the future this work can be extended to introduce a novel mechanism to resolve various security issues in healthcare IoT.

Chapter 9

Jayanta Mondal, KIIT University, India
Debabala Swain, KIIT University, India

Images unduly assist digital communication in this aeon of multimedia. During times a person transmits confidential images over a flabby communication network, sheer protection is an accost contention to preserve the privacy of images. Encryption is one of the practice to clutch the reticence of images. Image encryption contributes a preeminent bite to charter security for secure sight data communication over the internet. Our work illustrates a survey on image encryption in different domains providing concise exordium to cryptography, moreover, furnishing the review of sundry image encryption techniques.

Preface

Internet of Things (IoT) is the booming technology conquering the technologically compressed ball, the Globe. Changes are inevitable even to a common man in his daily activities and the technology is not exempted. Technology, exempted from vagaries will become extinct. Before Cloud computing conceals the globe, IoT swallowed the globe and cloud. IoT incorporates everything under the umbrella of Internet. 5G under study could provide the expected speed and along with IPv6 could enrich IoT to a better podium. At the same time IoT flags flap, intruders try to invade. Propaganda of IoT with its Quality of Service will also drive the researcher to focus on security breaches. IoT provides services to all the sectors including healthcare, vehicular network, industrial trades, Education, locating, tracking and monitoring household, smart cities etc. Exponential increase in the number of devices and the connectivity among them warns the IoT developers about the precautions to be measured on the data stored and retrieved.

Medical transcription in IoT can save the human life during emergencies. None will carry all the medical data always. In case of an accident, the stored data can be retrieved by the doctors and the current condition of the patient can be studied without undergoing multiple preliminary lab tests. At the same time, database should not be accessed by an ill-legitimate. Hence the intended or unintended security breach should be analyzed and an appropriate authentication and authorization mechanisms has to be deployed at the right ratio to protect the data. IoT in transportation is again a flair to track and monitor the smart vehicles. But if the speed of the vehicle is controlled and operated by an intruder, it would lead to malicious behavior.

IoT architecture has been proposed in multiple versions by different experts. IoT comprises many devices and layers. Each device has its own security concerns to be addressed and mitigated to avoid unsolicited activities.

Bursty growth, in Internet of Things (IoT) towards the peak, from the floor is owed by the ease of connectivity. Anything and everything can interconnect and communicate with each other in a smarter way. Devices became smarter, with embedded sensors make every device to talk and operate without human intervention. IoT can be deployed in all real time basic amenities, be it a child care, health care, appliances control, city surveillance or environmental change. IoT could make the human life simple and stress free but not threat free.

Fascinating features of IoT are devices can trigger a warning signal in an emergency situation, vehicles can be auto controlled, electrical appliances can be operated remotely and many more. Threat arises here, who is going to receive and respond to the emergent warning signal, the intended or the attacker. We are happy about automobile control with no think on what happens when the vehicle is controlled by an attacker.

Apart from invaders, illegal users, and misnomers IoT can also be faded away by the signals it receives from. IoT operations wholly depend on the signals received from sensors. Accuracy of sensor signal may be verified and confirmed with redundant sensors, leads to ambiguous values. Hence, IoT should focus on both precision, QoS and threats, Security.

We hope timely publication of this title could serve as an essential reference source, building on the available literature in the field of smart networks, IoT everywhere. It is trusted that this text will provide the resources necessary for students, academia, researchers and industrial experts those who always expect and experience technical challenges.

This book tries to analyze different IoT architecture versions and all possibilities of security breaches in detail. This book carries 10 chapters that address: (1) IoT Architecture; (2) Security Perspectives in IoT: Current Issues and Trends; (3) Security in Network Layer of IoT: Possible Measures to Preclude; (4) Security in Application Layer Protocols of IoT: Threats and Attacks; (5) Security in IoT Devices; (6) Security Threats in Autonomous Vehicles; (7) Intelligent Digital Forensics in the Era of IoT; (8) Mechanisms to Secure Communications in the IoT; (9) IoT in Healthcare: Breaching Security Issues; (10) A Contemplator on Topical Image Encryption Measures.

Chapter 1 discusses the importance of Internet of Things in various application areas. It has been elucidated that how IoT can be used effectively in the smart wireless networks. Most of the devices used in the IoT system are of sensor and actuator devices. The architectural model and communication layout of IoT is explicated through appropriate diagrams.

Chapter 2 focuses on the literature review through a thorough literature consolidation of the IoT and security perspectives. The extensive literature of the IoT and security perspectives provides a contribution to practitioners and researchers by revealing the issues and trends with the IoT and security perspectives in order to enhance organizational performance and reach strategic goals in global operations.

Chapter 3 lights upon the threats in the network layer of IoT, the new objects that enter the network are configured automatically. This characteristic makes IoT highly susceptible to security threats such as Disruption and Denial of Service (DoS), eavesdropping, problems in authentication and physical attacks on devices in different forms, are most common.

Chapter 4 uncovers the cyber-attacks, cyber threats at the application layer and provide the control mechanism or guidelines to combat cyber-attacks, especially in the application layer.

Chapter 5 provides a general survey of the prevailing attack types along with analysis of the underlying structures that make these attacks possible, which would help researchers in understanding the DDoS problem better.

Chapter 6 aims to examine the vulnerability of the systems present inside an autonomous vehicle, and propose solutions to the same. Currently, no official standards exist for the secure functioning of an autonomous vehicle, apart from the 'guidelines' released by the US DOT.

Chapter 7 introduces of internet of things (IoT) forensics, IoT application in forensics field. Art-of-states for IoT forensics are provided. The issues for IoT forensics are identified. Also, introduced the proposed data classification in IoT forensics protocol.

Chapter 8 focuses on existing protocols and different proposed mechanisms in literature to secure communications in the IoT.

Chapter 9 focuses on security by design: better collaboration among industry; manufacturers, regulators, and medical practitioners; a change in the regulatory approval paradigm, and encouraging feedback from patients and families who directly benefit from these devices.

Chapter 10 analyses the image encryption mechanisms which could help in healthcare record transmissions.

Hence, this book could attract academicians, researchers, advanced-level students, technology developers, and curriculum designers.

Chapter 1
IoT Architecture

H. Parveen Sultana
VIT University, India

ABSTRACT

Internet of Things (IoT) is an emerging area for the researchers. IoT with the combination of thing, gateway, and Internet perform any operation in a smart way. This chapter discusses the importance of Internet of Things in various application areas. It has been elucidated that how IoT can be used effectively in the smart wireless networks. Most of the devices used in the IoT system are of sensor and actuator devices. The architectural model and communication layout of IoT is explicated through appropriate diagrams. A 16 bit and 32 bit microcontroller based processors are used in the IoT devices to send and receive instructions from the machine to machine, people to people and people to machine. As and when changes or any variations occur in the smart environment suitable instructions are forwarded through gateway to execute corrective task.

DOI: 10.4018/978-1-5225-2296-6.ch001

INTRODUCTION

Internet of Thing (IoT) is a common term used to specify that how networked devices are helpful in communication. In most of the researches it has been shown that IoT has made the daily lives of human easier. The devices involved in the IoT structure are linked with the Internet to sense and generate data or information to interact with the whole world for disseminating it. On receipt of this information various actions are performed in different applications and tasks are executed effectively. Moreover IoT is not limited to any industrial application or any specific application area. In the recent tears it is noticed that IoT is a part of information security, transmission of data and an important communication channel in electronic devices. So IoT is a collection of smart objects as the price and size of electronic devices involved in it such as sensors and actuators are low and small. And also these devices consume less energy to perform any transmission as these devices are considered as smart devices.

These smart devices are capable to handle the situations or perform the actions with the help of interlinked functionalities which are already defined. These smart devices apply Internet services in a specified situation, so that human-machine interaction to be carried out in any digitized objects. This is a significant advantage for the smart devices of IoT to have enhanced interaction. IoT is more helpful in maintaining the tasks of smart devices in remote regions where human cannot intervene. This ensures that the real world situations can be perceived in unexpected levels by a manageable cost. Most of the critical scenarios or situations are handled automatically with the help of IoT to provide faster service and to improve the services of commercial applications. Actually in the year 1999, the caption "Internet of Things" became popular based on the work carried out in Auto-ID Centre at the Massachusetts Institute of Technology (MIT). This institute is famous for designing Radio Frequency IDentification (RFID) infrastructure. From the year 2005 it has been shown that how computers can operate from networked structure to network of interlinked smart objects. Most of the researchers proved that how real world had change the life style from RFID to IoTs in the conferences held in the year 2006 and 2007.

The question arises that in what way the IoT can be more useful to people. The following are the some of the technologies or equipments in which IoT can be applied.

- When IoT is linked with the wearable sensor devices, it sends cautionary messages on detection of critical situations.
- Helpful in parking vehicles with the sensors
- Assisting elderly people in home with sensor equipped devices

- Manage the home purchase orders
- Ensuing the daily activity schedules
- Providing safety mechanisms for the people who work in precarious environments
- Using intelligent mechanisms in the engines IoT saves fuel

All the devices such as motion sensors, lighting equipments and different kinds of home appliances connected with the Internet are customized to function in an IoT structure. In addition smart watches and smart glasses also a part of IoT networked system. All the above mentioned devices are operable with wireless standards such as Zigbee, WiFi and Bluetooth.

The Figure 1 shows how Internet of things is involved in various applications like biomedical applications, vehicular networking, healthcare systems and remotely operated systems in channel accessing.

BACKGROUND

IoT as Internet of Networks

IoT comprised of tiny, inexpensive networked devices that manage various applications which are added with security mechanisms. In IoT new objects are linked and

Figure 1. Layout of IoT communication

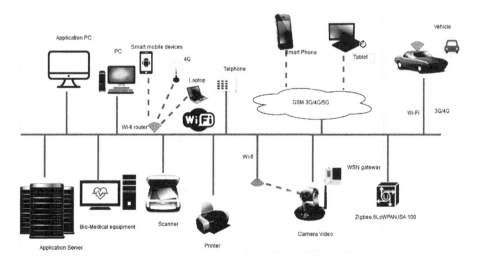

processed with the help of built-in sensors, through image recognition and enhanced communication. These improved functionalities provide additional opportunities for business applications to get more profit efficiently. This is possible only when IoT provides solutions using an integrated information and communications technology which includes electromechanical devices. The Figure 2 (Ovidiu & Peter, 2013) shows the convention of information and communications technology involved in IoT as Internet of networks.

IoT is not only an interconnection of networks but also a collection of interlinked smart devices of various sizes and types, home equipments, smart electronic devices, healthcare systems and industrial applications. Figure 2 depicts that all smart devices used in any application are interconnected to disseminate and transfer the information at any time through people to people communication, machine to machine communication and people to machine communication. IoT is a process of sensing, generating data, transferring data for further action and fetching responses from the tasks executed. From the year 2011, a huge revolution in the IoT technology had been noticed. As a future vision we can analyse that in year 2020 all tasks that are interlinked through Internet will be processed by a single application. As a result of this new technologies will be introduced for small or large scale industries to experience augmented services.

Figure 2. IoT as Internet of networks

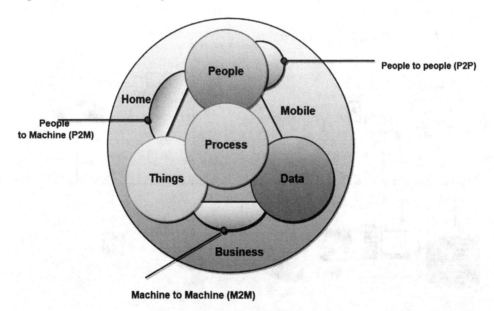

Components of IoT

From the last decade embedded systems take a lead in the design and development of Internet of things. To process innovative applications the devices with sensors and actuators which are interconnected with Internet are needed. These devices disseminate information among various platforms through integrated platform. To provide uninterrupted sensing, data collection and information sharing, IoT structure require four components such as:

- Sensor and actuator devices
- Wired or wireless network
- Internet
- Back-End services

The above Figure 3 (Micrium, 2014) depicts the components of IoT as embedded systems. In this structure the Sensor and actuator devices are considered as Things from IoTs, wired or wireless networks are local network such as Local Area Network (LAN), Personal Area Network (PAN) and Body Area Network (BAN). Local network has gateway which converts the communication protocol (proprietary) to Internet Protocol (IP) for seamless transmission of data. Bach-End services are provided on reception of instructions from the "Things". In response the remote server, portable computing devices (smart phones) or any business data systems perform actions or send suitable actuation commands to regulate the process in the specified networked system.

Figure 3. Components of IoT as embedded systems

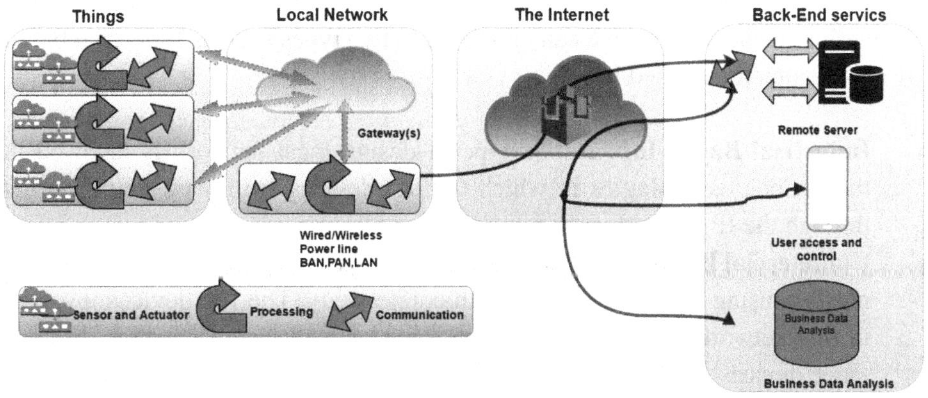

Figure 4. Architectural layout of IoT

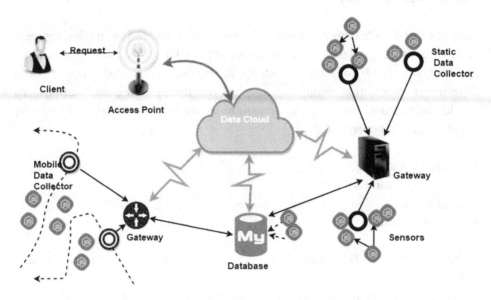

It has been noticed from the Figure 4 that data or instructions are generated or collected from the portable devices and sensors deployed in the structure. The forwarded data is either stored in a local database or maintained in the centralized database for future action. As soon as the servers have less network traffic, it will transmit the instruction or data to the client or to the static sensor cum actuator devices to perform actuation via the gateway. All the gateways perform the forwarding actions by linking with IP protocol.

Though the layout design of IoT looks so simple but it is not. IoT structure designing is a bit challenging task. Because the IoT architecture requires design components of type hardware and software as like in embedded systems. While considering the IoT design, we can classify into two types such as Industrial based IoT and Commercial based IoT.

- **Industrial Based IoT:** In this type of design local network is involved in the various technologies in which the IoT devices are linked with Internet through the IP network connection.
- **Commercial Based IoT:** This has wired or wireless connectivity for communication using Ethernet or Bluetooth connectivity. The IoT devices involved in this networking can communicate only with the local or short distance range devices.

The choice IoT devices for any communication technology decide how cost- effectively a system can be designed. In other words the design of any IoT structure is based on the costs and requirements of devices to be used. Let's take a design case of industry based IoT system say smart factory. This smart factory obviously requires sensor and actuator in more quantity which are deployed in several areas of factory region. Since it is a smart factory a wireless communication is suitable. The following Figure 5 (Micrium, 2014) shows how Wireless Sensor Network (WSN) is applied in the smart factory to connect with the Internet through any gateway used in it.

In the below diagram WSN as IoT is shown with the collection of WSN nodes which detect or monitor the environmental changes that occur in the smart factory such as change in the temperature, variation in sound level and dissimilarity in the pressure. Nowadays these WSN nodes comes with less cost and functions at low powered battery, it can be used more in number. As soon as WSN nodes detect these changes, it will generate data and transmit through various WSN nodes to the gateway for further action. WSN nodes are capable to retrieve and store energy from other sources like wind energy, solar system and thermal power.

The gateway is another type of WSN node called edge node which provides IP connectivity. This acts as a connector between the IP network and the WSN. This

Figure 5. WSN as IoT in smart network

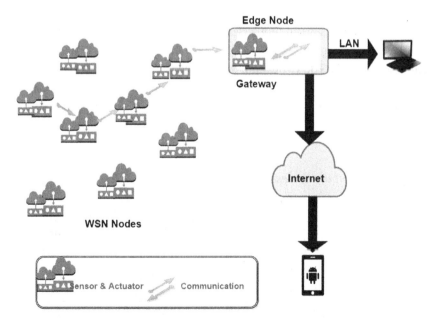

edge node forwards the generated data from the WSN nodes or stores the data in a local database for future action. To regulate the process of forwarding data for corrective action, IoT require WSN technologies like WiFi, IEEE 802.15.4, and 6LoW-PAN (Micrium, 2014). WiFi connection is common in every home or office that has Internet connectivity. WiFi connection can be availed at minimal power. Most of the smart systems uses IEEE 802.15.4 standard since it provides low power with short range connectivity.

The enhancement in IEEE 802.15.4 standard such as 802.15.4e and 802.15.4g used to improve the data transmission in smart applications. In embedded smart systems IPv6 over Low power Wireless Personal Area Network (6LoWPAN) (Micrium, 2014) configuration is used. Because in these systems the devices transmit information for a short period since it holds very small amount of data. 6LoWPAN performs the transmission effectively when the volume of data is small. The following Table 1 (Micrium, 2014) compares the wireless radio technologies in terms of frequency, range of data, transmission range, Battery life and power consumption used in IoT.

Advanced wireless technologies provide less power consumption solutions with the minimal cost for the technology enhancement. These technologies are helpful in designing intelligent devices for a new smart wireless structure. These smart devices have a long battery life attached with low-power radios. Through these solutions devices involved in the IoT structure retrieve energy via energy harvesting method. Design of new protocols allows for tasks to be performed automatically. The long pending operation where human cannot intervene is handled through mesh networking concept. This is possible only in machine to machine network communication. There are several industries that use low power wireless technologies such as 6LoWPAN, Zigbee IP, Wireless HART (Micrium, 2014), Wireless M-Bus (Micrium, 2014), ISA-100 (Micrium, 2014),etc. to execute automated operations. IoTs should be supported by Internet Protocol version 6(IPv6) to perform all the special and automated operations in IoT structure. IPv6 supports IoT devices for seamless communication locally and across the globe.

Table 1. Comparison of wireless radio technologies

Standard	Bluetooth	IEEE 802.15.4	WiFi
Frequency bandwidth	2.4 GHz	868/915 MHZ	2.4 GHZ to 5.8 GHZ
Data rate	723 Kbps	250 Kbps	11to 105 Mbps
Transmission Range	10 m	10 to 100 m	10 to 300 m
Battery Life	Rechargeable	Alkaline	Rechargeable
Power Consumption	Low	Very Low	High

Software Architecture of IoT

The term "Thing" in Internet of Thing is an embedded device that transmits the generated data and receives instructions as response to complete the task in any wireless network. The embedded devices might be electronic devices, health or fitness equipments, health monitoring devices and emergency response systems. As the things in IoTs are part of embedded system its functionality is based on software that uses small amount of memory and microcontrollers. Nowadays most of the embedded systems operate on android based systems which uses application processor for running any application dynamically. Micrium is a microcontroller based operating system which is often used in IoTs.

Since the prices of 32-bit microcontrollers have been slashed the Real-Time Operating System (RTOS) (Micrium, 2014) is a better choice for the development of IoT based applications. The RTOS adapt to compatible and extensible software that is run on IoT based systems. RTOS architecture has kernel, Graphical User Interface, File system, Universal Serial Bus stack and networking capability. RTOS with a 32-bit microcontroller has software architecture for IoT device as shown in the Figure 6 (Micrium, 2014).

The Intel and Advanced RISC Machine (ARM) (Micrium, 2014) architecture based processors are considered as best choices for development of IoT systems. Though these processers come with low cost in the market, but for all IoT devices this architecture is not sufficient. When network communication is across the globe, an effective and superior processing is required for designing IoT system. This is provided by ARM architecture based processors such as Cortex-M0 (Micrium, 2014) for IoT device design and ARM Cortex-M3/M4 (Micrium, 2014) or Cortex-A (Micrium, 2014) processors can be used for gateways involved in it. A better choice of processors for IoT system other than ARM processors are Renesas RL78 (Micrium, 2014) or RX100 (Micrium, 2014) for IoT device design and for gateway node design Renesas RX600 (Micrium, 2014) or RZ (Micrium, 2014) processors are more suitable.

All the above mentioned processors have extra flash memory and expandable RAM capacity at low cost. Nowadays there are several core architectures based processors that consume very less power compared to other processors available in the market. ARM is trying to design a near-threshold core architecture which consumes power nearer to the specified (threshold) voltage value. The embedded systems used for IoT applications run its software developed in C, C++ and Java. In advanced technologies JAVA developers had made a remarkable growth. So JAVA can be used as a programming language in the development of IoT device for any IoT application.

Figure 6. Software Architecture of IoT devices

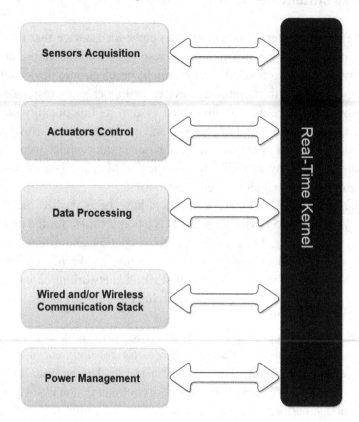

IoT Device and Gateway Design

The IoT device can run limited tasks with the help of single processor. To carry out several tasks at a time, a single processor cannot handle it. To do so two processors are required to initiate communication from any IoT device to the server in any wireless or wired network to perform any task or tasks. This is to ensure that transmission of data from IoT device through gateway to be executed successfully. An 8 or 16 bit processor is used in the design of IoT device to connect with the Internet (Gateway node) and a powerful 32-bit processor is used in wireless smart network for executing network interface. The following Figure 7 (Micrium, 2014) shows how IoT device is run with the 16-bit and 32-bit processors.

A gateway is an edge node that connects two different wireless (or wired) networks to transmit the information from one wireless system to another wireless (or wired) structure. Gateway is a bridge between the Internet and the smart wireless

IoT Architecture

Figure 7. IoT devices with two processors

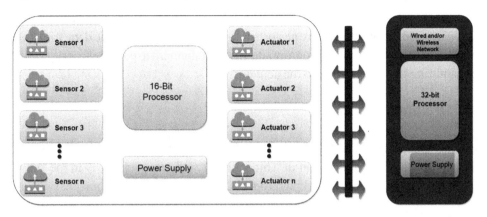

network which is called as proprietary network. For instance in smart home or smart office or smart hospital deployed with different IoT devices in different locations of its structure. All these IoT devices communicate with its own configured gateway for forwarding the information. According to network traffic in the system information is retained in the local database for future action. The following Figure 8 (Micrium, 2014) gives the overall design of gateway node.

Figure 8. Gateway nodes architecture

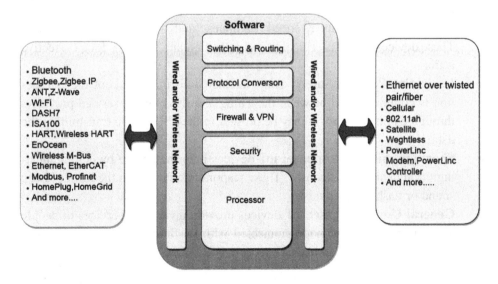

In the gateway node design there are several wireless technologies that connect with the other private wireless networks. This connectivity is to ensure that the software used in the architecture perform the operations of routing the data, forwarding instructions and applying appropriate protocol standard to provide security while transmitting the instructions to the actuators.

IoT Drivers

IoT has great impact on environment, society and commercial profit. This is due to the state, identity and region of Things in IoT. IoT involvement is in the fields of highway maintenance, Tracking products, smart office, smart home, harvesting (agriculture) and defence systems. All most in all fields of society IoT has created its effect extraordinarily. There are seven IoT value drivers recognized by (Fleisch, 2010) to show that IoT is most important in every stage of process or task to be executed in smart way. The following are the list of IoT drivers (Fleisch, 2010) which change the lives of people across the globe.

- **Simplified Instruction for Nearness Detection:** IoT devices transmit its identity while wandering in the sensing region of sensors. Once its identity is detected, an appropriate action is performed.
- **Instinctive Detection of Nearness:** When any two IoT devices fall below the level (threshold), the action is detected automatically. By knowing the type and location of IoT devices, it performs suitable action positively.
- **Sensor Detection Instinctively:** IoT devices receive generated data such as air pressure, temperature, speed, dampness and orientation from sensors. These devices sense its criticality and condition and forwards for a corrective action.
- **Instinctive Product Safety:** Authenticated Information about the transaction is communicated between the Thing and the Internet service providers through coding pattern. It may be present in the URL while transmitting the data.
- **Short and Simple Response:** IoT devices help the people by communicating through simple responses. These responses might be in the form of beep sound or flash light signals.
- **General User Response:** IoT devices provide invaluable services to people with the help of edge node connected with the Internet. In response users executes appropriate actions.

- **Mind Changing Responses:** With the combination of cyber and physical world, Things inform about the changes (like the car speed variants) occur in the environment or people.

The above mentioned seven IoT drivers are suitable for real-time IoT applications. Among these seven drivers first four IoT drivers are from machine-to-machine transmission and the rest three are from people-to-people communication.

Challenges Around IoT

Though IoT take a lead in the advancement of technologies, there are certain issues which prompts that whether the personal is data is secure or the health providers monitors the changes in the health related data or the battery of the devices need to be replaced. Though the portable devices connected with the Internet in a smarter way, there are certain technical challenges which say that there still more improvement required for the development of IoT system. People still need advancement in the IoT system which can rearrange and modify the wireless system according to the preferences and situations occur. The following are the some of the technological challenges (Mattern & Floerkemeier, 2010) that are to be discussed.

- **Scalability:** Though the devices (Things) operate in local structure but it also be extended to large-scale environments like oil or water plant industries.
- **Operate and Configure:** The smart devices programmed to change and rearrange the system in precarious situations. These changes should occur instinctively rather than periodically by the smart devices.
- **Interoperability:** The Things deployed in the IoT system hold different information according to its functionality. To transfer and communicate various types of information among the smart devices, a common standard or methodology to be implemented in the Internet Protocol standard of any Internet location.
- **Detection:** IoT is a collection of different smart devices, the actions to be taken by these devices have to identified and appropriate actuations to be carried out immediately. The status or functionalities of the Things can be obtained from the search engines which provide findings about the devices.
- **Sizes of Data:** Certain applications used in sensor networks have communication during irregular intervals. Whereas real-time applications used in industries store high voluminous data on centre servers which overload the Internet servers.

- **Data Elucidation:** The smart systems handled by the users are provided with some instructions to understand. The service providers interpret the raw data generated from the sensor node to convert into proper instructions to be performed in the application scenario.
- **Power Supply:** All portable devices cannot be connected with the power supply continuously. Since these devices have transmission range limited, often it require battery to be recharged. Sensor devices that consume less power (which is very minimal) are also need to be recharged at regular intervals by consuming energy from the surrounding environment. Though we have no battery equipped sensors, till date energy harvesting has not become famous method due to insufficient energy requirements that produce energy.
- **Secrecy and Security:** Internet provides so many security mechanisms while transmitting authenticated information. In spite of these mechanisms double level security check should be provided to access certain operations like corporate transactions which are handled by smart devices. Smart devices designed to get unaffected from snooping or hackers.
- **Error Handling:** Design of IoT system should be reliable and strong to handle and rectify any exceptions that occur. The IoT devices able to adapt to the variations occur during communication and transmit appropriate instructions.
- **Short-Range Transmission and Communication:** All IoT devices involved in the wireless network transmit or retrieve information from a short distance (even few centimetres). While performing transmission suitable Radio Frequency IDentification (RFID) devices or Near Field Communication (NFC) units to be used accordingly.
- **Wireless Standards:** Considering energy as an important factor in IoT, advanced narrow bandwidth standards of WPAN such as IEEE 802.15.4e and IEEE 802.15.4g, apart from existing less energy consuming wireless standards.

CONCLUSION

Internet of Things is an emerging area in which research potentials are more. IoT has changed the world's view from interconnection of computers to interconnection smart intelligent devices. IoT performs actions with the combination of sensors, actuators, gateway node and the Internet protocol. IoT is treated as embedded system since it uses powerful microcontroller based processors. These processors come low in cost and consume less energy. The architecture design of Thing in IoT and gateway node is explained. Also discussed how IoT drivers have changed the lifestyle of each individual connected with the smart wireless network. Though IoT has become popular in all fields like healthcare, agriculture harvesting, measuring variations in the vehicular networking, still faces certain challenges that need to be focused in future.

REFERENCES

Atzori, L., Iera, A., & Morabito, G. (2010). The internet of things: A survey. *Computer Networks*, *54*(15), 2787–2805. doi:10.1016/j.comnet.2010.05.010

Castellani, A., Bui, N., Casari, P., Rossi, M., Shelby, Z., & Zorzi, M. (2010, March). Architecture and protocols for the internet of things: A case study. In *Pervasive Computing and Communications Workshops (PERCOM Workshops), 2010 8th IEEE International Conference on* (pp. 678-683). IEEE. doi:10.1109/PERCOMW.2010.5470520

Coetzee, L., & Eksteen, J. (2011, May). The Internet of Things-promise for the future? An introduction. In *IST-Africa Conference Proceedings, 2011* (pp. 1-9). IEEE.

Fleisch, E. (2010). What is the internet of things? An economic perspective. Economics. *Management and Financial Markets*, *5*(2), 125.

Fleisch, E. (2010). *What is the Internet of things? An Economic Perspective*. Auto-ID Labs White Paper WP-BIZAPP-053. Retrieved from http://www. autoidlabs. org/uploads/media/AUTOIDLABS-WP-BIZAPP-53.pdf

Gubbi, J., Buyya, R., Marusic, S., & Palaniswami, M. (2013). Internet of Things (IoT): A vision, architectural elements, and future directions. *Future Generation Computer Systems*, *29*(7), 1645–1660. doi:10.1016/j.future.2013.01.010

Jain, D., Krishna, P. V., & Saritha, V. (2012). *A Study on Internet of Things based Applications*. arXiv preprint arXiv:1206.3891.

Mattern, F., & Floerkemeier, C. (2010). From the Internet of Computers to the Internet of Things. In *From active data management to event-based systems and more* (pp. 242–259). Springer Berlin Heidelberg. doi:10.1007/978-3-642-17226-7_15

Micrium. (2014). *IoT for Embedded Systems: The New Industrial Revolution*. Retrieved from https://www.micrium.com/iot/overview/

Ovidiu, V., & Peter, F. (2013). *Internet of Things: Converging Technologies for Smart Environments and Integrated Ecosystems*. Aalborg, Denmark: The River Publishers Series in Communications.

Sadeghi, A. R., Wachsmann, C., & Waidner, M. (2015, June). Security and privacy challenges in industrial internet of things. In *Proceedings of the 52nd Annual Design Automation Conference* (p. 54). ACM. doi:10.1145/2744769.2747942

Yogita, P., Nancy, S., & Yaduvi, S. (2016). Internet of Things (IoT): Challenges and Future Directions. *International Journal of Advanced Research in Computer and Communication Engineering.*, *5*(3), 960–964.

Zainab, H., Hesham, A., & Mahmoud, M. (2015). Internet of Things (IoT): Definitions, Challenges and Recent Research Directions. *International Journal of Computers and Applications*, *128*(1), 37–47. doi:10.5120/ijca2015906430

KEY TERMS AND DEFINITIONS

6LoWPAN: Low power Wireless Personal Area Network.
ARM: Advanced RISC Machine.
BAN: Body Area Network.
Gateway: It is an edge node that connects thing with the Internet.
IoT: Internet of Things.
IPv6: Internet Protocol version 6.
LAN: Local Area Network.
Local Network: Connecting PAN, BAN and LAN.
RFID: Radio Frequency Identification.
Thing: Portable sensor device which operate intelligently.
WSN: Wireless Sensor Network.

Chapter 2
Internet of Things and Security Perspectives:
Current Issues and Trends

Kijpokin Kasemsap
Suan Sunandha Rajabhat University, Thailand

ABSTRACT

This chapter reveals the overview of the Internet of Things (IoT); the IoT, Wireless Sensor Networks (WSNs), and Radio Frequency Identification (RFID); the technology of the IoT; the IoT and security concerns; the information security aspects of the IoT; the applications of the IoT in modern health care; and the implications of the IoT in the digital age. Organizations can utilize the IoT to gain the considerable cost savings by improving asset utilization, enhancing process efficiency, and increasing productivity in global operations. However, the IoT has its own challenges, such as the privacy of personal data, the lack of compatibility, and security breach. The chapter argues that utilizing the IoT and security techniques has the potential to enhance organizational performance and meet security requirements toward threat prevention in global operations.

DOI: 10.4018/978-1-5225-2296-6.ch002

INTRODUCTION

The Internet of Things (IoT) has been considered as one of the most promising paradigms that can allow people and objects to seamlessly interact (Zhao, Sun, & Jin, 2015). The significance of the IoT is made possible through enabling various technologies, such as wireless sensor networks (WSNs), mainly used for the sensing operations (Collotta & Pau, 2015). In the IoT, key nodes are represented by sensors, actuators, radio frequency identification (RFID) tags, smart objects, and servers connected to the Internet, which have the most diverse characteristics and capabilities (Atzori, Iera, & Morabito, 2010). A combination of Internet-connected devices, smart objects, sensors, and supplementary web-based services makes the IoT practically pervasive in various industries (Shelby & Bormann, 2011). IoT offers a potential to affect the economic activity across industries, influencing their strategic decisions, their investments, and their productivity (Borgia, 2014).

The rise of the IoT has important socio-technical implications for individuals, organizations, and society (Shin, 2014). With fast development and application, the IoT brings more opportunities to business (Rong, Hu, Lin, Shi, & Guo, 2015) and is characterized by heterogeneous technologies, which concur to the provisioning of innovative services in various application domains (Sicari, Rizzardi, Grieco, & Coen-Porisini, 2015). In this perspective, the satisfaction of security and privacy requirements plays an important role (Sicari et al., 2015). Security is crucial to the success of active networking especially when the current network is characterized by a dynamic nature and increasing distribution (Al-Saadoon, 2015). Together with the conventional security solutions, there is the need to provide the built-in security in the IoT devices themselves (i.e., embedded devices) in order to pursue dynamic prevention, detection, diagnosis, isolation, and countermeasures against successful breaches (Babar, Stango, Prasad, Sen, & Prasad, 2011).

This chapter focuses on the literature review through a thorough literature consolidation of the IoT and security perspectives. The extensive literature of the IoT and security perspectives provides a contribution to practitioners and researchers by revealing the issues and trends with the IoT and security perspectives in order to enhance organizational performance and reach strategic goals in global operations.

Background

With the rapid development of various communication technologies, more devices are able to access the Internet and to interact with it (Collotta & Pau, 2015). During the last three decades, tremendous work on the Internet has led to the growth of the IoT where intelligent interconnections are created among diverse objects for the globally integrated communication platform (Zheng, Simplot-Ryl, Bisdikian, &

Mouftah, 2011). The main vision of the IoT is that embedded devices, also known as smart objects, are becoming Internet Protocol (IP), which is enabled in an attempt to compute, organize, and communicate (Ashraf & Habaebi, 2015).

The IoT enables a full spectrum of machine-to-machine (M2M) communications, equipped with distributed data collection capabilities and connected through the cloud computing in order to facilitate centralized data analysis (Ponnusamy, Tay, Lee, Low, & Zhao, 2016). Cloud computing includes network access to storage, processing power, development platforms, and software (Kasemsap, 2015a). The advent of cloud computing services as well as their steady improvement in such areas as security and reliability make these solutions a logical choice for executives in the supply chain organizations who require the latest innovations, functionality, and efficiency as well as cost effectiveness (Kasemsap, 2015b).

It is important to validate the parties involved in M2M communication, while keeping the IoT constraints in mind (Ashraf & Habaebi, 2015). The recent advances in information technology (IT) enable the surrounding objects to use to exchange information using the IP (Manațe, Fortiş, & Moore, 2015). By putting intelligence into everyday objects, they are turned into smart objects able not only to collect information from the environment and control the physical world, but also to be interconnected, to each other, through the Internet to effectively exchange data and information (Borgia, 2014).

The requirement of virtual resource utilization and storage capacity necessitates making the IoT applications smarter (Alohali, 2016). The IoT describes a future computing scenario, where everyday physical objects will be connected to the Internet, and will be able to identify themselves to other devices (Chen, 2012). The IoT is a new communication paradigm in which the Internet is extended from the virtual world to interact with the objects of physical world (Souza & Amazonas, 2015) and affects the surrounding environment by acting as actuators (Miorandi, Sicari, Pellegrini, & Chlamtac, 2012). IoT technologies not only connect the specific industrial systems, but also stakeholders who connect with the IoT (Rong et al., 2015). The major challenge is to make these numerous objects seamlessly interact with each other (Efremov, Pilipenko, & Voskov, 2015).

FACETS OF THE INTERNET OF THINGS AND SECURITY PERSPECTIVES

This section provides the overview of the IoT; the IoT, WSNs, and RFID; the technology of the IoT; the IoT and security concerns; the information security aspects of the IoT; the applications of the IoT in modern health care; and the implications of the IoT in the digital age.

Overview of the Internet of Things

The Internet of Things (IoT) is a novel paradigm in the aspect of modern wireless telecommunication, which presents a wide variety of things, such as RFID tags, sensors, actuators, and cellular phones (Gubbi, Buyya, Marusic, & Palaniswami, 2013). The vision of the IoT enhances technology development by creating an interactive environment where smart objects are connected and can react to the environment (Luo et al., 2010). The IoT promises the new ways of interacting with physical objects, empowered by various kinds of digital extensions ranging from digital media linked with an object to sensors and actors attached to the object (Kröner, Haupert, & Barthel, 2015). The IoT provides a large amount of data, which can be shared or consumed by thousands of individuals and organizations around the world (Boubeta-Puig, Ortiz, & Medina-Bulo, 2014).

Within the IoT, objects autonomously operate to provide the specified services and accomplish the assigned tasks (Oriwoh & Williams, 2015). As the IoT services directly sense and control the physical world, it has the requirement of rapid response (Zhao et al., 2016). Being involved with a large number of devices, the IoT generates the massive data, which is real-time, dynamic, sparse, and highly heterogeneous (Zhao et al., 2015). The architecture of the IoT can be divided into three layers (i.e., perception layer, network layer, and application layer) (Zhao & Ge, 2013). The perception layer is responsible for object information, interfacing with the environment as well as the origin of sensor data. Network layer handles middleware implementations and communication from network to network.

Application layer in the IoT describes the schemes for reporting, big data, analytics, user interfacing, and data storage (Ashraf & Habaebi, 2015). Big data contains the very large sets of data that are produced by people using the Internet, and that can only be stored, understood, and utilized with the support of special tools and methods (Kasemsap, 2016a). When the adoption of big data is properly aligned to the business, existing governance structures can be easily adjusted to address security, assurance, and general approach to embracing new technologies (Kasemsap, 2017a).

Previous studies on the IoT focus on both technological aspects (Gubbi et al., 2013) and business applications, such as health care (Turcu & Turcu, 2013), surveillance (Miorandi et al., 2012), social networking (Atzori, Iera, Morabito, & Nitti, 2012), and logistic service (Karakostas, 2013). Others discussed the social aspects of the IoT technology, such as privacy (Roman, Zhou, & Lopez, 2013) and security (Alcaraz, Roman, Najera, & Lopez, 2013). The IoT brings tangible benefits to the environment, the society, individuals, and business with the creation of new intelligent applications, services, and products in various domains while ensuring the protection and privacy of information and content (Garcia-Morchon, Kuptsov, Gurtov, & Wehrle, 2013). The IoT-related multimedia and networking technologies permeate social relations, social institutions, industrial relations, and financial systems (Shaev, 2014).

The Internet of Things, Wireless Sensor Networks, and Radio Frequency Identification

The IoT refers to the expansion of the Internet technologies to include WSNs and smart objects by the extensive interfacing of distributed communication devices (Ashraf & Habaebi, 2015). In the last ten years, WSNs have triggered the intensive research activities which have produced a large body of literature, addressing legacy networking, such as routing protocol (Akkaya & Younis, 2005), transport protocols (Wang, Sohraby, Li, Daneshmand, & Hu, 2006), and topology control (Yu, Wang, Wang, & Yu, 2013). Numerous user authentication schemes have been proposed for the security of the WSNs (Turkanovic, Brumen, & Holbl, 2014). Concerning WSNs, most user authentication schemes concentrate on the establishment of a cryptographic key between the user and the base station or the gateway node. Asymmetric schemes represent the good foundations for the protected exchange of keys within a network, and require much more computational and communicational powers (Turkanovic et al., 2014).

With its capability to store and wirelessly communicate information as well as automatically identify and track objects in real time, RFID is considered as one of the enabling technologies of the IoT, and has to be equipped with a holistic security framework for a secure and scalable operation (Ray, Abawajy, & Chowdhury, 2014). RFID solutions can be utilized to reduce the operating costs through decreasing labor costs, enhancing automation, improving tracking and tracing, and preventing the loss of materials (Казстзар, 2017b). Although there are many security proto cols for RFID (Song & Mitchell, 2011), most of these protocols are vulnerable to various attacks and have serious shortcomings in scalability and customizability. The scalability and adaptability issues of the exiting security protocols are serious concerns for the wide adoption of RFID technology in many distributed applications (Trujillo-Rasua & Solanas, 2011).

Technology of the Internet of Things

The Bluetooth technology is used for sending data among devices located at a short distance (Borgia, 2014). Bluetooth utilizes 79 channels with a bandwidth of 1 MHz on the 2.4 GHz ISM band with a pseudo-random frequency hopping sequence (Collotta, Bello, & Mirabella, 2010). Bluetooth low energy (BLE), also known as Bluetooth 4.0, has a high potential in becoming an important technology for the IoT in terms of low power, low cost, and small devices (Collotta & Pau, 2015). BLE emerges due to the unsuitability of Wi-Fi, ZigBee, and other such technologies in order to provide networking with low power consumption, low cost, simplicity (Collotta, Messineo, Nicolosi, & Pau, 2014), and the ability to remain in a suspended state for the extended periods of time (Shrestha, Imtiaz, & Jasperneite, 2013).

Regarding the IoT technology, ZigBee, a pure wireless technology, is based upon the IEEE 802.15.4 standard for wireless personal area networks (WPANs). ZigBee is intended to be the low-cost and low-power wireless mesh network standard, allowing for the secure communication with a data rate of up to 250 kbps (Collotta & Pau, 2015). The near field communication (NFC) is a communication technology that enables devices to wirelessly share information by touching them together or bringing them into proximity (Borgia, 2014). NFC can be useful for sharing personal data (e.g., business cards, videos, and photos), making transactions, accessing information from smart posters, and providing credentials for the access control systems with a simple touch (Borgia, 2014).

The concept of mechatronics was introduced nearly 50 years ago in order to express and reflect the increasing utilization of computers for controlling mechanical processes and systems (Tomizuka, 2002). The recent development of the IoT is forcing mechatronics designers, practitioners, and educators to review the ways in which mechatronic systems and components are perceived, designed, and manufactured (Bradley et al., 2015). In particular, the role of mechatronic smart objects as part of the IoT-based system in which the structure is defined by context is resulting in an increasing emphasis on various issues, such as machine ethics, user interaction, and complexity.

The increasing number of connected devices which utilize the IoT technology and associated services is a real challenge to interoperability (Atanasov, Nikolov, Pencheva, Dimova, & Ivanov, 2015). Due to the large diversity of millions of devices, and the consequent distribution of their storage and data analysis resources in order to handle the problem of big data, the IoT requires interoperability at multiple levels (Kotis & Katasonov, 2013). The volume, velocity, and volatility of the IoT data impose the significant challenges to the existing information systems (Barnaghi, Wang, Henson, & Taylor, 2012). The realization of the IoT paradigm relies on the implementation of systems of intelligent objects with interoperability capabilities (Colistra, Pilloni, & Atzori, 2014).

One of the interoperability features concerns the cooperation among nodes toward a collaborative deployment of applications taking into account the available resources, such as electrical energy, memory, processing, and object capability to perform a given task, which are often limited (Colistra et al., 2014). The IoT has the limited resources in terms of processing capacity, memory, energy supply, and routing (Atzori et al., 2010). RPL is an Internet Protocol Version 6 (IPv6) distance vector routing protocol that operates on top of the IEEE 802.15.4 Physical and Data

Link Layers and is appropriate for low-power wireless networks with very limited energy and bandwidth resources (Fotouhi, Moreira, & Alves, 2015).

The Internet of Things and Security Concerns

It is required to secure the communication channels and to introduce the supporting security technologies in the IoT devices (O'Neill, 2014). Security represents a critical component for enabling the worldwide adoption of the IoT technologies and applications (Ashraf & Habaebi, 2015). Cryptography is the science of studying the information security (Alshaikhli & AlAhmad, 2015). Many IoT-related security researches have focused on network-based cryptographic mechanisms (Kothmayr, Schmitt, Hu, Brünig, & Carle, 2013), embedded security (Babar et al., 2011), distributed approaches for the IoT service provisioning (Roman et al., 2013), security solutions for applications (Chen et al., 2011) as well as system security frameworks (Pan, Paul, & Jain, 2011).

Ning et al. (2013) proposed the areas in cybersecurity and presented the security requirements to meet the IoT security-related requirements. However, the implementation of full IP security to protect mobile devices, the implementation of transport layer security (TLS), and the utilization of firewalls on each end device is rather restricted (Shelby & Bormann, 2011). The firewall is a network security system that monitors and controls the incoming and outgoing network traffic based on predetermined security rules (Boudriga, 2010). Furthermore, firewall implementation in the lower layers is inefficient as it can be directly overridden over the wireless channel (Ashraf & Habaebi, 2015).

Historically, IoT referred to RFID-based technologies where the security solutions have be managed in a vertically integrated ad hoc manner (Miorandi et al., 2012). The heterogeneity in technology required the specific security mechanisms to meet the security-related requirements. For the wide variety of the IoT devices today, there exists a huge tradeoff among performance, cost, and security which make security for the IoT a big challenge. IoT offers a wide range of areas where the security aspect is to be researched. Many components of IoT (e.g., the end devices) lack the high computing resources (Sehgal, Perelman, Kuryla, & Schonwalder, 2012). Mobahat (2010) indicated that the high computing resources have three major parts (i.e., information collection, transmission, and information processing) and are beneficial to the implementation of full IP security protocols.

There are many studies about the IoT-related security issues. Atzori et al. (2010) analyzed the IoT enabling technologies and existing middleware from an application point of view, and presented security and privacy regarding standardization activities. Weber (2010) explored the security and privacy challenges only under a legislative point of view, with particular attention to the European Commission directives. Miorandi et al. (2012) provided the main research contexts (e.g., impact areas, projects, and standardization activities) and challenges in the IoT, dealing with data confidentiality, privacy, and trust concerning security requirements.

Roman et al. (2013) investigated the advantages and disadvantages of centralized and distributed architectures in terms of security and privacy in the IoT with an analysis of the principal attack models and threats. Gubbi et al. (2013) provided an overview of various IoT aspects, such as the involved technologies, the applications, the cloud platforms, the architecture, the energy consumption issues, the quality of service, and data mining implications.

Information Security Aspects of the Internet of Things

Insider threat is one of the most complex problems in information security. Thus, it requires a sophisticated response to detect the subtle variations in the access patterns that separate the intentional misuse from the authorized utilization (Al-Khanjari & Nayyef, 2015). Ashraf and Habaebi (2015) indicated that the IoT-related information security perspectives include confidentiality, integrity, availability, privacy, and authenticity. Confidentiality guarantees that information is not revealed to unauthorized persons or processes during any communication transaction (Wrightson, 2012). Confidentiality is achieved by using the symmetric key cryptography where both sender node and receiver node significantly utilize a shared secret key, and the data is encrypted or decrypted using this shared secret key.

In current Internet, data owners can provide integrity and authentication when data is generated (Lee, Oh, & Jang, 2015). Integrity refers to the inability of modification of information by the unauthorized users (Wrightson, 2012). Data integrity solutions guarantee that an adversary cannot modify data in the transaction without the system detecting the change. The problem of data integrity can be solved by using symmetric cryptography, which helps to create signatures corresponding to the data under transmission. In IoT, asymmetric schemes are mostly employed for securing the initial process of symmetric key exchange and for enhancing data integrity. Availability ensures that the system's authorized users have the uninterrupted access to the information in the system (Wrightson, 2012). The whole systems along with all components should be functionally available, and capable to provide their services whenever required.

Privacy defines the rules under which data referring to individual users can be accessed. Yang and Fang (2011) indicated that the traditional privacy mechanisms are divided into two categories (i.e., discretionary access and limited access). Discretionary access addresses the minimum privacy risks, in order to prevent the disclosure or the cloning of sensitive data; whereas the limited access aims at limiting the security access to avoid the unauthorized attacks (Yang & Fang, 2011). Wei et al. (2014) implemented the privacy by batch verification, as well as prioritizing computation, auditing, and analysis. Regarding privacy requirement, both data protection and users personal information confidentiality have to be ensured, since devices may manage sensitive information (e.g., user habits). Privacy and security issues should be treated with a high degree of flexibility (Chaqfeh & Mohamed, 2012).

Evans and Eyers (2012) proposed the data tagging for managing privacy in the IoT. Using data tagging techniques taken from the information flow control, data representing network events can be tagged with several privacy properties; such tags allow the system to reason about the flows of data and preserve the privacy of individuals (Evans & Eyers, 2012). Focusing on the privacy protection in the IoT, Ukil et al. (2014) provided the privacy preserving data mining (PPDM) technique, minimizing the sensitive data disclosure probability and the sensitive content analysis. In PPDM technique, the user privacy awareness issue is highlighted, proposing a privacy management scheme which enables the user to estimate the risk of sharing sensitive data. PPDM technique aims at developing a robust sensitivity detection system, and is able to quantify the privacy content of the information (Ukil et al., 2014).

The goal of authenticity guarantees the legitimacy of the parties under consideration since it is necessary to ensure that communication data should derive from where it claims to derive from (Grover & Lim, 2015). With reference to security, data anonymity, confidentiality, and integrity need to be guaranteed, as well as authentication and authorization mechanisms in order to prevent the unauthorized users (e.g., humans and devices) to access the system (Sicari et al., 2015). Most IOT applications are based around the M2M communication with the user being a consumer of information or service rather than the initiator of operations (Hawrylak, Reed, Butler, & Hale, 2014). Petrov et al. (2014) proposed the NFC based authentication using an innovative way to tackle the problem of constrained resources in the IoT.

Zhao (2013) made use of a custom encapsulation mechanism (i.e., smart business security IoT application protocol), combining the cross-platform communications with encryption, signature, and authentication, in order to improve the IoT applications development capabilities by establishing a secure communication system among different things. Kothmayr et al. (2013) introduced the first fully implemented two-way authentication security scheme for IoT, based on the existing Internet standards, specifically the datagram transport layer security (DTLS) protocol, which is placed between transport and application layer. Palattella et al. (2013) indicated that this scheme is designed for IPv6 over Low power Wireless Personal Area Networks (6LoWPANs). The extensive evaluation, based on real IoT systems, shows that such the IoT architecture provides message integrity, confidentiality, and authenticity with enough affordable energy, end-to-end latency, and memory overhead (Sicari et al., 2015).

Roman et al. (2011) indicated that it is possible to classify the key management system (KMS) protocols in four major categories (i.e., key pool framework, mathematical framework, negotiation framework, and public key framework). Wu et al. (2011) proposed a transmission model with signature-encryption schemes, emphasizing the IoT security requirements (e.g., anonymity, trustworthy, and attack-resistance) by means of object naming service (ONS) queries. Root-ONS can authenticate the identities and platform creditability of local ONS servers (L-ONS) by a trusted authentication server (TAS), and the TAS gives a temporary certificate to validated L-ONS, which can apply for inquiry services many times with the certificate in the validated time (Sicari et al., 2015).

Applications of the Internet of Things in Modern Health Care

Rapid access to health care information through health IT can create the efficiencies in care by eliminating redundancies (Kasemsap, 2017c). The IoT enables the augmentation of objects, which provides a massive increase in information transfer, thus improving clinician perception (Michell, 2016). Combining RFID tag identification with structured and secure IoT solutions, individuals can establish the ubiquitous and quick access to any type of medical-related records, as long as they can secure all the Internet-mediated interactions (Laranjo, Macedo, & Santos, 2013).

The connected health vision is growing due to the availability of new technology enablers (e.g., low energy wireless standards and new sensor technologies) allowing for the development of connected personal health devices (Santos, Almeida, & Perkusich, 2015). Through the IoT, personal health devices can transmit data using the short-range wireless technologies, such as Bluetooth, NFC, and ZigBee, toward increasing the control of privacy and security issues in modern health care. Providing a continuous monitoring of the patients by using the IoT-related sensors can offer the early detection of risky situations for people suffering of cognitive and physical disabilities (Copie, Manațe, Munteanu, & Fortiș, 2015).

Through the IoT, patients can use the connected devices and services available on the Internet (Santos et al., 2015). The wide area network (WAN) interface utilizes the patient care device profiles, concerning privacy and security issues, to share the personal health data across different services. This interface definition is focused on data payload, message exchange, and security aspects of health information sharing across external networks, such as the Internet. In the IoT context, Bazzani et al. (2012) presented the IoT middleware with the practical case for health care.

Implications of the Internet of Things in the Digital Age

The IoT is considered as the developing tendency of network technology and refers to the networked interconnection of different kinds of objects (Shang, Zhang, & Chen, 2012). The adoption of the IoT has many potential benefits, including improvement in operational processes, value creation, cost reduction, and risk minimization based on transparency, traceability, adaptability, scalability, and flexibility (Chui, Löffler, & Roberts, 2010). Gubbi et al. (2013) indicated that businesses in the future will be influenced by the emerging IoT technologies and their applications can be summarized in four main areas (i.e., personal issue and home; enterprise; utilities; and mobile devices). There is a need for modern companies to think about how they can adopt the IoT to facilitate current businesses and market opportunities (Miorandi et al., 2012).

The IoT brings the smart supply chain to reality by employing RFID technologies, sensors, and data analytics to manage internal and external supply chain processes more intelligently (Lee, 2016). The advent of the IoT provides a new approach, enabling to collect, transfer, store, and share information on the logistics flow for better cooperation and interoperability among supply chain partners (Gnimpieba, Nait-Sidi-Moh, Durand, & Fortin, 2015). The industrial deployment of the IoT provides the development of an ideal platform for the decentralized management of warehouses (Reaidy, Gunasekaran, & Spalanzani, 2015).

Collaborative warehouse platforms are considered as the promising supply chain solutions in response to the volatile demand and the changing costs. There are many connections among partners, processes, products, and IT systems in the supply chain (Frohlich & Westbrook, 2001). These interconnections enable improved visibility, traceability, interoperability, and collaborative decision making among supply chain partners. This perspective implies utilizing the IOT infrastructure (Atzori et al., 2010) based on supply chain technologies, such as RFID technology, ambient intelligence, and real-time information (Reaidy et al., 2015).

In order to improve the processing efficiency and provide the most relevant information from the unprecedented amount of data according to user's query becomes a critical issue regarding privacy and security concerns (Zhao et al., 2015). Conventional searching technologies fall short of in the IoT, such as the architecture design of search engines, search locality, and scalability (Zhang, Yang, & Huang, 2011). The retrieval model for the application layer of the IoT (i.e., context-aware information retrieval) provides the suitable results for the user according to the user's physical state of the surrounding environment (Giannikos, Kokoli, Fotiou, Marias, & Polyzos, 2013).

Application development in the IoT is challenging because it involves dealing with a wide range of related issues, such as lack of separation of concerns, and lack of high-level of abstractions to address both the large scale and heterogeneity (Patel & Cassou, 2015). IoT applications execute on a network consisting of heterogeneous devices in terms of types (e.g., sensing, actuating, storage, and user interface devices), interaction modes, such as publish/subscribe (Eugster, Felber, Guerraoui, & Kermarrec, 2003), request/response (Berson, 1996), command (Andrews, 1991), and different platforms (e.g., Android and mobile operating system). Stakeholders have to address the issues that are attributed to different life cycles phases, including development, deployment, and maintenance (Bischoff & Kortuem, 2007).

FUTURE RESEARCH DIRECTIONS

The classification of the extensive literature in the domains of the IoT will provide the potential opportunities for future research. Digital libraries comprise digital collections, services, and infrastructure to educationally support the lifelong learning, research, and conservation of the recorded knowledge (Kasemsap, 2016b). Data mining plays a key role in organizing huge amount of data and condensing it into valuable information (Kasemsap, 2016c). Web mining techniques can be applied with the effective analysis of the clearly understood business needs and requirements (Kasemsap, 2017d). Business process modeling is the documentation of a business system using a combination of text and graphical notation (Kasemsap, 2016d). Business intelligence involves creating any type of data visualization that provides the insight into a business for the purpose of making a decision or taking an action (Kasemsap, 2016e). An examination of linkages among the IoT, digital libraries, data mining, web mining, business process modeling, and business intelligence in global operations would seem to be viable for future research efforts.

CONCLUSION

This chapter highlighted the overview of the IoT; the IoT, WSNs, and RFID; the technology of the IoT; the IoT and security concerns; the information security aspects of the IoT; the applications of the IoT in modern health care; and the implications of the IoT in the digital age. Regarding the IoT, the Internet connectivity and smart devices significantly present organizations with tremendous opportunity to create innovative products and services, reduce operational costs, and enhance additional revenue streams. The IoT is driven by a combination of forces, including the exponential growth of smart devices, the confluence of low-cost technologies (e.g., sensors, wireless networks, big data, and computing power), pervasive connectivity, and massive volumes of data.

Organizations can utilize the IoT to gain the considerable cost savings by improving asset utilization, enhancing process efficiency, and increasing productivity in global operations. The IoT encourages the communication between devices. Through the IoT, the physical devices are able to stay connected and the total transparency is available with greater quality. The unparalleled data generated by the IoT devices has the potential to create benefits for product manufacturers, supporting organizations and consumers. The IoT-driven innovations are expected to increase return on research and development (R&D) investments, reduce time to market, and enhance additional sources of revenue from new business models and opportunities.

Although the IoT offers the huge value potential, organizations must overcome the significant challenges, such as the lack of interoperable technologies and standards, data and information management issues, privacy and security concerns, and the skills to manage the growing complexity of the IoT. Before the potential of the IoT can be realized, organizations must deal with the shortcomings in IT standards, skill sets, and data management capabilities. Utilizing the IoT and security techniques has the potential to enhance organizational performance and meet security requirements toward threat prevention in global operations.

REFERENCES

Akkaya, K., & Younis, M. (2005). A survey on routing protocols for wireless sensor networks. *Ad Hoc Networks*, *3*(3), 325–349. doi:10.1016/j.adhoc.2003.09.010

Al-Khanjari, Z. A., & Nayyef, A. A. (2015). Real time internal intrusion detection: A case study of embedded sensors and detectors in e-government websites. In A. Al-Hamami & G. Waleed al-Saadoon (Eds.), *Handbook of research on threat detection and countermeasures in network security* (pp. 48–65). Hershey, PA: IGI Global. doi:10.4018/978-1-4666-6583-5.ch004

Al-Saadoon, G. M. (2015). Automatic intrusion detection and secret multi agent preservation using authentication measurement network threat. In A. Al-Hamami & G. Waleed al-Saadoon (Eds.), *Handbook of research on threat detection and countermeasures in network security* (pp. 33–47). Hershey, PA: IGI Global. doi:10.4018/978-1-4666-6583-5.ch003

Alcaraz, C., Roman, R., Najera, P., & Lopez, J. (2013). Security of industrial sensor network-based remote substations in the context of the Internet of Things. *Ad Hoc Networks*, *11*(3), 1091–1104. doi:10.1016/j.adhoc.2012.12.001

Alohali, B. (2016). Security in Cloud of Things (CoT). In Z. Ma (Ed.), *Managing big data in cloud computing environments* (pp. 46–70). Hershey, PA: IGI Global. doi:10.4018/978-1-4666-9834-5.ch003

Alshaikhli, I. F., & AlAhmad, M. A. (2015). Cryptographic hash function: A high level view. In A. Al-Hamami & G. Waleed al-Saadoon (Eds.), Handbook of research on threat detection and countermeasures in network security (pp. 80–94). Hershey, PA: IGI Global. doi:10.4018/978-1-4666-6583-5.ch006 doi:10.4018/978-1-4666-6583-5.ch006

Ashraf, Q. M., & Habaebi, M. H. (2015). Autonomic schemes for threat mitigation in Internet of Things. *Journal of Network and Computer Applications*, *49*, 112–127. doi:10.1016/j.jnca.2014.11.011

Atanasov, I., Nikolov, A., Pencheva, E., Dimova, R., & Ivanov, M. (2015). An approach to data annotation for Internet of Things. *International Journal of Information Technology and Web Engineering*, *10*(4), 1–19. doi:10.4018/IJITWE.2015100101

Atzori, L., Iera, A., & Morabito, G. (2010). The Internet of Things: A survey. *Computer Networks*, *54*(15), 2787–2805. doi:10.1016/j.comnet.2010.05.010

Atzori, L., Iera, A., Morabito, G., & Nitti, M. (2012). The Social Internet of Things (SIoT) – When social networks meet the Internet of Things: Concept, architecture and network characterization. *Computer Networks*, *56*(16), 3594–3608. doi:10.1016/j.comnet.2012.07.010

Babar, S., Stango, A., Prasad, N., Sen, J., & Prasad, R. (2011). *Proposed embedded security framework for Internet of Things (IoT)*. Paper presented at the 2nd International Conference on Wireless Communication, Vehicular Technology, Information Theory and Aerospace & Electronic Systems Technology (Wireless VITAE 2011), Chennai, India.

Barnaghi, P., Wang, W., Henson, C., & Taylor, K. (2012). Semantics for the Internet of Things: Early progress and back to the future. *International Journal on Semantic Web and Information Systems*, *8*(1), 1–21. doi:10.4018/jswis.2012010101

Bazzani, M., Conzon, D., Scalera, A., Spirito, M., & Trainito, C. (2012). *Enabling the IoT paradigm in e-health solutions through the VIRTUS middleware*. Paper presented at the 2012 11th IEEE International Conference on Trust, Security and Privacy in Computing and Communications (TrustCom 2012), Liverpool, United Kingdom. doi:10.1109/TrustCom.2012.144

Berson, A. (1996). *Client/Server architecture*. New York, NY: McGraw–Hill.

Bischoff, U., & Kortuem, G. (2007). *Life cycle support for sensor network applications*. Paper presented at the 2nd International Workshop on Middleware for Sensor Networks (MidSens 2007), Newport Beach, CA. doi:10.1145/1376860.1376861

Borgia, E. (2014). The Internet of Things vision: Key features, applications and open issues. *Computer Communications*, *54*, 1–31. doi:10.1016/j.comcom.2014.09.008

Boubeta-Puig, J., Ortiz, G., & Medina-Bulo, I. (2014). Approaching the Internet of Things through integrating SOA and complex event processing. In Z. Sun & J. Yearwood (Eds.), *Handbook of research on demand-driven web services: Theory, technologies, and applications* (pp. 304–323). Hershey, PA: IGI Global. doi:10.4018/978-1-4666-5884-4.ch014

Boudriga, N. (2010). *Security of mobile communications*. Boca Raton, FL: CRC Press.

Bradley, D., Russell, D., Ferguson, I., Isaacs, J., MacLeod, A., & White, R. (2015). The Internet of Things: The future or the end of mechatronics. *Mechatronics*, *27*, 57–74. doi:10.1016/j.mechatronics.2015.02.005

Chaqfeh, M. A., & Mohamed, N. (2012). *Challenges in middleware solutions for the Internet of Things*. Paper presented at the 2012 International Conference on Collaboration Technologies and Systems (CTS 2012), Denver, CO. doi:10.1109/CTS.2012.6261022

Chen, D., Chang, G., Jin, L., Ren, X., Li, J., & Li, F. (2011). *A novel secure architecture for the Internet of Things*. Paper presented at the 5th International Conference on Genetic and Evolutionary Computing (ICGEC 2011), Xiamen, China. doi:10.1109/ICGEC.2011.77

Chen, Y. (2012). *Challenges and opportunities of Internet of Things*. Paper presented at the 17th Asia and South Pacific Design Automation Conference (ASP-DAC 2012), Sydney, Australia. doi:10.1109/ASPDAC.2012.6164978

Colistra, G., Pilloni, V., & Atzori, L. (2014). The problem of task allocation in the Internet of Things and the consensus-based approach. *Computer Networks*, *73*, 98–111. doi:10.1016/j.comnet.2014.07.011

Collotta, M., Bello, L. L., & Mirabella, O. (2010). *An innovative frequency hopping management mechanism for Bluetooth-based industrial networks*. Paper presented at the 5th International Symposium on Industrial Embedded Systems (SIES 2010), Trento, Italy. doi:10.1109/SIES.2010.5551385

Collotta, M., Messineo, A., Nicolosi, G., & Pau, G. (2014). A self-powered Bluetooth network for intelligent traffic light junction management. *WSEAS Transactions on Information Science and Applications*, *11*, 12–23.

Collotta, M., & Pau, G. (2015). Bluetooth for Internet of Things: A fuzzy approach to improve power management in smart homes. *Computers & Electrical Engineering*, *44*, 137–152. doi:10.1016/j.compeleceng.2015.01.005

Copie, A. Manaţe, B., Munteanu, V. I., & Fortiş, T. (2015). An Internet of Things governance architecture with applications in healthcare. In F. Xhafa, P. Moore, & G. Tadros (Eds.), Advanced technological solutions for e-health and dementia patient monitoring (pp. 322–344). Hershey, PA: IGI Global. doi:10.4018/978-1-4666-7481-3.ch013

Efremov, S., Pilipenko, N., & Voskov, L. (2015). An integrated approach to common problems in the Internet of Things. *Procedia Engineering*, *100*, 1215–1223. doi:10.1016/j.proeng.2015.01.486

Eugster, P., Felber, P., Guerraoui, R., & Kermarrec, A. (2003). The many faces of publish/subscribe. *ACM Computing Surveys*, *35*(2), 114–131. doi:10.1145/857076.857078

Evans, D., & Eyers, D. (2012). *Efficient data tagging for managing privacy in the Internet of Things*. Paper presented at the 2012 IEEE International Conference on Green Computing and Communications (GreenCom 2012), Besançon, France. doi:10.1109/GreenCom.2012.45

Fotouhi, H., Moreira, D., & Alves, M. (2015). mRPL: Boosting mobility in the Internet of Things. *Ad Hoc Networks*, *26*, 17–35. doi:10.1016/j.adhoc.2014.10.009

Frohlich, M. T., & Westbrook, R. (2001). Arcs of integration: An international study of supply chain strategies. *Journal of Operations Management*, *19*(2), 185–200. doi:10.1016/S0272-6963(00)00055-3

Garcia-Morchon, O., Kuptsov, D., Gurtov, A., & Wehrle, K. (2013). Cooperative security in distributed networks. *Computer Communications*, *36*(12), 1284–1297. doi:10.1016/j.comcom.2013.04.007

Giannikos, M., Kokoli, K., Fotiou, N., Marias, G. F., & Polyzos, G. C. (2013). *Towards secure and context-aware information lookup for the Internet of Things*. Paper presented at the International Conference on Computing, Networking and Communications (ICNC 2013), San Diego, CA. doi:10.1109/ICCNC.2013.6504160

Gnimpieba, D. R., Nait-Sidi-Moh, A., Durand, D., & Fortin, J. (2015). Using Internet of Things technologies for a collaborative supply chain: Application to tracking of pallets and containers. *Procedia Computer Science*, *56*, 550–557. doi:10.1016/j.procs.2015.07.251

Grover, K., & Lim, A. (2015). A survey of broadcast authentication schemes for wireless sensor networks. *Ad Hoc Networks*, *24*, 288–316. doi:10.1016/j.adhoc.2014.06.008

Gubbi, J., Buyya, R., Marusic, S., & Palaniswami, M. (2013). Internet of Things (IoT): A vision, architectural elements, and future directions. *Future Generation Computer Systems*, *29*(7), 1645–1660. doi:10.1016/j.future.2013.01.010

Hawrylak, P. J., Reed, S., Butler, M., & Hale, J. (2014). The access of things: Spatial access control for the Internet of Things. In M. Matin (Ed.), *Handbook of research on progressive trends in wireless communications and networking* (pp. 189–207). Hershey, PA: IGI Global. doi:10.4018/978-1-4666-5170-8.ch007

Karakostas, B. (2013). A DNS architecture for the Internet of Things: A case study in transport logistics. *Procedia Computer Science*, *19*, 594–601. doi:10.1016/j.procs.2013.06.079

Kasemsap, K. (2015a). The role of cloud computing adoption in global business. In V. Chang, R. Walters, & G. Wills (Eds.), *Delivery and adoption of cloud computing services in contemporary organizations* (pp. 26–55). Hershey, PA: IGI Global. doi:10.4018/978-1-4666-8210-8.ch002

Kasemsap, K. (2015b). Adopting cloud computing in global supply chain: A literature review. *International Journal of Social and Organizational Dynamics in IT*, 4(2), 49–62. doi:10.4018/IJSODIT.2015070105

Kasemsap, K. (2016a). Mastering big data in the digital age. In M. Singh & D. G. (Eds.), *Effective big data management and opportunities for implementation* (pp. 104–129). Hershey, PA: IGI Global. doi:10.4018/978-1-5225-0182-4.ch008

Kasemsap, K. (2016b). Mastering digital libraries in the digital age. In E. de Smet & S. Dhamdhere (Eds.), *E-discovery tools and applications in modern libraries* (pp. 275–305). Hershey, PA: IGI Global. doi:10.4018/978-1-5225-0474-0.ch015

Kasemsap, K. (2016c). Multifaceted applications of data mining, business intelligence, and knowledge management. *International Journal of Social and Organizational Dynamics in IT*, 5(1), 57–69. doi:10.4018/IJSODIT.2016010104

Kasemsap, K. (2016d). The roles of business process modeling and business process reengineering in e-government. In J. Martins & A. Molnar (Eds.), *Handbook of research on innovations in information retrieval, analysis, and management* (pp. 401–430). Hershey, PA: IGI Global. doi:10.4018/978-1-4666-8833-9.ch015

Kasemsap, K. (2016e). The fundamentals of business intelligence. *International Journal of Organizational and Collective Intelligence*, 6(2), 12–25. doi:10.4018/IJOCI.2016040102

Kasemsap, K. (2017a). Software as a service, Semantic Web, and big data: Theories and applications. In A. Turuk, B. Sahoo, & S. Addya (Eds.), *Resource management and efficiency in cloud computing environments* (pp. 264–285). Hershey, PA: IGI Global. doi:10.4018/978-1-5225-1721-4.ch011

Kasemsap, K. (2017b). The role of radio frequency identification in modern libraries. In I. Management Association (Ed.), Identity theft: Breakthroughs in research and practice (pp. 174–200). Hershey, PA: IGI Global. doi:10.4018/978-1-5225-0808-3.ch009

Kasemsap, K. (2017c). Analyzing the role of health information technology in global health care. In N. Wickramasinghe (Ed.), *Handbook of research on healthcare administration and management* (pp. 287–307). Hershey, PA: IGI Global. doi:10.4018/978-1-5225-0920-2.ch017

Kasemsap, K. (2017d). Mastering web mining and information retrieval in the digital age. In A. Kumar (Ed.), *Web usage mining techniques and applications across industries* (pp. 1–28). Hershey, PA: IGI Global. doi:10.4018/978-1-5225-0613-3.ch001

Kothmayr, T., Schmitt, C., Hu, W., Brünig, M., & Carle, G. (2013). DTLS based security and two-way authentication for the Internet of Things. *Ad Hoc Networks*, *11*(8), 2710–2723. doi:10.1016/j.adhoc.2013.05.003

Kotis, K., & Katasonov, A. (2013). Semantic interoperability on the Internet of Things: The semantic smart gateway framework. *International Journal of Distributed Systems and Technologies*, *4*(3), 47–69. doi:10.4018/jdst.2013070104

Kröner, A., Haupert, J., & Barthel, R. (2015). Digital object memory. In M. Khosrow-Pour (Ed.), *Encyclopedia of information science and technology* (3rd ed.; pp. 7605–7613). Hershey, PA: IGI Global. doi:10.4018/978-1-4666-5888-2.ch749

Laranjo, I., Macedo, J., & Santos, A. (2013). Internet of Things for medication control: E-health architecture and service implementation. *International Journal of Reliable and Quality E-Healthcare*, *2*(3), 1–15. doi:10.4018/ijrqeh.2013070101

Lee, I. (2016). A conceptual framework of the Internet of Things (IoT) for smart supply chain management. In I. Lee (Ed.), *Encyclopedia of e-commerce development, implementation, and management* (pp. 1177–1189). Hershey, PA: IGI Global. doi:10.4018/978-1-4666-9787-4.ch084

Lee, J., Oh, S., & Jang, J. W. (2015). A work in progress: Context based encryption scheme for Internet of Things. *Procedia Computer Science*, *56*, 271–275. doi:10.1016/j.procs.2015.07.208

Luo, Z., Lai, M., Cheung, M., Han, S., Zhang, T., Luo, Z., & Tipoe, G. et al. (2010). Developing local association network based IoT solutions for body parts tagging and tracking. *International Journal of Systems and Service-Oriented Engineering*, *1*(4), 42–64. doi:10.4018/jssoe.2010100104

Manațe, B., Fortiș, F., & Moore, P. (2015). An architecture to implement the Internet-of-Things using the Prometheus methodology. *International Journal of Distributed Systems and Technologies*, *6*(4), 1–20. doi:10.4018/IJDST.201510010

Michell, V. A. (2016). The Internet of Things and opportunities for pervasive safety monitored health environments. In *E-health and telemedicine: Concepts, methodologies, tools, and applications* (pp. 1568–1605). Hershey, PA: IGI Global. doi:10.4018/978-1-4666-8756-1.ch079

Miorandi, D., Sicari, S., Pellegrini, F. D., & Chlamtac, I. (2012). Internet of Things: Vision, applications and research challenges. *Ad Hoc Networks*, *10*(7), 1497–1516. doi:10.1016/j.adhoc.2012.02.016

Mobahat, H. (2010). *Authentication and lightweight cryptography in low cost RFID*. Paper presented at the 2nd International Conference on Software Technology and Engineering (ICSTE 2010), San Juan, Puerto Rico. doi:10.1109/ICSTE.2010.5608776

Ning, H., Liu, H., & Yang, L. T. (2013). Cyber-entity security in the Internet of Things. *Computer*, *46*(4), 46–53. doi:10.1109/MC.2013.74

ONeill, M. (2014). The Internet of Things: Do more devices mean more risks? *Computer Fraud & Security*, *2014*(1), 16–17. doi:10.1016/S1361-3723(14)70008-9

Oriwoh, E., & Williams, G. (2015). Internet of Things: The argument for smart forensics. In M. Cruz-Cunha & I. Portela (Eds.), *Handbook of research on digital crime, cyberspace security, and information assurance* (pp. 407–423). Hershey, PA: IGI Global. doi:10.4018/978-1-4666-6324-4.ch026

Palattella, M., Accettura, N., Vilajosana, X., Watteyne, T., Grieco, L., Boggia, G., & Dohler, M. (2013). Standardized protocol stack for the Internet of (important) Things. *IEEE Communications Surveys and Tutorials*, *15*(3), 1389–1406. doi:10.1109/SURV.2012.111412.00158

Pan, J., Paul, S., & Jain, R. (2011). A survey of the research on future Internet architectures. *IEEE Communications Magazine*, *49*(7), 26–36. doi:10.1109/MCOM.2011.5936152

Patel, P., & Cassou, D. (2015). Enabling high-level application development for the Internet of Things. *Journal of Systems and Software*, *103*, 62–84. doi:10.1016/j.jss.2015.01.027

Petrov, V., Edelev, S., Komar, M., & Koucheryavy, Y. (2014). *Towards the era of wireless keys: How the IoT can change authentication paradigm*. Paper presented at the 2014 1st IEEE World Forum on Internet of Things (WF-IoT 2014), Seoul, South Korea. doi:10.1109/WF-IoT.2014.6803116

Ponnusamy, V., Tay, Y. P., Lee, L. H., Low, T. J., & Zhao, C. W. (2016). Energy harvesting methods for Internet of Things. In V. Ponnusamy, N. Zaman, T. Low, & A. Amin (Eds.), *Biologically-inspired energy harvesting through wireless sensor technologies* (pp. 51–70). Hershey, PA: IGI Global. doi:10.4018/978-1-4666-9792-8.ch003

Ray, B. R., Abawajy, J., & Chowdhury, M. (2014). Scalable RFID security framework and protocol supporting Internet of Things. *Computer Networks, 67*, 89–103. doi:10.1016/j.comnet.2014.03.023

Reaidy, P. J., Gunasekaran, A., & Spalanzani, A. (2015). Bottom-up approach based on Internet of Things for order fulfillment in a collaborative warehousing environment. *International Journal of Production Economics, 159*, 29–40. doi:10.1016/j.ijpe.2014.02.017

Roman, R., Alcaraz, C., Lopez, J., & Sklavos, N. (2011). Key management systems for sensor networks in the context of the Internet of Things. *Computers & Electrical Engineering, 37*(2), 147–159. doi:10.1016/j.compeleceng.2011.01.009

Roman, R., Zhou, J., & Lopez, J. (2013). On the features and challenges of security and privacy in distributed Internet of Things. *Computer Networks, 57*(10), 2266–2279. doi:10.1016/j.comnet.2012.12.018

Rong, K., Hu, G., Lin, Y., Shi, Y., & Guo, L. (2015). Understanding business ecosystem using a 6C framework in Internet-of-Things-based sectors. *International Journal of Production Economics, 159*, 41–55. doi:10.1016/j.ijpe.2014.09.003

Santos, D. F. S., Almeida, H. O., & Perkusich, A. (2015). A personal connected health system for the Internet of Things based on the constrained application protocol. *Computers & Electrical Engineering, 44*, 122–136. doi:10.1016/j.compeleceng.2015.02.020

Sehgal, A., Perelman, V., Kuryla, S., & Schonwalder, J. (2012). Management of resource constrained devices in the Internet of Things. *IEEE Communications Magazine, 50*(12), 144–149. doi:10.1109/MCOM.2012.6384464

Shaev, Y. (2014). From the sociology of things to the "Internet of Things". *Procedia: Social and Behavioral Sciences, 149*, 874–878. doi:10.1016/j.sbspro.2014.08.266

Shang, X., Zhang, R., & Chen, Y. (2012). Internet of Things (IoT) service architecture and its application in e-commerce. *Journal of Electronic Commerce in Organizations, 10*(3), 44–55. doi:10.4018/jeco.2012070104

Shelby, Z., & Bormann, C. (2011). *6LoWPAN: The wireless embedded Internet*. Hoboken, NJ: John Wiley & Sons.

Shin, D. (2014). A socio-technical framework for Internet-of-Things design: A human-centered design for the Internet of Things. *Telematics and Informatics, 31*(4), 519–531. doi:10.1016/j.tele.2014.02.003

Sicari, S., Rizzardi, A., Grieco, L. A., & Coen-Porisini, A. (2015). Security, privacy and trust in Internet of Things: The road ahead. *Computer Networks*, *76*, 146–164. doi:10.1016/j.comnet.2014.11.008

Song, S., & Mitchell, C. J. (2011). Scalable RFID security protocols supporting tag ownership transfer. *Computer Communications*, *34*(4), 556–566. doi:10.1016/j. comcom.2010.02.027

Souza, A. M. C., & Amazonas, J. R. A. (2015). An outlier detect algorithm using big data processing and Internet of Things architecture. *Procedia: Computer Science*, *52*, 1010–1015.

Tomizuka, M. (2002). Mechatronics: From the 20th to 21st century. *Control Engineering Practice*, *10*(8), 877–886. doi:10.1016/S0967-0661(02)00016-3

Trujillo-Rasua, R., & Solanas, A. (2011). Efficient probabilistic communication protocol for the private identification of RFID tags by means of collaborative readers. *Computer Networks*, *55*(15), 3211–3223. doi:10.1016/j.comnet.2011.05.013

Turcu, C. E., & Turcu, C. O. (2013). Internet of Things as key enabler for sustainable healthcare delivery. *Procedia: Social and Behavioral Sciences*, *73*, 251–256. doi:10.1016/j.sbspro.2013.02.049

Turkanovic, M., Brumen, O., & Holbl, M. (2014). A novel user authentication and key agreement scheme for heterogeneous ad hoc wireless sensor networks, based on the Internet of Things notion. *Ad Hoc Networks*, *20*, 96–112. doi:10.1016/j. adhoc.2014.03.009

Ukil, A., Bandyopadhyay, S., & Pal, A. (2014). *IoT-privacy: To be private or not to be private*. Paper presented at the 2014 33rd IEEE International Conference on Computer Communications (INFOCOM 2014), Toronto, Canada. doi:10.1109/INFCOMW.2014.6849186

Wang, C., Sohraby, K., Li, B., Daneshmand, M., & Hu, Y. (2006). A survey of transport protocols for wireless sensor networks. *IEEE Network*, *20*(3), 34–40. doi:10.1109/MNET.2006.1637930

Weber, R. H. (2010). Internet of Things: New security and privacy challenges. *Computer Law & Security Report*, *26*(1), 23–30. doi:10.1016/j.clsr.2009.11.008

Wei, L., Zhu, H., Cao, Z., Dong, X., Jia, W., Chen, Y., & Vasilakos, A. V. (2014). Security and privacy for storage and computation in cloud computing. *Information Sciences*, *258*, 371–386. doi:10.1016/j.ins.2013.04.028

Wrightson, T. (2012). *Wireless network security: A beginner's guide*. New York, NY: McGraw–Hill.

Wu, Z. Q., Zhou, Y. W., & Ma, J. F. (2011). A security transmission model for Internet of Things. *Jisuanji Xuebao/Chinese Journal of Computers, 34*(8), 1351–1364.

Yang, J., & Fang, B. (2011). Security model and key technologies for the Internet of Things. *Journal of China Universities of Posts and Telecommunications, 8*(2), 109–112. doi:10.1016/S1005-8885(10)60159-8

Yu, J., Wang, N., Wang, G., & Yu, D. (2013). Connected dominating sets in wireless ad hoc and sensor networks: A comprehensive survey. *Computer Communications, 36*(2), 121–134. doi:10.1016/j.comcom.2012.10.005

Zhang, D., Yang, L. T., & Huang, H. (2011). *Searching in Internet of Things: Vision and challenges*. Paper presented at the 9th International Symposium on Parallel and Distributed Processing with Applications (ISPA 2011), Busan, South Korea. doi:10.1109/ISPA.2011.53

Zhao, F., Sun, Z., & Jin, H. (2015). Topic-centric and semantic-aware retrieval system for Internet of Things. *Information Fusion, 23*, 33–42. doi:10.1016/j.inffus.2014.01.001

Zhao, K., & Ge, L. (2013). *A survey on the Internet of Things security*. Paper presented at the 9th International Conference on Computational Intelligence and Security (CIS 2013), Chengdu, China. doi:10.1109/CIS.2013.145

Zhao, S., Cheng, B., Yu, L., Hou, S., Zhang, Y., & Chen, J. (2016). Internet of Things service provisioning platform for cross-application cooperation. *International Journal of Web Services Research, 13*(1), 1–22. doi:10.4018/IJWSR.2016010101

Zhao, Y. (2013). *Research on data security technology in Internet of Things*. Paper presented at the 2nd International Conference on Mechatronics and Control Engineering (ICMCE 2013), Dalian, China. doi:10.4028/www.scientific.net/AMM.433-435.1752

Zheng, J., Simplot-Ryl, D., Bisdikian, C., & Mouftah, H. T. (2011). The Internet of Things. *IEEE Communications Magazine, 49*(11), 30–31. doi:10.1109/MCOM.2011.6069706

ADDITIONAL READING

Bandyopadhyay, S., Sengupta, M., Maiti, S., & Dutta, S. (2011). Role of middleware for Internet of Things: A study. *International Journal of Computer Science and Engineering Survey*, 2(3), 94–105. doi:10.5121/ijcses.2011.2307

Benssalah, M., Djeddou, M., & Drouiche, K. (2014). Security enhancement of the authenticated RFID security mechanism based on chaotic maps. *Security and Communication Networks*, 7(12), 2356–2372. doi:10.1002/sec.946

Carretero, J., & Garcia, J. D. (2014). The Internet of Things: Connecting the world. *Personal and Ubiquitous Computing*, 18(2), 445–447. doi:10.1007/s00779-013-0665-z

Chang, J. Y. (2015). A distributed cluster computing energy-efficient routing scheme for Internet of Things systems. *Wireless Personal Communications*, 82(2), 757–776. doi:10.1007/s11277-014-2251-8

Clarke, J., Gritzalis, S., Zhou, J., & Roman, R. (2014). Protecting the Internet of Things. *Security and Communication Networks*, 7(12), 2637–2638. doi:10.1002/sec.1174

Deng, H., Zhang, B., Li, C., Huang, K., & Liu, H. (2012). MAX–MIN aggregation in wireless sensor networks: Mechanism and modeling. *Wireless Communications and Mobile Computing*, 12(7), 615–630. doi:10.1002/wcm.1000

Ding, Y., Zhou, X. W., Cheng, Z. M., & Lin, F. H. (2013). A security differential game model for sensor networks in context of the Internet of Things. *Wireless Personal Communications*, 72(1), 375–388. doi:10.1007/s11277-013-1018-y

Forsstrom, S., & Kanter, T. (2014). Continuously changing information on a global scale and its impact for the Internet-of-Things. *Mobile Networks and Applications*, 19(1), 33–44. doi:10.1007/s11036-013-0479-2

Hsieh, H. C., Hsieh, W. H., & Chen, J. L. (2015). Mobile IMS integration of the Internet of Things in ecosystem. *Wireless Personal Communications*, 80(2), 819–836. doi:10.1007/s11277-014-2043-1

Hu, W., & Cheng, T. (2015). Simulative research on the function of Internet of Things basing on the changing of topological structure. *Multimedia Tools and Applications*, 74(19), 8445–8454. doi:10.1007/s11042-013-1615-5

Liu, Y., Chen, Z., Lv, X., & Han, F. (2014). Multiple layer design for mass data transmission against channel congestion in IoT. *International Journal of Communication Systems*, 27(8), 1126–1146. doi:10.1002/dac.2399

Lopez, T. S., Ranasinghe, D. C., Harrison, M., & McFarlane, D. (2012). Adding sense to the Internet of Things. *Personal and Ubiquitous Computing, 16*(3), 291–308. doi:10.1007/s00779-011-0399-8

Luo, M., Tu, M., & Xu, J. (2014). A security communication model based on certificateless online/offline signcryption for Internet of Things. *Security and Communication Networks, 7*(10), 1560–1569. doi:10.1002/sec.836

Manches, A., Duncan, P., Plowman, L., & Sabeti, S. (2015). Three questions about the Internet of Things and children. *TechTrends, 59*(1), 76–83. doi:10.1007/s11528-014-0824-8

Mustafee, N., & Bessis, N. (2015). The Internet of Things: Shaping the new Internet space. *Concurrency and Computation, 27*(8), 1815–1818. doi:10.1002/cpe.3483

Najera, P., Roman, R., & Lopez, J. (2013). User-centric secure integration of personal RFID tags and sensor networks. *Security and Communication Networks, 6*(10), 1177–1197. doi:10.1002/sec.684

Nataliia, L., & Elena, F. (2015). Internet of Things as a symbolic resource of power. *Procedia: Social and Behavioral Sciences, 166*, 521–525. doi:10.1016/j.sbspro.2014.12.565

Qiu, T., Sun, W., Bai, Y., & Zhou, Y. (2013). An efficient multi-path self-organizing strategy in Internet of Things. *Wireless Personal Communications, 73*(4), 1613–1629. doi:10.1007/s11277-013-1270-1

Rapti, E., Karageorgos, A., & Gerogiannis, V. C. (2015). Decentralised service composition using potential fields in Internet of Things applications. *Procedia Computer Science, 52*, 700–706. doi:10.1016/j.procs.2015.05.079

Sun, Y., Bie, R., Thomas, P., & Cheng, X. (2014). Advances on data, information, and knowledge in the Internet of Things. *Personal and Ubiquitous Computing, 18*(8), 1793–1795. doi:10.1007/s00779-014-0789-9

Tsai, C. W., Lai, C. F., Chiang, M. C., & Yang, L. T. (2014). Data mining for Internet of Things: A survey. *IEEE Communications Surveys and Tutorials, 16*(1), 77–97. doi:10.1109/SURV.2013.103013.00206

Wang, Y., Zhang, L., Huang, Y., Zhao, B., & Zhao, C. (2013). Service community construction method of Internet of Things based on semantic similarity. *Journal of Electronics (China), 30*(1), 49–56. doi:10.1007/s11767-013-2121-7

Wortmann, F., & Fluchter, K. (2015). Internet of Things. *Business & Information Systems Engineering, 57*(3), 221–224. doi:10.1007/s12599-015-0383-3

Wu, T. Y., Liaw, G. H., Huang, S. W., Lee, W. T., & Wu, C. C. (2012). A GA-based mobile RFID localization scheme for Internet of Things. *Personal and Ubiquitous Computing, 16*(3), 245–258. doi:10.1007/s00779-011-0398-9

Xia, F., Yang, L. T., Wang, L., & Vinel, A. (2012). Internet of Things. *International Journal of Communication Systems, 25*(9), 1101–1102. doi:10.1002/dac.2417

Xu, L., He, W., & Li, S. (2014). Internet of Things in industries: A survey. *IEEE Transactions on Industrial Informatics, 10*(4), 2233–2243. doi:10.1109/TII.2014.2300753

Zhou, L., & Chao, H. C. (2011). Multimedia traffic security architecture for the Internet of Things. *IEEE Network, 25*(3), 35–40. doi:10.1109/MNET.2011.5772059

KEY TERMS AND DEFINITIONS

Computer: The electronic machine that is used for storing, organizing, and finding words, numbers, and pictures, for doing calculations, and for controlling other machines.

Internet: The worldwide computer network that provides the information on many subjects and enables users to exchange the messages.

Network: A number of computers that are connected together so that they can share the information.

Radio Frequency Identification: A method of tracking and identifying the objects by affixing the very small radio transmitters that contain chip and antenna.

Sensor: The device that is utilized to record that something is present or that there are the changes in something.

Technology: The utilization of scientific knowledge to solve the practical problems, especially in industry and commerce.

The Internet of Things: All the different devices, including computers, phones, wearable technology, and smart systems, that are able to connect to each other utilizing the Internet.

Wireless Sensor Network: A group of specialized transducers with the communications infrastructure for monitoring and recording the conditions at various locations.

Chapter 3
Security in Network Layer of IoT:
Possible Measures to Preclude

B. Balamurugan
VIT University, India

Dyutimoy Biswas
VIT University, India

ABSTRACT

The internet of things (IoT) is an imminent model in the field of wireless telecommunications. It is also considered as a third wave of information technology after the Internet and mobile communication. Basically, IoT is a wireless interconnected network of variety of objects such as radio frequency identification (RFID) tags, sensors, actuators, mobile phones and other types of wireless devices. It has extensible application in the areas such as public security, infrastructure development, modern agriculture, environment protection, urban management, healthcare, enhanced learning, and business service, among others. IoT is a self-configuring wireless network of sensors where the primary goal of establishing connection is to offer interconnectivity of various objects. The concept of IoT was coined by the Auto-Id center of the Massachusetts Institute of Technology (MIT) in 1999

DOI: 10.4018/978-1-5225-2296-6.ch003

INTRODUCTION

Internet of things (IoT) is an amazing, if not the most powerful technological invention of the last couple of decades, providing superior power to the hands of human race. The most promising aspect of IoT is that this technology is still budding and has immense potential to kick-start a new, fully coordinated technological era. In IoT, 'things' or devices communicate between each other over wireless networks. Therefore, while developing algorithms and techniques for IoT, the standards and rules set for wireless networks, which are essentially different from that of wired networks, are taken into consideration. Since IoT is still in its inception stage, its usage is still limited within the scope of the enterprises and not very common in consumer market. Therefore, unlike the high speed network where computers communicate with other computers where aspects of 'security breaches' is dealt by the programmers and developers for ages, and many robust techniques for this purpose have been built and used, in IoT, with fewer, if not zero, number of cases of security breaches have occurred, apart from standard techniques, it's a challenge for the engineers to develop techniques, both on hardware and software levels, to secure the future of IoT (Kelly et al., 2013; Babar et al., 2010; Alam, Sarfraz, Chowdhury, & Noll, 2011; Barnaghi et al., 2012).

In IoT, the new objects that enter the network are configured automatically. This characteristic makes IoT highly susceptible to security threats. Among several kinds of threats in an IoT network, Disruption and Denial of Service (DoS), eavesdropping, problems in authentication and physical attacks on devices in different forms, are most common.

Therefore, it is essential to devise security measures without interfering with the operation of the IoT network. Also, robust and bug free analytical tools and algorithms should be employed that will detect malicious and unethical activity, whilst improving service offered to the customers. Generally, the intrusion detection and prevention systems and enhancement of packet security by incorporating suitable fields in packet header are the security measures associated with the Layer 3 of wireless networks (Babar et al., 2010; Zargar et al., 2013; Savola, Reijo, Abie, & Sihvonen, 2012).

SECURITY ISSUES

Ensuring security for the IoT devices has been the most challenging task. Combining a strong cryptography with a highly constrained environment, under the condition of limited energy consumption, since most of the devices are battery operated, and little or no maintenance time makes it extremely difficult. That IoT can achieve intelligent address resolution, track location, monitor and manage devices makes it vulnerable to security threats, as a lot of applications run simultaneously. The security threats commonly found in high speed networks may pose similar menace to IoT, but, in reality, owing to the the low processing power and less storage capacity that are characteristic of devices used in IoT, the protocols designed for higher processing power and greater storage capacity cannot be directly implemented in IoT. With the data moving freely between world wide network of devices, security measures and solutions must be readily available so that users can operate without fear of data manipulation. Therefore, the security measures must be incorporated while designing the device after a proper predictive analysis and not to be treated and adopted for troubleshooting purposes only. At the same time, the choice of security measures should not be made at the cost of compromising users' satisfaction. For the number of intrusion points in a heterogeneous network having billions and possibly trillions of edge devices, the core system requires an equally efficient protection system (Casado, Lander, & Philippas Tsigas, 2009; Babar et al., 2010).

The various security issues that should be provided by a secure network layer for wireless networks are as follows:

1. **Confidentiality:** It ensures that the user information is guarded from unauthorized access. Typically, this is achieved by using symmetric key cryptography for encrypting with a shared secret key. Symmetric key algorithms can be of 2 types, i.e. stream ciphers and block ciphers (Medaglia, Carlo Maria, & Alexandru Serbanati 2010; Weber, 2010).
2. **Semantic Security:** It ensures that no partial information about the plaintext can be extracted by observing the cipher text. A special mode of operation and an initialization vector are often used to provide randomization (Alam, Sarfraz, Chowdhury, & Noll, 2011; Le et al., 2012; Barnaghi et al., 2012).
3. **Integrity:** It prevents the packet modification during transmission. A message integrity code (MIC) or a checksum in each packet is used to achieve integrity. The MIC is computed through a cryptographic hash function that detects malicious altering or accidental transmission errors. Checksums are used to detect only transmission errors (Babar et al., 2010; Heer et al. 2011).
4. **Authenticity:** Data authenticity ensures that the legitimate user should only be able to receive the message, while any unauthorized attempt to gain access to the message is rejected. For this purpose, a message authentication code (MAC) is included in each packet. The MAC is computed using a shared secret key which could be the same key used to encrypt the plaintext. MAC also provides integrity (Babar et al., 2010; Ukil, Arijit, Jaydip Sen, & Sripad Koilakonda, 2011; Park, Jiye, Saemi Shin, and Namhi Kang, 2013).

Introducing a far-sighted and simultaneous security standards and procedures will help in establishing and implementing a universally secured and trusted network of systems and devices. Currently available security systems provide a patchwork of solutions for different kinds of systems. Authenticating identity and privilege in different platforms and applications should be done universally and automatically. When there are flaws and exploitations, standard protocols must be devised for automatic updation of security software in the new systems as well as evolved systems to minimize further damage (Casado, Lander, & Philippas Tsigas, 2009; Babar et al., 2013; Park, Jiye, Saemi Shin, and Namhi Kang, 2013).

THE NETWORK LAYER OF IoT

The Layer 3 of Low Power and Lossy Networks (LLNs) corresponds the Network Layer in OSI or TCP/IP model. In the next subsection 3.1, an analysis regarding the threats related to the Layer 3 of IoT has been done and in subsection 3.2, the architecture i.e. the techniques and protocols related to this layer and corresponding security provisions are discussed.

Security Breaches in Network Layer

Security Breaches Taxonomy

Selective Forwarding Attack

This attack takes place when packets are selectively forwarded with the purpose of disrupting routing paths and filtering any protocol. DoS (Denial of Service) type of attack falls under this category. In RPL the attacker can forward all RPL control messages and drop the rest of the traffic. A possible remedy can be creating a disjoint or dynamic path between the parent and the children. Another solution can be to use an encryption technique where the attacker will not able to identify the traffic flow. A Heartbeat protocol, originally used to detect disruption in network topology, can be used as a defender against a selective forwarding attack. IDS solution is given in the End to End packet loss adaptation algorithm for detection of selective forwarding attack. Such attacks need to be detected and removed, as the RPL self-healing does not correct the topology (Pongle, Pavan, and Gurunath Chavan, 2015; Karlof, Chris, and David Wagner, 2003; Yu, Bo, and Bin Xiao, 2006).

Sinkhole Attack

In sinkhole type attacks the attacker node creates a beneficial path to attract many nearby nodes to route traffic through it. This attack does not disrupt the operation of the network but it can become very powerful when combined with other attacks. The IDS system provides the solution to this attack by proposing an evaluated parent fail-over and a rank authentication technique. The rank authentication technique relies on the one way hash technique, where the root begins to generate hash values by choosing random ones, and broadcasts it in DIO messages. All the nodes calculate the hash values using the previously received ones and again broadcast it using DIO message in an iterative process. With the assumption that malicious node fails to calculate the hash value, it simply broadcasts the received DIO message. Each node stores the hash value received by its parent along with number of hops in the path. When the root node broadcasts a random number securely, a given node can verify its parent's rank using the intermediate hops number. The parent fail-over technique uses the UNS (unheard nodes set) field in the DIO message indicating that the nodes are in a sinkhole-compromised path. If the node receives the DIO message containing its ID in UNS, it adds its parent in black list. Like in selective forwarding, RPL does not have the self-healing capacity against the sinkhole attack, too (Pongle, Pavan, and Gurunath Chavan, 2015; Karlof, Chris, and David Wagner, 2003; Ngai, Edith CH, Jiangchuan Liu, & Michael R. Lyu, 2006).

Clone ID Attack

Here, the attacker node replicates the identity of other node to gain access to traffic destined to or through victim node. This attack can be minimized by tracking the number of instances of each identity, thereby ultimately detecting cloned ones. If the geographical locations of the nodes are stored at 6BR along with their identity, one can use that information to differentiate between the original node and the cloned/malicious one. Other distributed technique is by using distributed hash table (DHT) (Pongle, Pavan, and Gurunath Chavan, 2015; Xiao et al., 2006).

Hello Flooding Attack

For joining the network a node broadcasts an initial message known as HELLO message. An attacker can introduce himself as a neighbour node to multiple nodes by broadcasting HELLO messages with strong routing metrics and enter into a network. In RPL, DIO messages referred to as HELLO messages, and are used to publicise information about DODAG. This attack can be avoided by using the link-layer metric as a parameter while selecting the default route. A different route is chosen when it fails to receive link-layer acknowledgements. An alternate solution might be to utilise the geographical distance, by determining the criterion that a given node should not select the ones which lie beyond their transmission range. This attack, when alone, cannot exist for a prolonged period of time in a RPL network, as it is removed by the RPL's Global and Local repair mechanism. However, when combined with other attacks, it remains an undetected threat to security (Pongle, Pavan, and Gurunath Chavan, 2015; Karlof, Chris, and David Wagner, 2003; Pathan, Al-Sakib Khan, Hyung-Woo Lee, and Choong Seon Hong, 2006).

Wormhole Attack

The main purpose of the wormhole attack is to disrupt the network topology and the traffic flow. This attack occurs when a tunnel is created between two given attackers, A and B and transmitting selective traffic through it. Wormhole attacks can be prevented by using the construction of Markle tree authentication. As opposed to the normal tree in RPL which spans from the root node to leaf ones, the Markle tree spans in reverse, viz. from the leaves to the root. It utilises the ID of a node and the public key for calculating hash. Each parent is identified by its children nodes. Authentication of a given node begins from the root node up to the node itself. If any node fails to authenticate, the children nodes avoid the wrong parent selection (Pongle, Pavan, and Gurunath Chavan, 2015; Karlof, Chris, and David Wagner, 2003; Hu, Yih-Chun, Adrian Perrig, and David B. Johnson, 2003).

Sybil Attack

Sybil attack is somewhat similar to the clone ID attack, in that the malicious node uses several identities on the same physical node. Using this attack large parts of a network can be taken under control without deploying physical nodes. The Sybil attacks have been identified in social domain of Internet of Things and stated defence against these attacks. The Sybil attack on RPL however is not evaluated yet (Pongle, Pavan, and Gurunath Chavan, 2015; Douceur, 2002; Newsome et al., 2004).

Black Hole Attack

In the Black Hole attack, the attacker node drops all data packets silently, which is analogous to a hole that sucks in everything. In this way, all packets in the network routing through that node are dropped. The Black hole attack was tested on a 6LoWPAN network, where the Contiki RPL was used in the Cooja simulator. The attack test bed comprises of 3 scenarios, viz.

1. A network topology not facing an attack.
2. A selective forwarding attack (which is a special case of Black Hole attack) in a network.
3. A purely Black hole attack in a network.
4. To simulate malicious activity, some modifications are made in Contiki OS such that the data packets from neighbouring nodes are completely dropped by the malicious node. The attacking node continues to take part in the route formation by consistently sending DIO packets. After the case study, the author inferred the following:
   a. Increased number of DIO messages reflects instability in the network.
   b. The scenario with the malicious node sending self-generated data packets shows 8% increase in the total number of DIO packets exchanged between nodes.
   c. When the malicious node does not generate any data packets, lesser number of DIO messages is exchanged.
   d. Data packets suffer delay in presence of malicious activity in the network.
   e. The delay for data packets generated by malicious nodes is 4.3 times higher than that of data packets from a clear network (Pongle, Pavan, and Gurunath Chavan, 2015; Le et al., 2012).

Denial of Service Attack

The Denial of service or the Distributed denial of service attack is an attempt to make resources unavailable to its intended user. In RPL this attack can be brought about using the IPv6 UDP packet flooding. Many malicious nodes can coordinate to cause the Distributed denial of service attack, making it is difficult to identify the malicious nodes. In an attempt to prevent this attack, the IDS system has proposed the framework for detection of DOS attack in 6LoWPAN. The architecture integrates the IDS into the network framework developed within the EU FP7 project ebbits. At the security layer of ebbits the DoS protection module is added. IDS probe nodes are located in the network which send periodically, the traffic in 6LoWPAN through wired connections to the IDS system. The DoS protection manager receives the alerts from IDS system and takes the network-related information from the other modules of the network manager layer to confirm the occurrence of the attack. The IDS sends the jamming information of the attack to the Dos protection manager. The presence of jamming information at the modules of network manager of ebbits indicates the presence of the attack (Pongle, Pavan, and Gurunath Chavan, 2015; Babar et al., 2010; Zargar, Saman Taghavi, Jyoti Joshi, and David Tipper, 2013).

Any event that reduces, disrupts or completely eliminates a network's communication services can be categorized as a DoS attack. For any information network, 'device availability' is the most important factor. DoS attacks target 'network availability' by preventing normal communication between network devices to access the services provided. Therefore, DoS attacks are considered to be an important security issue. These attacks can be initiated from remote places with mere commands, and, combined with advanced tools, attackers can even perform distributed DoS attacks, which are proven to affect big networks. It is very difficult to identify a DoS attack before the service becomes unavailable. DoS attacks range from simple jamming attack to sophisticated attacks as mentioned below (Pongle, Pavan, and Gurunath Chavan, 2015; Garcia-Morchon et al., 2013).

Jamming

Jamming is the process of transmitting a radio signal to interfere with the radio frequencies being used by the sensor network. It can be performed either continuously or intermittently. In both the cases, the network suffers from considerable damage. A jamming attack is usually carried out during the 'operational phase'. It occurs at the link-level by sending forged packets which create collisions, causing legitimate packets to get dropped (Pongle, Pavan, and Gurunath Chavan, 2015; Kozlov, Denis, Jari Veijalainen, and Yasir Ali, 2013).

Cloning of Things

This takes place during the 'manufacturing process', as well as during the 'operational phase'. In the first case, an internal attacker can substitute a genuine *thing* with a similar, pre-programmed *thing* for unauthorized purposes. During the 'operational phase', a node can be captured and replicated, a type of attack commonly known as node-replications attacks. Node capture could further lead to attacks such as extracting security parameters and firmware replacement attacks (Pongle, Pavan, and Gurunath Chavan, 2015; Garcia-Morchon et al., 2013).

Eavesdropping

This vulnerability is evident in 'operational phase' of all wireless communications. If security parameters like key materials and configurations are exchanged as clear messages, an attacker could retrieve these messages just by passively listening to the operating channel. The attacker could exploit them to join the network as a legitimate node and perform further attacks. At a later period, this could lead to a man-in-the-middle attack (Pongle, Pavan, and Gurunath Chavan, 2015; Garcia-Morchon et al., 2013).

Routing Attack

The information that is routed in IoT can be spoofed, altered or replayed in order to create routing loops, attract or repel network traffic, extend or shorten source routes, etc. Other possible routing attacks include flooding, sinkhole attack, selective forwarding, wormhole attack, and sybil attack . Attacks based on 6LoWPAN such as packet fragmentation attacks and RPL protocol such as rank attacks, local-repair attacks, back-off attack are also possible (Pongle, Pavan, and Gurunath Chavan, 2015; Garcia-Morchon et al., 2013).

Alteration and Spoofing Attack

1. **Rank Attack:** In RPL rank value increases as one goes from the root to the child node. By changing this value, an attacker may attract a child node for selecting as a parent one, or improve some other metric, and can thus attract large traffic going toward the root. The classification of this attack can be made based on the duration (continuous or discontinuous) and update or no update of DIO information, into four types and evaluated in RPL environment against network QOS parameters. The consequences of rank attack are as follows:
    a. Forming an un-optimized path
    b. Forming a loop without any detection.
    c. Forming an optimized path which exists in the topology but is never used.
    d. Decreasing the packet delivery ratio and changing the end-to-end delay a little as the number of attackers increases.
    e. The topology concerning the malicious node is also expected to change. Should the routing information be updated in the DIO, their neighbours will have to update their topology as well, leading to the creation of more control overheads.

To prevent the rank attack, VeRA (Version number and Rank Authentication), a new security service for preventing the misbehaving node from decreasing rank values is employed. VeRA prevents publishing an illegitimate decreased rank by generating the hash chaining using a random number chosen by the root node. The new hash chain generated is nothing but the rank. The attacker cannot change the rank value as he requires the previous hash chain value to generate a new one, as rank authentication is used which is provided by the root node consisting of the MAC (Message Authentication Code) over the maximum rank hash value and the next version number as the key. The VeRA schema further goes on to prevent two attacks, viz., the Rank Hash Chain Forgery attack and the Rank Replay attack. However, as

VeRA is only 2-backward-secure, it is vulnerable to the Rank Chain Forgery attack. To mitigate this backward-secure approach, a modification is made in which a simple challenge-response procedure is followed and the authentication of the rank hash chains is provided using an encryption chain instead of MACs. In each rank update, VeRA discloses the cryptographic credentials needed to verify the advertisements from all the parent nodes. This attack is mitigated using the Challenge-Response Scheme. TRAIL (Trust Anchor Interconnection Loop), a generic scheme for topology authentication in the RPL, detects and prevents topological inconsistencies by enabling each node to validate its upward path to the root, while also detecting the rank spoofing on it. It also minimizes exchange of network messages and consumption of node resource (Pongle, Pavan, and Gurunath Chavan, 2015; Le et al., 2012).

2. **Version Attack:** This attack takes place by publishing the higher version number in the DODAG tree. When nodes receive the new higher version number through the DIO message they start the process of forming a new DODAG tree. This can cause a new, un-optimized topology to be generated, thus creating inconsistencies in topology. The loops and rank inconsistencies created by the attack are generally located in the vicinity of the attacker. The VeRA schema prevents this attack by verifying the version number using a digital signature and MAC. The attack increases control overhead by 18 times the normal, thereby affecting energy consumption and channel availability. It also reduces the delivery ratio of packets by up to 30% and nearly doubles the end-to-end delay in a network. An attacker located at a large distance from the root causes the highest increase in overhead, and the highest packet loss (Pongle, Pavan, and Gurunath Chavan, 2015; Mayzaud, 2014).

3. **Local Repair Attack:** In this type of attack, the attacker periodically sends local repair messages without facing any problem with connectivity. This causes local repair around the nodes which intercept the local repair message. This attack creates more impact on delivery ratio than any other type of attack, generating more control packets and increasing the end-to-end delay. During construction, the dropping of packets occurs from the previous topology. It also exhausts the energy of node unnecessarily (Pongle, Pavan, and Gurunath Chavan, 2015; Le et al., 2012).

4. **Neighbour Attack:** In this attack the malicious node broadcasts DIO messages that it received without adding any further information itself. The node which receives these types of messages might think that its new neighbour node sent this DIO message. The victim nodes try to select the node that is not in range, as a parent node and changes the route to the farther neighbours.

This attack is somewhat similar to the wormhole attack with the special case of selectively forwarding of DIO messages. This attack affects the network QOS parameters, slightly increasing the end-to-end delay and deviating a little from the network topology, without significantly affecting control overhead and without changing the packet delivery ratio. When combined with other attacks, this attack can be dangerous (Pongle, Pavan, and Gurunath Chavan, 2015; Rghioui, Anass, Mohammed Bouhorma, and Abderrahim Benslimane, 2013).

5. **DIS Attack:** The DIS (DODAG Information Solicitation) message is used by a new node to get the information about the topology before joining the RPL network. In this type of attack malicious nodes periodically send the DIS messages to its neighbours. When the DIS messages are broadcast by the attacker, the receiver nodes receive them and reset the DIO timer to create the false impression that something went wrong with the topology around it. When the attacker unicasts the DIS message the receiver node sends the DIO message back, indicating that the sender is willing to join the network. Two ways of sending DIS messages may not affect delivery ratio, but DIS multicast attacks showed the greatest increase in end-to-end delay. This attack generates more control overhead and exhausts more energy (Pongle, Pavan, and Gurunath Chavan, 2015).

6. **Replay Attack:** This attack occurs when the attacker retransmits or delays a package or data that is yet to be received by the destination host, through an established session in order to gain an undue access and obtain the trust of the system. In this process it mainly manipulates the authentication process, by destroying the validity of certification (Pongle, Pavan, and Gurunath Chavan, 2015; Khoo, 2011).

NETWORK LAYER ARCHITECTURE

IEEE 802.15.4

IEEE 802.15.4 MAC Layer Overview

The IEEE 802.15.4 standarddefines the physical and the Media Access Control (MAC) layers for low rate, wireless, personal area networks. It considers 2 types of network nodes, i.e. full function devices (FFDs) and reduced function devices

(RFDs) on both peer-to-peer and star networks. A FFD works as the coordinator of the network and it is the reference device for all the other RFD nodes that have lower resource and communication capabilities (Piro, Giuseppe, Boggia, & Grieco, 2014; Sajjad, Muhammad, & Yousaf, 2014).

The IEEE 802.15.4e specification introduces some amendments to the 802.15.4 standard. Among its key features there is the time synchronized channel hopping (TSCH), i.e. a novel MAC protocol which better supports multi-hop communications in emerging industrial applications.

IEEE 802.15.4 Security Standards

The IEEE 802.15.4 standard offers a set of security measures in Low Power and Lossy Networks. At the MAC layer, it defines a set of procedures and parameters. Single variables and tables stored at this layer can be used to protect and authenticate packets by adopting techniques based on symmetric key cryptography. To handle security features, the IEEE 802.15.4 standard defines a specific Auxiliary Security Control field within the MAC header. It is made by three sub-fields: the Security Control, which explains the security level and the key identification mode chosen by the sender; the Frame Counter, used to protect the message from replay attacks; and the Key Identifier, to identify the key for encrypting and authenticating the packet by using the Key Source and Key Index variables. Moreover, this information is made available into the MAC frame whenever the Security Enabled flag in the Frame Control field of the MAC header is set to TRUE. When a device intends to send or receive a protected MAC frame, it executes the outgoing frame security or the incoming frame security procedures, respectively, by exploiting security related attributes stored at the MAC layer. Consequently, particular atten tion will be devoted only to a sub set of them, i.e., the macSecurityLevelTable, the macKeyTable, and the macDeviceTable. First of all, it is important to remark that 8 security levels have been defined by considering the following configurations: "unsecured" (i.e., level 0), "only authenticated" (i.e., from level 1 to level 3), "only encrypted" (i.e., level 4), and "encryption with authentication" (i.e., from level 5 to level 7). A specific security level should be guaranteed for each kind of message (i.e., beacon, command frame, data packet, and ACK). The related information is stored in the macSecurityLevelTable, made by a set of SecurityLevelDescriptor elements providing information about the frame type which it refers to, the minimal expected/required security level, the set of allowed security levels, and a Boolean flag indicating if the minimal security service may be overridden by a given device. A dedicated key can be used for each remote device and for each type of MAC frame. To achieve this objective, the macDeviceTable is created to store information about devices which a given node can interact with, for a secure communication. Finally, all keys are organized in the macKeyTable, where each keyDescriptor element contains the key, the set of devices that can use it, a list of KeyUsageDescriptor indicating which frame may be protected with this key, and other parameters (e.g., KeySource and keyIndex) which uniquely identify the key. During the outgoing frame security procedure, the node identifies the key that is to be used during the encryption process (for this, the Key Identifier announced by the upper layer is considered), protects the MAC payload according to the selected Security Level, creates the Auxiliary Security Control field, and reassembles the whole packet. Similarly, when a device receives a protected MAC frame, it identifies the key to exploit during the decryption process, verifies whether the Security Level chosen by the sender is correct, and then decrypt the payload (Piro, Giuseppe, Boggia, & Grieco, 2014; Sajjad, Muhammad, & Yousaf, 2014).

Figure 1. IEEE 802.15.4 MAC and auxiliary security header format

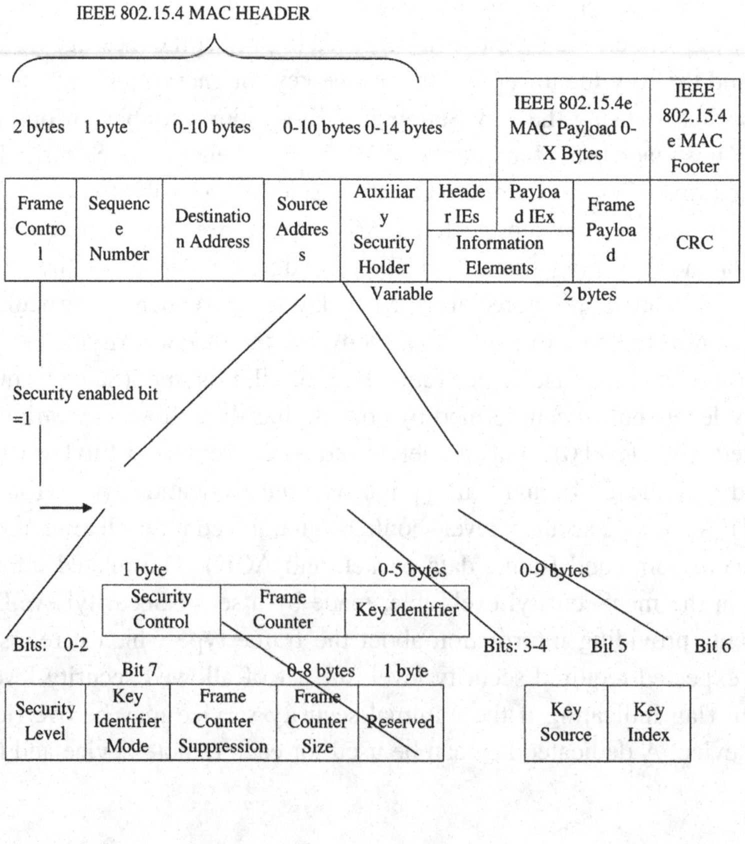

Unfortunately, in spite of what the standard describes, namely the procedures and parameters to be adopted for handling secured MAC frames with a high level of accuracy, it does not clarify some crucial aspects, such as the initialization of a secure IEEE 802.15.4 domain, the generation and the exchange of keys, instructions about building the macKeyTable and defining the way the entire system may react when a new device (that does not either support security capabilities, or is not able to synchronize itself with the existing secure domain) wants to join the IEEE 802.15.4 network (Piro, Giuseppe, Gennaro Boggia, and Luigi Alfredo Grieco, 2014; Sajjad, Syed Muhammad, and Muhammad Yousaf, 2014).

The Back off attack: In this kind of attack, the attacker, desiring maximum of access to the medium, executes variety of tactics such as the intentional selection of low back- off time. The attacker attacks the Contention Access Period by attempt-

Figure 2. IEEE 802.15.4e MAC and auxiliary security header format

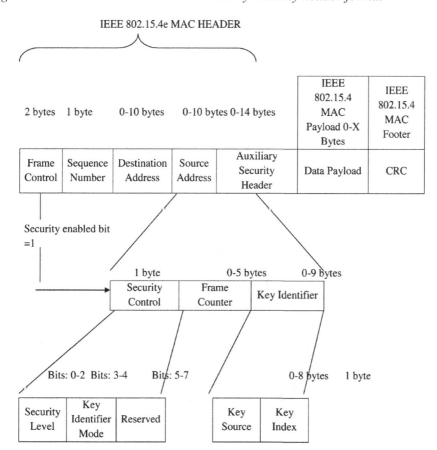

Figure 3. GTS allocation process

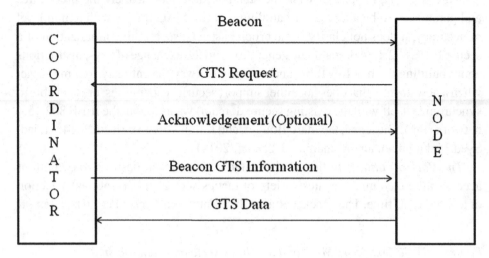

Figure 4. GTS deallocation process

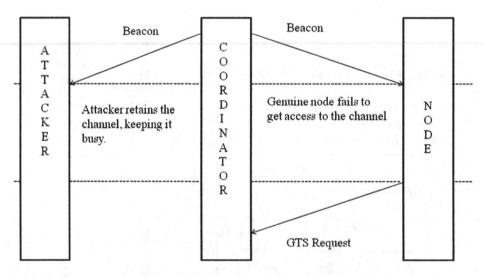

ing to choose a low back-off time to retain the channel permanently busy. This kind of attack deprives the legitimate nodes from sending requests of GTS slot as illustrated in Figure 5 (Piro, Giuseppe, Gennaro Boggia, and Luigi Alfredo Grieco, 2014; Sajjad, Syed Muhammad, and Muhammad Yousaf, 2014).

Figure 5. Back-off manipulation attack

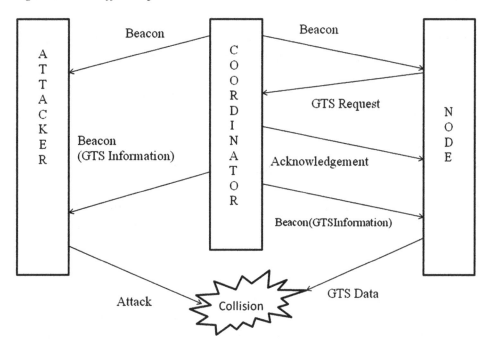

Figure 6. Back-off manipulation attack causing collision

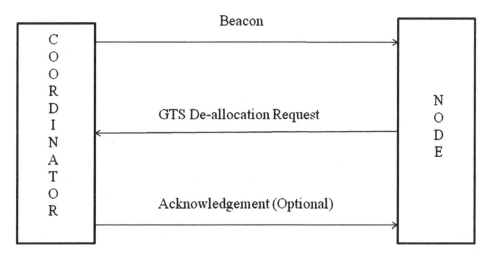

IETF 6LoWPAN, 6TiSCH and RPL

The Internet Engineering Task Force (IETF), has recently been dedicating consider-able efforts to construct the definition of standard protocols for IoT networks. As a consequence, three working group were created to address these issues, namely 6LOWPAN (The IPv6 over LOw power Wireless Personal Area Networks), ROLL (Routing Over Low power and Lossy Networks) and CORE (Constrained RESTful Environments).

6LoWPAN Technology and Security Overview

The reference protocol concerning the network layer of the internet is the Internet Protocol (IP), but it is not suitable for the sensor networks composed of resource constrained devices. 6LoWPAN (Low Power Personal Area Network) has been designed particularly to ensure the interoperability of the sensor networks and the internet (Accettura, Nicola, and Giuseppe Piro, 2014; Le et al., 2012; Rghioui, Anass, Mohammed Bouhorma, and Abderrahim Benslimane, 2013).

With the rapid development of wireless communication technologies, viz. machine-to-machine (M2M) communications, an essential part of the Internet of Things (IoT), allows both wireless and wired systems to monitor environments without human intervention. To extend the use of M2M applications, the standard of Internet Protocol version 6 (IPv6) over Low power Wireless Personal Area Net-works (6LoWPAN), developed by The Internet Engineering Task Force (IETF), is applied into M2M communication to enable IP based M2M sensing devices to connect to the open Internet (Accettura, Nicola, and Giuseppe Piro, 2014; Le et al., 2012; Rghioui, Anass, Mohammed Bouhorma, and Abderrahim Benslimane, 2013).

6LoWPAN integrates IP-based infrastructure and WSNs by specifying how IPv6 packets are to be routed in constrained networks having IEEE 802.15.4 specifica-tions. Owing to the limited payload size of the link layer in 6LoWPAN networks, the 6LoWPAN standard also defines fragmentation and reassembly of datagram. The IEEE 802.15.4 frame size may exceed the Maximum Transmission Unit (MTU) size of 127 bytes for big application data, in which case additional fragment(s) are needed. 6LoWPAN networks are connected to the Internet through the 6BR (6LoW-PAN Border Router) which is analogous to a sink in a WSN. The 6BR performs compression/decompression and fragmentation/assembly operations involving IPv6 datagrams (Accettura, Nicola, and Giuseppe Piro, 2014; Le et al., 2012; Rghioui, Anass, Mohammed Bouhorma, and Abderrahim Benslimane, 2013).

The security proof provided by the Protocol Composition Logic (PCL) and the formal verification provided by the Simple Promela Interpreter (SPIN) both reveal that the proposed scheme in 6LoWPAN could enhance the security functionality with the ability to prevent malicious attacks like replay attacks, man-in-the-middle attacks, impersonation attacks and Sybil attacks, among others (Accettura, Nicola, and Giuseppe Piro, 2014; Le et al., 2012; Rghioui, Anass, Mohammed Bouhorma, and Abderrahim Benslimane, 2013).

The IETF IPv6 over Low power Wireless Personal Area Networks WG (6LOW-PAN WG) has recently standardized 6LoWPAN as an adaptation layer capable of "Internet-connect"-ing multi-hop wireless networks based on low power link-layer communication technologies. Among others, the IEEE802.15.4 physical layer allows a maximum frame length equal to 127 bytes. The IPv6 default minimum MTU size being 1280 bytes, a no-fragmented IPv6 packet might be too large to accommodate in an IEEE802.15.4 frame. Moreover, the overhead created due to the 40-bytes long IPv6 header would waste the limited bandwidth available at the PHY layer. Hence, the adoption of IPv6 on top of a low-power WPAN is not straightforward, and poses strong requirements for the optimization of this adaptation layer. In this regard, 6LoWPAN provides some interesting features that allows IEEE802.15.4-smart devices to be equipped with IPv6 connectivity, thus solving a number of issues, viz., handling network auto-configuration, supporting applications with a huge number of devices (and addresses), facilitating the internet-working with other IP-based infrastructures as proposed in the IoT vision. To elaborate, 6LoWPAN is an intermediate layer between IPv6 and IEEE 802.15.4 MAC levels, which enables link-layer forwarding and fragmentation. It can also compress IPv6 headers and Next Headers, by suppressing redundant information that can be inferred from other layers in the communication stack. Other benefits provided by 6LoWPAN include the auto-configuration of IPv6 addresses, the reduction of routing and management overhead, the adoption of lightweight application protocols (or novel data encoding techniques), and the support for security mechanisms (Accettura, Nicola, and Giuseppe Piro, 2014; Le et al., 2012; Rghioui, Anass, Mohammed Bouhorma, and Abderrahim Benslimane, 2013).

6TiSCH Technology and Security Overview

In order to cope with large multi-hop, resource-constrained and IPv6-compliant Low-power and Lossy Networks (LLNs) based on IEEE802.15.4 radios, novel protocols have been standardized within the IETF. The recent IEEE802.15.4e Time slotted Channel Hopping (TSCH) MAC amendment has been effective in meeting the requirements of industrial applications, by reducing idle listening and improving reliability in the presence of narrow-band interference and multi-path fading. To integrate this new powerful MAC within the framework of IPv6-based LLN protocols, a new IETF working group has been defined, viz. the "IPv6 over the TSCH mode of IEEE 802.15.4e" (6TiSCH) (Accettura, Nicola, and Giuseppe Piro, 2014; Palattella, et al., 2014).

RPL Technology and Security Overview

RPL stands for "Routing Protocol for Low Power and Lossy Networks". Mainly designed keeping the multipoint-to-point communication in mind, it can also support point-to-point and point-to-multipoint communications. RPL topology forms the DODAG (Destination Oriented Directed Acyclic Graph), which contains only one route. The root node, also known as the sink node, initiates the formation of the topology by broadcasting the DIO (DODAG Information Object) messages. The nodes receiving the DIO message select the path connecting the parent to the sender having the rank value calculated with respect to the parents' rank value, among other parameters. The rank value calculation parameters can be decided by the network owner. The nodes continue to broadcast the DIO messages and form

Box 1. 6TiSCH stack

IETF CoAP	
UDP	
IPv6	IETF RPL
IETF 6LoWPAN	
IEEE802.15.4e-2012 MAC	
IEEE 802.15.4-2006PHY	

the tree topology (Accettura, Nicola, and Giuseppe Piro, 2014; Wallgren, Linus, Shahid Raza, and Thiemo Voigt, 2013).

The need for a routing protocol which would be able to manage IoT-compliant multi-hop LLNs has triggered the development of the IETF Routing Over Low power and Lossy networks WG (ROLL WG) . This has led to the advent of the IPv6 Routing Protocol for LLNs (RPL), recently standardized in RFC 6550. RPL is a gradient-based distance vector routing protocol that eases the formation and the management of networks based on short-range and low-power links. It can support a wide variety of link layers, including ones that are constrained, potentially lossy, or typically utilized in conjunction with host or router devices that have very limited resources. More specifically, the RPL has been designed to fulfill the typical requirements of a LLN in building/home automation, industrial environments, and urban applications. Furthermore, it strictly adheres to the IPv6 architecture, in that a gradient is set up and maintained using signaling messages which are carried as options of IPv6 Router Advertisements. In the most typical of RPL scenarios, only a few LLN sinks are capable of coordinating a large set of smart wireless devices through multihop paths. To elaborate, the RPL organizes a network topology like a Directed Acyclic Graph (DAG) which is partitioned into one or more Destination Oriented DAGs (DODAGs), each graph rooted at a LLN sink. A DAG is built based on path costs, which in turn represent a combination of link and node metrics/constraints, like available energy resources, workload, throughput, latency and reliability. Therefore, RPL minimizes the costs incurred to reach any LLN sink (from any device) through an Objective Function, which can be defined in many ways so as to support a very high level of flexibility with respect to the operating conditions. In order to be applicable in a wide range of LLN application domains, the RPL protocol specification has been specifically decoupled from the definitions of objective functions and routing metrics. RPL topologies are constructed using an information dissemination mechanism which enables minimal configuration in the devices and allows them to operate autonomously. To establish paths towards the roots, each RPL node multicasts, periodically and link-locally, DAG Information Option (DIO) messages which carry information about its position with respect to the LLN sink (i.e., the rank), the objective function, IDs, and so forth. To avoid redundancies and to control the signaling overhead, the trickle algorithm triggers a new DIO message for each node, but only when the overall amount of control packets previously sent in the neighbourhood of the said node is small enough. The RPL also allows information to be propagated downwards along the DODAGs, using the Destination Advertisement Object for handling downward routes. Lastly, it manages security at the networking layer. Therefore, a RPL device may indeed operate in three security modes:

1. Unsecured, i.e. employing no security mechanism;
2. Preinstalled, i.e. assuming that a node has pre-installed keys used to protect the RPL messages; and
3. Authenticated, i.e. when nodes retrieve keys from an authentication authority.

Generally speaking, data confidentiality and message integrity are both offered through the AES-128 encryption scheme for pre-installed and authenticated configurations. In this regard, the ROLL WG has been investigating additional countermeasures against threats and attacks that might compromise security at the networking layer.[5]

CONTIKI OS

The Contiki is an open source, easy portable and multitasking operating system used in Wireless Sensor Networks (WSN). Written in C Language, this operating system is suitable for microcontrollers possessing a small amount of memory. It can work on a mere 2 KB of RAM and 40 KB of ROM. One of the most important features of the Contiki is that it can dynamically load applications or services at runtime. Its configurable design has three security modes, viz., confidentiality, authentication and integrity. It has been designed to balance low energy consumption and security, while restricting itself to a small amount of memory. [1][7]

ZIGBEE

ZigBee is one of the global standards of communication protocol that builds on the physical layer and MAC according to definitions of IEEE 802.15.4 for WPAN. The security in ZigBee networks is provided by 128 bit symmetric encryption keys. Its network layer supports both tree and mesh topology.

ZigBee chips are typically integrated with radios and microcontrollers that have between 60 to 256 KB flash memory.

ZigBee IP Specifications

- Security services are at both network (i.e., Network Level Security) and application (i.e., Application Level Security) layers;
- A dedicated entity, namely Zigbee Device Object (ZBO) is deployed, which is in charge of handling security functionalities in a device;

Box 2. ZigBee stack

ZigBee Application Layer
ZigBee Network Layer
IEEE802.15.4-2011 MAC
IEEE802.15-2006PHY

Box 3. ZigBee IP stack

IETF CoAP	
UDP	
IPv6	IETF RPL
IETF 6LoWPAN	
IEEE802.15.4-2011 MAC	
IEEE802.15.4-2006 PHY	

- Two operational modes are used, i.e., high-security and low-security, that differ among them for the length of the key adopted to protect messages;
- Key distribution and joining procedures are handled, in a centralized fashion, by the Trust Center;
- Three different keys are used, viz., the Master Key, which is used to finalize authentication procedures, the Network Key, which is used to protect management messages, and the Link Key, which is exploited to protect the communication between a couple of devices.

RFID

One of the key technologies under IoT is RFID (Radio Frequency Identifier). In fact, the concept of IoT was born when Kevin Ashton of MIT bounded the RFID information with the internet in the year 1999 (Deng 2012; Xiao et al., 2006; Khoo, 2011).

RFID Technology Overview

The Radio Frequency IDentification (RFID) technology is a kind of an automatic diagnosis technology which emerged in 1990s. It realizes non-contact information transmission and recognition by radio-frequency signal through the space coupling. A typical RFID system consists of an RFID tag, a reader and the application systems. It can mark objects uniquely in the form of code data that is preserved in the RFID tag. The tag mainly consists of an antenna, a resonant capacitance and an IC chip. The reader usually contains a radiofrequency signal launch unit, a radio frequency receiving element and a control unit. Additionally, many readers may also possess an additional connection equipment aim to transmit the data it received to another system for further processing or for storage. The antenna is used to generate magnetic flux (Deng 2012; Xiao et al., 2006; Khoo, 2011).

The Sensing Layer

The process of acquiring and recognizing information takes place in the sensing layer, where the RFID system and the WSN are fused. It is called the EPC sensor network, as an innovation for IoT. The outstanding advantage of this network in the application, is that not only can it gain the objects' environment information, but it can also distinguish between different objects precisely. It may also expand the RFID system's scope of recognition: the smart node technology that is the integrated RFID reader and the WSN node. It can gather the information about the objects' environment precisely, and determine the objects' exhaustive position. As the anti-jamming capacity of the RFID is not high, and as the effective reading distance of a passive RFID technology is

less than 10 m, an EPC sensor network can enable the effective identification range to 100 m, while also expanding the scope of application of the RFID technology thereby. The primary applications of the RFID technology in the EPC global "IoT" system are the EPC encoding, EPC RFID systems and the EPC information network system, where the EPC encoding technology is used in the RFID tags. The encoding of IoT should follow the "one object with

only one code" principle, so as to not only manage every object but also to track them at any time vis-a-vis realizing the classified queries, statistical applications and e-commerce according to the specific categories and information it contains regading the objects . The EPC encoding technology satisfies these requirements, where the EPC RFID system is the module that collects the codes automatically, whereas the EPC information network system formed by the

local and global Internet network is the module that conducts the information management and flow (Deng 2012; Xiao et al., 2006; Khoo, 2011).

Information Acquisition

The EPC sensor network is used in the sensing layer. This fusion technology may be divided into 4 kinds: a. RFID tags with sensors, b. RFID tags with WSN nodes, c. RFID readers and WSM nodes and d. RFID readers and WSN base stations. The first two kinds are responsible for the manufacture and design of RFID tags, while the technical costs are higher in the fourth way. The RFID reader and the WSN node integrated to a smart node,

are adopted in this structure. The smart node can both read EPC tags data and gather objects' surrounding information completely. This EPC sensor network can be realized easily, and it can highlight the prominent characteristics of the system after the fusion (Deng 2012; Xiao et al., 2006; Khoo, 2011).

RFID Security

There are four main hidden impediments involved with RFID information security, namely the RFID tag information security, the wireless communication information security, the network transmission information security, information storage and processing security.

1.   To enhance the RFID tag information security, the data shield should be strengthened to make the related data forgery-proof.
2.   With respect to the wireless communication security, the research on the communication protocol strategy and network communication confirmation strategy should be strengthened, for example, the exclusive communication protocol should realize a higher security rank effectively, while the related confirmation mechanism established may enforce the communication security.
3.   The control and information encryption strategy should also be improved to enhance the security in the network-level.
4.   The application of the advanced cloud computation technology in the IoT, helped enhancing the information storage and processing security (Deng 2012; Xiao et al., 2006; Khoo, 2011).

CONCLUSION

IoT connected objects with embedded sensors, connected vehicles, health monitoring equipments, and other examples can generate an enormous amount of data, some of which may constitute personal data. There are many significant issues, related to providing control to the users on the distribution of their data through IoT connections have already been discussed. Adequate mechanisms should be deployed to control the flow of data and to enforce policies implementing existing regulations and users' preferences. These mechanisms should be flexible and scalable in order to support the wide range of technologies used in IoT infrastructure.

Middleware services are a novel approach that support the implementation, maintenance, and operation of IoT-based applications through provision of a platform that:

1.   Shields hardware heterogeneity in sensor networks;
2.   Coordinates and distributes activities to sensor nodes;
3.   Performs data filtering, aggregation and storage; and
4.   Significantly enhances the development of diverse applications (Mhlaba, Admire, and Muthoni Masinde, 2015).

With the advent of IoT, in the near future, most of our daily activities will eventually be dependent more and more on technology. Therefore, since the technology is evolving fast, the consumers should also be cognizant of how this issue applies to their daily life for their own security. However, along with security, two more aspects i.e., Privacy and Trust also play a significant role towards this issue.

Privacy issues are particularly relevant in healthcare, and there are many innovative healthcare applications that fall within the realm of IoT. We may cite, among others, the tracking of medical equipment in a hospital, the monitoring of vital statistics for patients at home or in an assisted living facility in this regard. In this scenario, it is essential to verify device ownership and the owner's identity while also decoupling the device from the owner. Shadowing is a mechanism that has been proposed to achieve this objective. Digital shadows enable the users' objects to act on their behalf, storing a virtual identity that contains information about their attributes (Securing the Internet of Things: A Proposed Framework, n.d.; Medaglia, Carlo Maria, and Alexandru Serbanati, 2010; Kozlov, Denis, Jari Veijalainen, and Yasir Ali, 2012).

Identity management in IoT may offer new opportunities to increase security by combining diverse authentication methods for humans and machines. For example, bio-identification combined with an object within the personal network might be used to open a door (Securing the Internet of Things: A Proposed Framework, n.d.).

Trust, on the other hand is an abstract concept that can shield concrete structure, and can provide uniform decision-making for heterogeneous and multi-domain IoT (Lize, Gu, Wang Jingpei, and Sun Bin, 2014).

Lastly, with all said and done, the ultimate responsibility rests with us to come up with a solution to secure the IoT network as efficiently and as economically as possible, to make the IoT functional and accessible to the masses.

REFERENCES

Accettura, N., & Piro, G. (2014). Optimal and secure protocols in the IETF 6TiSCH communication stack. *Industrial Electronics (ISIE), 2014 IEEE 23rd International Symposium on*. IEEE.

Alam, S., & Mohammad, M. R. (2011). Chowdhury, and Josef Noll. "Interoperability of security-enabled internet of things. *Wireless Personal Communications*, *61*(3), 567–586. doi:10.1007/s11277-011-0384-6

Babar, S. (2010). *Proposed security model and threat taxonomy for the internet of things (IoT). In Recent Trends in Network Security and Applications* (pp. 420–429). Springer Berlin Heidelberg.

Barnaghi, P., Wang, W., Henson, C., & Taylor, K. (2012). Semantics for the Internet of Things: Early progress and back to the future. *International Journal on Semantic Web and Information Systems*, *8*(1), 1–21. doi:10.4018/jswis.2012010101

Bormann, Carsten, Ersue, & Keranen. (2014). Terminology for Constrained-Node Networks. No. RFC 7228.

Casado, L., & Tsigas, P. (2009). *Contikisec: A secure network layer for wireless sensor networks under the contiki operating system. In Identity and Privacy in the Internet Age* (pp. 133–147). Springer Berlin Heidelberg.

Deng, N. (2012). RFID Technology and Network Construction in the Internet of Things. *Computer Science & Service System (CSSS), 2012 International Conference on*. IEEE.

Douceur, J. R. (2002). *The sybil attack. In Peer-to-peer Systems* (pp. 251–260). Springer Berlin Heidelberg. doi:10.1007/3-540-45748-8_24

Garcia-Morchon. (2013). *Security Considerations in the IP-based Internet of Things*. Academic Press.

Heer, T., Garcia-Morchon, O., Hummen, R., Keoh, S. L., Kumar, S. S., & Wehrle, K. (2011). Security Challenges in the IP-based Internet of Things. *Wireless Personal Communications*, *61*(3), 527–542. doi:10.1007/s11277-011-0385-5

Hu, Perrig, & Johnson. (2003). Packet leashes: a defense against wormhole attacks in wireless networks. *INFOCOM 2003. Twenty-Second Annual Joint Conference of the IEEE Computer and Communications. IEEE Societies* (Vol. 3). IEEE. doi:10.1109/ICACT.2006.206151

Karlof, C., & Wagner, D. (2003). Secure routing in wireless sensor networks: Attacks and countermeasures. *Ad Hoc Networks*, *1*(2), 293–315. doi:10.1016/S1570-8705(03)00008-8

Kelly, Tebje, Suryadevara, & Mukhopadhyay. (2013). Towards the implementation of IoT for environmental condition monitoring in homes. *IEEE Sensors Journal*, *13*(10), 3846–3853.

Khoo, B. (2011). RFID as an enabler of the internet of things: issues of security and privacy. *Internet of Things (iThings/CPSCom), 2011 International Conference on and 4th International Conference on Cyber, Physical and Social Computing*. IEEE. doi:10.1109/ICT4M.2013.6518912

Kozlov, D., Veijalainen, J., & Ali, Y. (2012). Security and privacy threats in IoT architectures. *Proceedings of the 7th International Conference on Body Area Networks*. ICST (Institute for Computer Sciences, Social-Informatics and Telecommunications Engineering).

Le, A., Loo, J., Lasebae, A., Aiash, M., & Luo, Y. (2012). 6LoWPAN: A study on QoS security threats and countermeasures using intrusion detection system approach. *International Journal of Communication Systems*, *25*(9), 1189–1212. doi:10.1002/dac.2356

Lize, G., Jingpei, W., & Bin, S. (2014). Trust management mechanism for Internet of Things. *Communications, China*, *11*(2), 148–156. doi:10.1109/CC.2014.6821746

Mayzaud, A. (2014). *A study of rpl dodag version attacks. In Monitoring and Securing Virtualized Networks and Services* (pp. 92–104). Springer Berlin Heidelberg.

Medaglia, C. M., & Serbanati, A. (2010). *An overview of privacy and security issues in the internet of things. In The Internet of Things* (pp. 389–395). Springer New York.

Mhlaba, A., & Masinde, M. (2015). Implementation of middleware for Internet of Things in asset tracking applications: In-lining approach. *Industrial Informatics (INDIN), 2015 IEEE 13th International Conference on*. IEEE. doi:10.1109/EMTC.2014.6996650

Newsome, J. (2004). The sybil attack in sensor networks: analysis & defenses.*Proceedings of the 3rd international symposium on Information processing in sensor networks*. ACM. doi:10.1145/984622.984660

Ngai, Liu, & Lyu. (2006). On the intruder detection for sinkhole attack in wireless sensor networks. *Communications, 2006. ICC'06. IEEE International Conference on* (Vol. 8). IEEE.

Palattella, M. R. (2014). *6TiSCH Wireless Industrial Networks: Determinism Meets IPv6. In Internet of Things* (pp. 111–141). Springer International Publishing.

Park, J., Shin, S., & Kang, N. (2013). Mutual Authentication and Key Agreement Scheme between Lightweight Devices in Internet of Things. *The Journal of Korean Institute of Communications and Information Sciences*, *38*(9), 707–714. doi:10.7840/kics.2013.38B.9.707

Pathan, A.-S. K., Lee, H.-W., & Hong, C. S. (2006). Security in wireless sensor networks: issues and challenges. *ICACT 2006. The 8th International Conference* (Vol. 2). IEEE.

Piro, G., Boggia, G., & Grieco, L. A. (2014). A standard compliant security framework for ieee 802.15. 4 networks. *Internet of Things (WF-IoT),2014IEEE World Forum on*. IEEE.

Pongle, P., & Chavan, G. (2015). A survey: Attacks on RPL and 6LoWPAN in IoT. *Pervasive Computing (ICPC),2015International Conference on*. IEEE. doi:10.1109/PERVASIVE.2015.7087034

Preiss, T. (2014). Implementing dynamic address changes in contikios. *Information Society (i-Society), 2014 International Conference on*. IEEE.

Rghioui, A., Bouhorma, M., & Benslimane, A. (2013). Analytical study of security aspects in 6LoWPAN networks. *Information and Communication Technology for the Muslim World (ICT4M), 20135th International Conference on*. IEEE.

Sajjad, S. M., & Yousaf, M. (2014). Security analysis of IEEE 802.15. 4 MAC in the context of Internet of Things (IoT). *Information Assurance and Cyber Security (CIACS), 2014Conference on*. IEEE.

Savola, R. M., Abie, H., & Sihvonen, M. (2012). Towards metrics-driven adaptive security management in e-health IoT applications. *Proceedings of the 7th International Conference on Body Area Networks*. ICST (Institute for Computer Sciences, Social-Informatics and Telecommunications Engineering). doi:10.4108/icst.bodynets.2012.250241

Sciancalepore, S. (2014). On securing IEEE 802.15. 4 networks through a standard compliant framework.*Euro Med Telco Conference (EMTC)*. IEEE.

Securing the Internet of Things. A Proposed Framework. (n.d.). Retrieved January 2, 2015, from http://www.cisco.com/web/about/security/intelligence/iot_framework.html#1

Ukil, A., Sen, J., & Koilakonda, S. (2011). Embedded security for Internet of Things. Emerging Trends and Applications in Computer Science (NCETACS), 2011 2nd National Conference on. IEEE.

Wallgren, L., Raza, S., & Voigt, T. (2013). Routing Attacks and Countermeasures in the RPL-based Internet of Things. *International Journal of Distributed Sensor Networks*.

Weber, R. H. (2010). Internet of Things–New security and privacy challenges. *Computer Law & Security Report, 26*(1), 23–30. doi:10.1016/j.clsr.2009.11.008

Xiao, Y. (2006). Security and privacy in RFID and applications in telemedicine. *Communications Magazine, IEEE, 44*(4), 64–72. doi:10.1109/MCOM.2006.1632651

Yu, B., & Xiao, B. (2006). Detecting selective forwarding attacks in wireless sensor networks. *Parallel and Distributed Processing Symposium, 2006. IPDPS 2006. 20th International*. IEEE.

Zargar, S. T., Joshi, J., & Tipper, D. (2013). A survey of defense mechanisms against distributed denial of service (DDoS) flooding attacks. *IEEE Communications Surveys and Tutorials, 15*(4), 2046–2069. doi:10.1109/SURV.2013.031413.00127

Chapter 4
Security in Application Layer Protocols of IoT:
Threats and Attacks

Jasmine Norman
VIT University, India

Paul Joseph
VIT University, India

ABSTRACT

IoT is an acronym for Internet of Things. It is the revolutionary area that transforms the digital world into a device world. IoT helps in not only fulfilling human requirements, but also they act as a communication medium between humans and electronic devices. The birth of IoT started in early 2000s, but since then, it is an amazing fact that now at least 65% of devices are connected with IoT technology with the term "smart" in their prefix and it would be up by 30% at the end of 2016 (Gartner Survey, 2015). Since then, many security issues were raised, and have been risen all these years due to the flaws in that devices. This made attackers to take advantage over that devices and started controlling them. This chapter studies IoT application layer protocols, services offered and gives an idea of existing cyber attacks and threat. In addition, the authors give the possible attacks on the IoT devices, in particular at application layer, and give the necessary precautions to overcome the cyber attacks both for consumers and vendors.

DOI: 10.4018/978-1-5225-2296-6.ch004

INTRODUCTION

The Internet of Things is an embedded technology where the physical objects interact with each other and provide a connected environment. These physical objects form a smart atmosphere wherein they offer flexible intelligent services. This smart atmosphere has the potential to affect every domain and the quality of life of individuals. The steadily expanding organizing abilities of devices and regular gadgets utilized as a part of the home, office hardware, versatile and wearable innovations, vehicles, whole industrial facilities and supply chains, and even urban foundation, open up a tremendous playing field of chances for business change and consumer loyalty. Kevin Ashton (1999) has found "The Internet of Things or IoT has a potential to change the world, pretty much as the Internet did. Possibly all the more so". The main objective of this chapter is to uncover the cyber-attacks, cyber threats at the application layer and provide the control mechanism or guidelines to combat cyber-attacks, especially in the application layer.

IoT is as of now incorporated over a few ranges where innovation reception is accelerating. The key ranges of driving IoT mix are:

- Smart life
- Health care
- Smart versatility
- Smart city
- Smart producing
- Machine
- Automobile industry

Amidst all promises, IoT has also emerged as the internet of insecurity things. IoT has complicated the communication mode by an indirect individual to individual communication through machines which makes it more vulnerable to different kind of attacks. Personal communication and business data transfer through cloud serve as a door for attackers. At the present scenario, the number of physical objects or devices connected to the internet outnumbers the people connected to the internet. According to a recent survey, 70 percent of these devices are vulnerable. The attackers use sophisticated mechanisms to exploit the vulnerabilities. Apart from using the public networks, they also use smart cars, phones, refrigerators and any smart object to launch the attack. While the IoT has entered everyday life to an ever increasing extent, security dangers relating to IoT are developing and evolving quickly.

BACKGROUND

Latest usage of IoT in automobile zone changed the user and the programmer's perception. Automobiles with IoT are associated through versatile remotes through the web, which can be handled by the remotes to change atmospheric conditions, for breaking framework and to control. Because of this, Fiat (1.5 lakh cars) and some different companies have reviewed their creative automobiles on account of flaws in their product. Programmers assaulted those with packet flooding component and took control of the climatic instrument control. IoT in refrigerators made attackers set the temperatures at adverse conditions and make them shaky, which affected the compressor. IoT in smart TVs opened an entryway broadly for assailants to introduce malware and download movies or tunes from their sellers. Each of these attacks is done through system associated devices uniquely through the application layer of the devices. Recently every cyber-attack that happened either in IoT or ordinary systems was executed through application layer as this layer collaborates with the both sides. In this chapter, the authors describe the application layer protocols and its design, its vulnerabilities and cyber-attacks through this layer. To comprehend digital assaults in IoT, one must require foundation information of the application layer, its protocols, communication mode, services offered and the attack mediums.

PROTOCOLS AND SERVICES OFFERED IN IOT:

IoT devices are having either 3 layered protocols or multiprotocol architecture based on its usage. But the common layer offered in every IoT device is the Application layer- the layer residing above all the remaining layers. The application layer helps users to interact with the IoT devices either through the mobile app or through a web interface. It is the layer through which the user sends commands to the device and receives signals from the device. It is also the layer through which all the cyber-attacks and cyber threats happen in IoT devices. According to Karagiannis (2015), so far no standard protocol or standard interface is being implemented in the application layer. Research by Eldridge & Lyman (2015), Aziz (2016) states that for the past two decades, four protocols have been widely used in the application layer based on four categories:

1. Device to Device communication (D-D)
2. Device to server communication (D-S)
3. Server to device communication (S-D)
4. Server to server communication (S-S)

Based on the categories above, the following protocols are widely used:

1. MQTT (D2S)
2. XMPP (D2S)
3. DDS (D2D)
4. REST/HTTP (S2S)

The following section briefs each protocol with the vulnerabilities in them.

1. MQTT

MQTT stands for MQ telemetry transport and is a machine to machine IoT protocol, designed for lightweight publishing and subscribing messaging transport that is advantageous in remote location. It is designed based on the hub and spoke architecture and also resembles client-server model in TCP connections. In this, each and every sensor acts as a client and connects to a server, also called as a broker (broker is a server that routes published messages to subscribers /sensors). It is a message oriented protocol in which each and every message is made into fragments of 2 bytes each and allows clients to have N*-N* (many-many) communication technique. MQTT frame: The maximum size is four octets and the format is given in Figure 1.

Figure 1. Frame format for MQ telemetry transport protocol

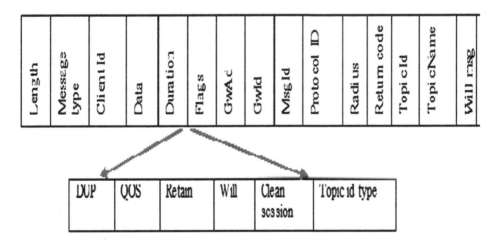

Disadvantages:
- ◦ Message loss
- ◦ Duplication of Message
- ◦ Performance degradation due to QOS
- ◦ DNS poisoning due to transmission through TCP/IP through gateways or hubs
- ◦ Redundancy of data results in bandwidth wastage, as bandwidth plays vital role in IoT devices
- ◦ Cannot be trusted due to possible loss of the message.
- ◦ As it uses four major control packets like CONNECT, PUBLISH, SUBSCRIBE, DISCONNECT, if an attacker sends packet flood with CONNECT AND DISCONNECT control packet, it might result in an overhead of IoT device and would be vulnerable.

2. XMPP

According to XMPP (2016), XMPP stands for extensible messaging and presence protocol, developed for instant messaging to connect people through text messages initially. It also runs on TCP stack and uses an XML text format. It supports both publish-subscribe and request-response architecture such that it is most useful for nearer communications. In XMPP architecture, a requesting device (client) with a unique name communicates with another client with a solitary name through an affiliated server. Each and every client/device implements the client form (request) of the protocol, where the server provides the routing capability. If different servers are to be contacted, then with the help of gateways, they are connected. XMPP is elongated to include publish-subscribe systems, making it a good choice for information that is handed to a central server and then distributed to numerous IoT devices at once. It is decentralized, and authentication can be built in by using a centralized XMPP server. XMPP protocol is explained in Figure 2 followed by the disadvantages.

Disadvantages:
- ◦ As it allows multiple logins for a user, username enumeration is possible.
- ◦ Due to multiple logins, the account lockout mechanism is not provided in this protocol, in which there is a chance of occurrence of dictionary and brute force attacks followed by random chosen number attack.
- ◦ As it uses XML messages, xml messages cause additional overhead due to a lot of headers and tags.

Figure 2. XMPP protocol overview

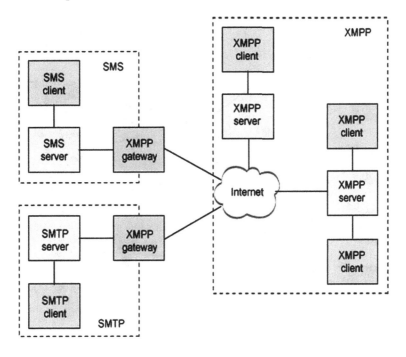

- ◦ In addition, XML overhead causes IoT device more power consumable which is the most drawback of IoT.
- ◦ No end- end encryption used while contacting servers or other devices.
- ◦ Doesn't support QoS, which is a real deal-breaker for applications.

3. DDS

DDS is an acronym for Data Distribution service for real-time systems. According to Esposito (n.d), it is a device to device bus communication, in which data-bus controls updates and services for the devices in the network. It defines two sublayers: publish- subscribe and data-local reconstruction sublayers. The publish –subscribe ensures the responsibility of the message reaching to the subscribers while the second is arbitrary and allows a simple integration of DDS in the application layer. Publisher layer is engaged for sensory data dispensation. Data writer collaborates with the publishers to agree to the data and changes to be sent to the subscribers. It supports four protocols, namely TCP/IP, RTPS/UDP, UDP/IP, multicast and supports numerous QoS services. The overview of DDS protocol is shown in Figure 3.

Figure 3. An overview of Data Distribution Service protocol

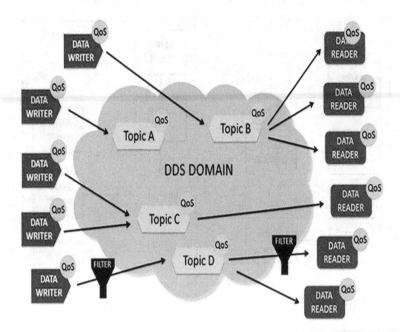

Limitations:

- Since it uses IP multicast, this architecture is also limited to known de-plorability and scalability limits.
- DDS violates the "stateless" perspective of IP protocols.
- IP multicasting breaks down to filter approaching packets beyond a few multicast groups, such that DDS does not scale to a large number of groups
- Since IP multicast has limitations for the regulatory mechanism for traf-fic pool, DDS could not work effectively with IP multicast.
- DDS is vulnerable to sudden traffic bursts, which causes overhead and compromises with the attacker.
- Vast services of QoS are used and so latency is very less in DDS (QoS ∝ Latency)
- Usage of Bus communication helps only through asymmetric and serial transmission of requests and responses.
- Implementation of DDS is expensive in common.

4. REST/HTTP

Castellani (2010) survey defines REST as for Representational State transfer and HTTP stands for hypertext transfer protocol. REST is a stateless, client-server, cacheable transmission protocol designed for network application IoT's. It uses the built-in accept header of HTTP (GET, POST, PUT, DELETE) to indicate the format of the data that it contains. The content type can be XML or JSON (JavaScript Object Notation) and confide in the HTTP server and its disposition. REST is by then a significant part of the IoT device because it is backed by all the monetary M2M cloud platforms. Furthermore, it can carry out in a smartphone and smart handheld appliances easily because it only feels a necessity for an HTTP library which is accessible for all the Operating Systems (OS) disposal. For security reasons, it uses HTTPS with SSL/TLS certificates for authentication. Since it doesn't use QoS, high latency is achieved. IoT and the possible vulnerabilities through these devices are explained in Figure 4.

Disadvantages:
- ◦ Attackers have already proved that the SSL certificate is vulnerable.
- ◦ Since REST uses XML type data, it results in traffic overload and traffic congestion.
- ◦ Java script is the best platform for the attackers to attack any device through flash programming or flash advertisements.
- ◦ It is continuously in contact with the servers, which helps an attacker to attack while he checks and monitor the network traffic.
- ◦ Finally, http/rest is vulnerable to DNS poison servers of which get and post methods can be injected with phishing or malware code.

According to the survey of OWASP (2015), it is obvious that these protocols are not sufficient in addressing the challenges posed by IoT. Apart from the protocol services and limitations, vulnerabilities through various mediums are given in Figure 5.

CYBER ATTACKS AT THE APPLICATION LAYER

There have been constant warnings from security experts about cyber threats for years. Even though in the 2014 Black Hat conference, the main focus was on IoT threats, there is negligible attention paid as the users have not understood the consequences.

Figure 4. Possible vulnerabilities through various mediums

Medium	Vulnerabilities
Device Memory	Clear content usernames Clear content passwords Outsider qualifications Encryption keys
Device Interfaces	Firmware extraction Privilege escalation Reset to uncertain state Evacuation of capacity media Physical Tamper resistance Gadget Serial number exposure
Device Web Interface	SQL injection Cross-site scripting Cross-site Request Forgery Username list Frail passwords Account lockout Known default credentials
Device Firmware	Hardcoded credentials Sensitive Data/URL exposure Encryption keys (Symmetric, Asymmetric) Firmware rendition show and/or last overhaul date Backdoor accounts Defenceless services (web, ssh, tftp)
Device Network Services	Administrator/Client command line interface Injection, DoS Decoded Services Buffer Overflow, DDoS Device Firmware OTA update block Replay assault
Local Data Storage	Unencrypted information Information encrypted with known keys Lack of trustworthiness checks Use of static same encryption/decryption key
Cloud Web Interface	SQL injection Cross-site scripting, CS Request Forgery Username enumeration, Weak passwords Account lockout Vulnerable password recovery mechanism Second-factor/OTP authentication
Mobile Application	Implicitly trusted by device or cloud Account lockout, fragile password Known default credentials Delphic data repository Transport encryption Diffident password recovery mechanism Two-factor authentication
Authentication/Authorization	Authentication/Authorization related values (session key, token, cookie, etc.) Reusing of a session key, token, etc. Device to device authentication (D-D) Device to mobile authentication (D-M) Device to cloud authentication (D-C) Mobile to cloud authentication (M-C) Web application to cloud authentication Lack of dynamic authentication
Privacy	User data exposure User/device location disclosure Differential privacy

Figure 5. Threats/attacks/vulnerabilities in their reality

Vulnerabilities	Meaning
Username Enumeration	To collect a set of legitimate usernames by associating with the authentication mechanism
Weak Passwords	Not following the standard password mechanism like the combination of Capital and lower alphabets, numbers and special symbols.
Account Lockout	Ability to keep sending confirmation endeavours after 3 - 5 fizzled login endeavours
Two-factor Authentication	Lack of two-factor confirmation systems, for example, a security token or finger capture mark.
Denial of Service	Service can be assaulted in a way that refuses assistance to that administration or the whole device.

This section covers the prominent cyber-attacks at the application level layer.

1. Botnet/ Thingbots
2. Man in the Middle attacks
3. Denial of Service
4. Identity Theft attack
5. DNS Flood
6. HTTP Flood.
7. Attacks over Wireless Connectivity.
8. Cloud Attacks
9. Malware Attacks

1. Botnet Attacks

A botnet is a system of frameworks joined together for remotely taking control and for disseminating malware. Controlled by botnet administrators by means of Command-and-Control-Servers (C&C Server), they are utilized by hoodlums on a greater scale for some things: taking private data, misusing the internet managing an account information, DDoS-assaults or for spam and phishing messages.

Botnets and in addition Thingbots comprise of a wide range of gadgets, all associated with each other – from PCs, portable workstations, cell phones and tablets to now additionally those "shrewd" devices. These things have two fundamental attributes in like manner: they are web-empowered and they can exchange information consequently by means of a system. Hostile to spam innovation can spot pretty dependable on the off chance that one machine sends a huge number of comparative messages, yet it's a great deal harder to spot if those messages are being sent from different devices that are a piece of a botnet. They all have one objective: sending a huge number of email solicitations to an objective with the expectation that the stage crashes while attempting to adapt to the massive measure of solicitations.

2. Man in the Middle Attacks

It is the attack in which the aggressor or interloper hopes to interfere with the interchanges between the two trusted frameworks or gadgets. It is very unsafe on the grounds that both the gatherings trust that their correspondence is reliable, however out of sight the assailant gets all the first message and begins a discussion with the gatherings as though he is a true blue gathering. This sort of assault is discovered regularly in Smart Tv's, smart vehicles which are worked on some working frameworks with web availability empowered. This attack mainly questions the integrity of the communication and integrity of the communicator parties.

3. Denial of Service

The name itself uncovers of making inaccessibility of asset to a real gathering with the expectation of criminal personality. It is additionally resort to as smokescreen for contrasting malignant exercises and to bring down the secure applications. DoS and DDoS are the same sort of assaults yet DoS is the assault from single web association with surge the objective with fake solicitations, though DDoS is the assault from gathering of tainted frameworks commonly a botnet and surge the solicitation to such an extent that the gadget can't hold every one of the solicitations on the double, and gets to be depleted with its assets and open to aggressor. When all is said in done, DoS assaults are measured in term of Request per second(RPS). In the event that an IoT gadget gets more than 20rps, then it no additionally withstanding to assaults.

4. Identity Theft Attack

This is the most common attack happen to every smart-user because of their negligent or inappropriate behaviour/careless safekeeping of interconnected devices.

The identity theft concentrates either on IoT device or IoT user to get information regarding either device id, device ip, device firmware version, device credentials etc. or information regarding user name, user account details, the user associated smart appliances etc. Generally, this common cyber-attack is performed on smart watches, smart apps for IoT devices in mobile etc. This attack could lead into further more aggressive like stealing from bank accounts associated, bypassing authentications, permanent blocking of that user against his own device.

5. DNS Flood

DNS flood is a sort of Distributed Denial of Service (DDoS) assault in which the assailant targets one or more Domain Name System (DNS) servers having a place with a given zone, endeavouring to hamper determination of asset records of that zone and its sub-zones. In a DNS flood assault, the guilty party tries to overbear a given DNS server (or servers) with obviously substantial activity, overpowering server assets and obstructing the servers' capacity to guide honest to goodness solicitations to zone assets.

DNS surge assault is viewed as a variation of the UDP surge assault, since DNS servers depend on the UDP convention for name determination, and is a Layer 3 assault. With UDP-based queries (dissimilar to TCP inquiries), a full circuit is never settled, and subsequently caricaturing is all the more effectively refined. The DNS flood attack is shown in Figure 6.

6. HTTP Flood

HTTP flood is a sort of Distributed Denial of Service (DDoS) assault in which the assailant abuses apparently legitimate HTTP GET or POST applications to attack a web server or application. HTTP surge assaults are volumetric assaults, frequently utilizing a botnet "zombie armed force"— a gathering of Internet-associated PCs, each of which has been perniciously assumed control, for the most part with the help of malware like Trojan Horses.

A refined Layer attack, HTTP floods doesn't utilize deformed packets, spoofing or reflection systems, but depend upon less transmission amplitude than different attacks to cut down the focused on hand or server. Accordingly, they request more top to bottom comprehension about the focused on hand or application, and every assault must be exceptionally made to be compelling. This makes HTTP flood assaults altogether harder to recognize and block.

Figure 6. Incapsula mitigates a massive DNS flood, peaking at over 25 million packets per second Source: Incapsula, 2016

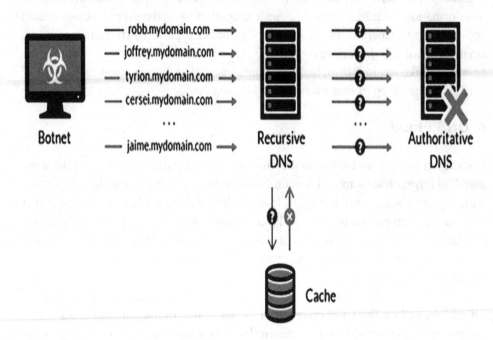

In addition to the general cyber-attacks, the accompanying is the application layer attacks with examples:

- DoS attacks (ping of death, teardrop)
- DDoS assaults (DNS surge)
- HTTP Floods (HTTP get, HTTP post).
- Slow assaults (Slow Loris or Rudy).
- DNS Query flood assault

7. Attacks over Wi-Fi/Ethernet IEEE802.11

Now a day, each and every IoT device is equipped either with internal Bluetooth or wifi hardware and associated with device id along with IP. Since IPV6 supports trillions of billions of ip addresses, every IoT device is assigned with IPV6 address. Though wifi connection supports more than four security schemes, the common security scheme used is either WPA or WPA2. Of course, in reality, both of them are vulnerable to attackers and in special WPA and WPS are most vulnerable to cyber attackers. These devices through the wifi connect to the internet either directly or by either gateways and hubs and communicate to the remote server. Research according to Barcena and Ballano (2015), shows that there are two common modes for smart home devices under this category:

1. Cloud polling (smart device is in continuous communication with the cloud server, waits for commands and updates at regular intervals).
    -MITM attack-ARP protocol poisoning-intercepting HTTPS connection
2. Direct connection (Some devices use explicit connections to disseminate with a hub in the homogeneous network). For example, a device/mobile app may be able to examine the regional network for visible devices and discover them by monitoring every internet protocol address for an explicit port. Another mechanism is to use the Simple Service Discovery Protocol/SSDP --Universal Plug and Play /UPNP protocol to identify the devices.

8. Cloud Attacks

Survey according to Barcena and Ballano (2015), most of the devices are attached to cloud servers at the back end for continuous monitoring. The most vulnerable condition is cloud doesn't provide a stronger password, rather than it allows 4digit pin, which can be broken through a brute force attack or randomly chosen number attack. It only allows users to communicate with the server either by means of a mobile application directly or by means of web application interfaces. The security weakness and the corresponding attack vectors with their severity is given in the Figure 7.

Secondly, no alternate authorization like OTP (one-time password) for authentication and very poor methods for password recovery mechanism. Normal attacks which are possible on cloud servers are also possible on IoT cloud servers to a great extent. Since smart cities, smart home or eco appliances rely on cloud servers, the prominence for the cloud attacks is utmost notable. The recent cloud attacks like CelebGate, JPMorgan, Amazon cloud are added advantages for enthusiastic attackers.

9. Malware Attacks

Malware is the program code specially injected with malicious and suspicious instructions to destroy the device or to take control over the device. This attack is possible through a USB device as some of the manufacturers are providing IoT

Figure 7. Attack vector and impact of cloud IoT
Source: OWASP, 2016; Daniel, 2015

Threat Agents	Attack vectors	Security Weakness		Technical impacts	Business impacts
Application Specific	Exploitability Average	Prevalence common	Detectability easy	Impact severe	Application/business specific
Consider any one who has access to internet	Attacker uses multiple vectors like insufficient authentication, lack of transport encryption and account enumeration to access data or control over cloud. Attack will most come from internet	An insecure cloud interface is present when easy to guess credentials that are used or account enumeration is possible. Insecure cloud interfaces are easy to discover by simple reviewing the connection to cloud interface and identifying if SSL is in use or by using password reset mechanism to identify valid accounts which can lead to account enumeration		Insecure cloud interface leads to compromise of user data and control over the device	Data could be stolen or modified and control over the devices are assumed. Could the business harm customers or harm its brand?

with USB hubs and in cyber-attack fashion, this malware can be injected directly either into a device or can be injected into a web server through which the device and application sends and receive commands. Malware can be seen often in smart Tv's, smart refrigerators which work on some operating systems. Recent prototype ransomware malware poses organisations and business individuals a very big challenge. Ransomware is one of the sophisticated malware code ever written, which brought millions of dollars loss, when injected into IoT devices- take full control of them, encrypt all the data and apply encrypted update to the IoT firmware.

PREVENTION OF CYBER-ATTACKS IN IOT

Being the main attack front for the attackers, the application layer security should be the major concern when designing IoT applications. Security and privacy issues should be addressed in each phase of the software development life cycle. IoT applications should have security incorporated in the design, analysis, implementation and testing phases. After the release, if vulnerabilities are discovered, it will prove to be very expensive for the business. So in designing strategies and policies to cope up is important. Anticipating cyber threats by using forensic tools help to counter the attacks. By following best practices and standards the attacks can be minimized. The organization risk assessment and management should be redefined to match the emerging threats. Security should be an integral part of the application not as an added feature. Finally, there are tools available such as IBM Security AppScan and Cisco IoT System Security which help in combating the threats and vulnerabilities.

On a whole, the following precautions can make IoT devices more secure and less prone to attackers.

- Implementing second-factor authorization either like OTP or fingerprint scan etc.
- Account lockout mechanism must be implemented if more than 3sucessive login fails.
- Vendors must urge their customers to change the default four-digit pin code/passcode.
- Communication between server and devices must be in encrypted form of at least lightweight cryptography like ECC (Elliptical Curve Cryptography)
- Manufacturers must design their chips such that reverse engineering is impossible for attackers.

FUTURE RESEARCH DIRECTIONS

So far we have seen the protocols, their services, attacker medium and different cyber-attacks in IoT devices. Though the roots of IoT devices have been found in 1998, now it became a physical device that communicates with other devices, servers and as well as human beings also. Right from the birth of IoT devices, development, security implementation and cyber-attacks are equally raised. With new security and new protocols, vendors have been targeting consumers about their device's security. The same way the new cyber-attacks are happening more and more. So far, when a person observes the cyber-attacks apart from physical attacks, 90% of them are done through the vulnerabilities present in protocols, services and communication mediums. In a nutshell, the application layer acts as an interface to access devices as well as it acts as a gateway to cyber attackers to attack the device. Though different protocols for different layers are there, the authors have concentrated on application layer itself as it acts a medium for both communication and present vulnerabilities. Instead of suggesting new protocols with security, if existing protocols are modified with better security mechanisms, it will make a good impact on the applications and thus will support the business. Many security reports, antivirus vendors, and business advisors state that the rise of IoT devices will be multiplied more in the coming years and there is high need of implementing complex low powered security mechanisms in these devices. The researchers should concentrate on the points listed below.

1. Light weight data protection algorithms
2. Tamper resistant devices
3. Antivirus for tiny devices
4. Open Source Tools such as CISCO IoT system security
5. Address the protocol vulnerabilities
6. Standardize protocols

CONCLUSION

This chapter discussed the application layer protocols, threats and cyber-attacks. The security and privacy concerns of IoT are really challenging as the physical devices are tamper resistant, which increases the vulnerability at many points. Since these devices are very small, the security controls need to be reinvented. Data protection techniques and malware detection and prevention methods should be developed for the tiny devices. In an alarming note, a survey by Gartner predicts 25% of cyber-attacks will involve the internet of things (IoT) by 2020. Unfortunately, there is no match in the security supplies to face the demand. Unless the research community contributes to the success of the digital world, the consequences will be very severe. It will not end with only data theft, but will affect the very presence of human beings.

REFERENCES

Atzori, L., Iera, A., Morabito, G., Esposito, C., Khan, R., Khan, S. U. S., & Ny, O. B. et al. (2016). The Internet of Things the Internet of Things. *Computer Networks*, *3*(257521), 678–683. doi:10.5480/1536-5026-34.1.63

Barcena, M. B., & Wueest, C. (2015, March). *Insecurity in the Internet of Things.* Symantec Corporation. Retrieved from https://www.symantec.com/content/dam/symantec/docs/white-papers/insecurity-in-the-internet-of-things-en.pdf

Castellani, A. P., Bui, N., Casari, P., Rossi, M., Shelby, Z., & Zorzi, M. (2010). Architecture and protocols for the internet of things: A case study. *2010 8th IEEE International Conference on Pervasive Computing and Communications Workshops, PERCOM Workshops 2010*, (pp. 678–683). http://doi.org/ doi:10.1109/PERCOMW.2010.5470520

Gartner. (2015). *Gartner Survey on IoT*. Retrieved from http://www.gartner.com/newsroom/id/3165317

Karagiannis, V., Chatzimisios, P., Vazquez-Gallego, F., & Alonso-Zarate, J. (2015). A Survey on Application Layer Protocols for the Internet of Things. *Transaction on IoT and Cloud Computing*, *3*(1), 11–17. doi:10.5281/ZENODO.51613

Miessler, D. (2015). Securing the Internet of Things: Mapping Attack Surface Areas Using the OWASP IoT Top 10.*RSA Conference*.

Owasp. (2013). OWASP Top 10 - 2013. *OWASP Top 10*, 22.

[OWASP. (2016). *OWASP Internet of Things Project - OWASP*. Retrieved from https://www.owasp.org/index.php/OWASP_Internet_of_Things_Top_Ten_Project#tab=OWASP_Internet_of_Things_Top_10_for_2014

Rose, K., Eldridge, S., & Lyman, C. (2015, October). The internet of things: an overview. *Internet Society*, 53. http://doi.org/10.1017/CBO9781107415324.004

Toms, L. (2016). 5 Common Cyber Attacks in the IoT - Threat Alert on a Grand Scale. *GlobalSign Blog*. Retrieved from https://www.globalsign.com/en/blog/five-common-cyber-attacks-in-the-iot/

ADDITIONAL READING

Bhattacharya, D. (2015). IOT Multiprotocols in Application layer. In O. International (Ed.), *Internet of things applications covering industrial domain*. San Fransico, USA: International, OMICS. Retrieved from http://industrialautomation. conferenceseries.com/

Cisco. (2015). IoT Threat Environment. *An Overview of the IoT Threat Landscape with Risk-Based Security Program Recommendations: A White Paper on IoT*, 1–10.

European Research Cluster on The Internet of Things. (2015). Internet of Things: IoT Governance, Privacy and Security Issues. *European Research Cluster on the Internet of Things*, *128*. doi:10.1002/dac.2417

E&Y. (2015). Cybersecurity and the Internet of Things. *E&Y*, (March), 1–15.

Gubbi, J., Buyya, R., & Marusic, S. (n.d.). 13- Internet of Things (IoT) A vision, architectural elements, and future directions, 1–28.

Item, K. (2016). 11 Internet of Things (IoT) Protocols You Need to Know About » DesignSpark, 1–7. Retrieved from http://www.rs-online.com/designspark/electronics/ knowledge-item/eleven-internet-of-things-iot-protocols-you-need-to-know-about

Karagiannis, V., Chatzimisios, P., Vazquez-Gallego, F., & Alonso-Zarate, J. (2015). A Survey on Application Layer Protocols for the Internet of Things. *Transaction on IoT and Cloud Computing*, *3*(1), 11–17. doi:10.5281/ZENODO.51613

Khan, R., Khan, S. U., Zaheer, R., & Khan, S. (2012). Future internet: The internet of things architecture, possible applications and key challenges. *Proceedings - 10th International Conference on Frontiers of Information Technology, FIT 2012*, 257–260. http://doi.org/ doi:10.1109/FIT.2012.53

Miessler, D. (2015). Securing the Internet of Things: Mapping Attack Surface Areas Using the OWASP IoT Top 10. *RSA Conference*.

Roman, R., Najera, P., & Lopez, J. (2011). Securing the Internet of Things (IoT). *IEEE Computer*, *44*(9), 51–58. doi:10.1109/MC.2011.291

Wang, C., Daneshmand, M., Dohler, M., Mao, X., Hu, R. Q., & Wang, H. (2013). Guest Editorial - Special issue on internet of things (IoT): Architecture, protocols and services. *IEEE Sensors Journal*, *13*(10), 3505–3508. doi:10.1109/JSEN.2013.2274906

Wiki, I. (2016). IoT Applications with the Examples. Retrieved from the http://internetofthingswiki.com/iot-applications-examples/541/

Xu, T., Wendt, J. B., & Potkonjak, M. (2014). Security of IoT systems: Design challenges and opportunities. *2014 IEEE/ACM International Conference on Computer-Aided Design (ICCAD)*, 417–423. http://doi.org/ doi:10.1109/ICCAD.2014.7001385

Chapter 5
Security in IoT Devices

N. Jeyanthi
VIT University, India

Shreyansh Banthia
VIT University, India

Akhil Sharma
VIT University, India

ABSTRACT

An attempt to do a comparison between the various DDoS attack types that exist by analysing them in various categories that can be formed, to provide a more comprehensive view of the problem that DDoS poses to the internet infrastructure today. Then DDoS and its relevance with respect to IoT (Internet of Things) devices are analysed where attack types have been explained and possible solutions available are analysed. This chapter does not propose any new solutions to mitigating the effects of DDoS attacks but just provides a general survey of the prevailing attack types along with analysis of the underlying structures that make these attacks possible, which would help researchers in understanding the DDoS problem better.

DOI: 10.4018/978-1-5225-2296-6.ch005

INTRODUCTION

Distributed Denial of Service attacks pose an imminent threat to the internet infrastructure, where the frequency of these attacks have increased in recent times many folds. Attackers constantly modify their attacking techniques to work around defence mechanisms in place, leaving the researchers to play catch-up with them. There is no silver bullet solution to this problem because each attack fundamentally differs from the other with respect to the part of the network system that it attacks, the way it attacks, the resources with which it attacks etc. With so many variables in place it's tough categorise solutions to these problems.

Now coming to DDoS attacks and their relation to IoT devices we have a scenario where according to IDC, the IoT market will hit evaluation of $7.1 trillion in revenue by 2020. Gartner predicts the IoT devices base to expand to 26 billion units by 2020. This gives us a perspective on the importance of IoT in our futures but at the same time this technology is susceptible to exploitation because of the security gaps that exist in the communication technologies that these devices employ.

We hope that this survey would go a long way in simplifying the myriad categories of attacks that are possible, thereby helping the research community to direct their research towards specific targets, enabling this focussed effort to make a bigger impact.

TAXONOMY OF THE DDOS ATTACK METHODS

Classifying by Degree of Automation

1. **Manual Attacks:** The offender physically try to find inaccessible machines for susceptibility, splits them, then proposes the attack code, and after charges the outset of the attack (Mirkovic & Reiher, 2002). After all the actions, it leads to progression of semi-automated attacks of DDoS.
2. **Semi-Automatic Attack:** The DDoS Network comprises of handler and specialist slave machines. The select, misuse and taint stages are automated. In the utilization stage, the offender species the attack sort, on-set, span and the casualty by means of the handler to specialists. Attacker tries to set up scripts for scanning and fitting of the attack code, then he uses those machines to define the type of attack and the address of the victim (Mirkovic & Reiher, 2002).

3. **Direct Communication:** Attack in type is done through strong-coding of IP address of handler machines in the attack code that is later introduced on the agent side (Houle & Weaver, 2001). The agent and handler mechanisms need to know each other's ID keeping in mind the end goal to impart. Every operator then reports its status to the handlers, who store its IP address in a record for later correspondence (Mirkovic & Reiher, 2002).

4. **Indirect Communication:** Through this attack a level of duplicity is expanded for the serviceability of a DDoS network. Late attacks give the case of utilizing IRC channels for specialist/handler correspondence. The utilization of IRC administrations replaces the capacity of a handler, since the IRC channel offers adequate namelessness to the offender.

5. **Attacks with Random Scanning:** Every composed host inquiry random addresses within the IP address area (Paxson & Weaver, 2003). This probably creates a high traffic volume since several machines research the same addresses. (CRv2) performed random scanning.

6. **Attacks with Hit-list Scanning:** A machine acting hit-list scanning finds all addresses from an outwardly provided list (Paxson & Weaver, 2003). When it finds the harmful machine, it will send one-half of the initial hit-list to the receiver and keeps the other half of the hit-list. This method grants for nice propagation speed (due to exponential spread) and no collisions throughout the scanning section.

7. **Attacks with Permutation Scanning:** In this scanning method, major composed machines share a typical pseudo-random permutation of the IP address area; every IP address is structured to the index during this permutation. A machine starts finding by using the index got from its IP address as a start line. Whenever it sees an already infected machine, it chooses a brand new random begin point (Mirkovic, Prier & Reiher, 2002).

Classifying by Exploited Vulnerability

There are two sub-categories under this section, protocol attacks and Brute-force attacks.

1. Protocol attacks abuse a particular element or execution bug of some convention introduced at the casualty so as to devour abundance measures of its assets (Mirkovic & Reiher, 2002). Illustrations incorporate the TCP SYN attack, the CGI request attack and the confirmation server attack (Seltzer, 2014) In the confirmation server attack, the attacker make use of the fact that the indication process of validation consumes notably more resources than fake signature generation.

2.   Brute force attacks are performed by starting a boundless measure of apparently genuine transactions (Seltzer, 2014). Since an upstream system can typically convey higher traffic volume than the victim system can handle, this depletes the victim's assets.

Classifying by Attack Rate Dynamics

1.   **Continuous Rate Attacks:** The majority of identified attacks deploy an eternal rate mechanism. Once the onset is commanded, agent machines generate the attack packets with full force. This quick packet flood disrupts the victim's services quickly, and then finally ends up in attack detection (Wang, 2006).
2.   **Variable Rate Attacks:** These are more guarded in their engagement, which they vary the rate of attack to avoid detection and response. Based on the rate modification mechanism attacks with increasing rate and unsteady rate are differentiated below:
3.   **Increasing Rate Attacks:** Attacks that have a bit by bit increasing rate result in a slow exhaustion of victim's resources. A phase transition of the victim may be therefore gradual that its services degrade slowly over an extended fundamental measure, so delaying detection of the attack (Wang, 2006).
4.   **Fluctuating Rate Attacks:** Attacks that have a unsteady rate modify the attack rate supported the victim's behaviour, often relieving the result to avoid detection (Mirkovic & Reiher, 2002). At the acute finish, there's the instance of pulsing attacks. Throughout pulsing attacks, agent hosts sporadically abort the attack and resume it at a later time.

CLASSIFYING BY IMPACT

Classified by Activity Level: Preventive Mechanism

The goal of preventive mechanisms is either to eliminate the likelihood of DDoS attacks altogether or to alter potential victims to endure the attack while not denying services to legitimate clients.

Attack avoidance mechanisms modify the system configuration to eliminate the prospect of a DDoS attack. They secure based on the target.

System or framework security methods increment the general security of the framework, guarding against ill-conceived gets to the machine, expelling application bugs and updating protocol establishments to avert interruptions and abuse of the framework.

Protocol security address the issue of terrible design of protocol. Numerous protocols contain operations that are modest for the customer yet costly for the server. Such protocols can be abused to draining the assets of a server by starting huge quantities of concurrent transactions (Cisco, 2008)

1. **Reactive Mechanism:** Reactive mechanisms attempt to reduce the impact of associate degree attack on the victim. So as to achieve this goal they have to find what type of attack and reply to it.
2. **Mechanisms with Pattern Attack Detection:** The kind of methods that spread out the pattern detection store the signatures of known type attacks in a data storage system. Every communication will be monitored and compared with data storage entries to find the occurrences of DDoS attacks. Drawback of this method is that it can only predict known attacks and it cannot be used for new attacks (Mirkovic & Reiher, 2002).
3. **Mechanisms with Anomaly Attack Detection:** The kind of mechanism which spread out inconsistency detection have a normal system behaviour. Advantage is that it can used for unknown attacks.
4. **Mechanisms with Hybrid Attack Detection:** It combines the pattern and anomaly-based detection, by using the data about attacks found by anomaly detection and to discover unique attack signs and then updates the storage system (Incapsula, 2016).
5. **Mechanisms with Third-Party Attack Detection:** Methods that dispose an unbiased observer detection do not handle the detection process themselves, but depend on a message comes from outside that signals the occurrence of the attack and provides characterization of the attack (Incapsula, 2016).

Based on response strategy we define reactive methods as:

1. **Agent Identification Methods:** This methodology give the victim with data regarding the identity of the machines that are acting the attack (Incapsula, 2016). This information will then be combined with alternative response approaches to mitigate the impact of the attack.
2. **Rate-Limiting Mechanisms:** These methods enforce a rate limit on a stream that has been characterised as vicious by the detection mechanism. Rate limiting may be an easy response technique that's typically deployed once the detection method features a high level of false positives or cannot exactly characterize the attack stream. The disadvantage is that they permit some attack traffic through, therefore very high scale attacks would possibly still be effective even though all traffic streams are rate-limited (Meena & Jadon, 2014).

Table 1. Comparison table of various DDOS attacks

Type of attacks 1)Volumetric Attack	2) Reflected Attack	3) UDP Flood	4) Ping Of Death	5) TCP SYN Flood	6) Slowloris
How it is being done: Attacker sends large traffic to overwhelm the bandwidth of the site.	Sends a request to an IP that will yield a big response, spoof the source IP to that of the actual victim.	Attacker send's UDP datagrams to victim with spoofed source address.	The victim is attacked by sending corrupt packets that could fail the system.	Attacker creates many half-open connections to target - Send SYN packet -Ignore SYN+ACK response.	It accomplishes this by creating connections to the aimed server, but sending only a partial request to it.
Major Causes: Causes a large amount of traffic congestion.	Causes the site to be slow down with requests until the server resources are exhausted.	Disturbs random ports on the intended host with IP packets also contains UDP datagrams. Also, threats the firewalls.	Damage the local area networks. Server can freeze, reboot or crash.	Target is to exploit server CPU memory. To crash the system.	This ultimately excess the maximum connection pool, and leads to denial of additional connections from legitimate clients.
Possible way of doing: Usually botnets or traffic from spoofed IPs generating high bps/pps traffic volume.	Usage of a possibly legitimate third party component to send the attack traffic to a victim.	Attacked host will receive the junk-filled UDP packets to ports, get reply with ICMP destination unreachable packet.	Sends data packets above the max. Limit (65,536 bytes) that TCP/IP allows.	Attacker sends repeated SYN packets to every port on the targeted server, may be using a fake IP address.	Attack will hold as many connections to the target web server open for as long as possible.
Example: Phishing, click fraud through BOTNET.	Example: Reflective DNS response attack.	Example: UDP Unicorn	Example: C:\ windows>ping -l 65600. It might hang the victim's computer as it crosses max. limit.	Example: On SunOS this may be done by the command: netstat -a -f inet. Large number of connections in the state "SYN_ RECEIVED" could indicate that the system is being attacked.	Example: Sending incomplete request by slowloris: "GET /$rand HTTP/1.1\r\n" "Host: $sendhost\r\n" "Content-length: 32\r\n";

3. **Reconfiguration Mechanisms:** These strategies modify the structure the inter-mediate network to either add additional resources to the sufferer or to separate the attack machines. Examples: reconfigurable overlay networks asset replication kind of services, attack segregation methods (Meena & Jadon, 2014).

CLASSIFICATION OF DDOS ATTACKS BASED ON THE LAYER IN THE NETWORK THAT IS AFFECTED

This part of chapter exhaustively compares types of DDOS attacks on the basis of layers. It also tells there how attacker attacks, discusses the attack mechanism and the after effects of them. It also gives the examples of attack on each type of layers. Here we briefly discuss the attacks on the basis of level and then we will gradually talk about attacks in the layers (Li, Zhou, Li, Hai & Liu, 2011)

DDOS attack can attack on different levels namely:

1. Network device level
2. OS level
3. Application level
4. Protocol feature level

Network Device Level: It consists of data link layer and physical layer. In this level attacker uses the weak points of a router to attack and hence takes down the system (Xie & Yu, 2009)

OS level: In this level the attacker takes the advantage of the vulnerability of the OS features and hence they are more effective as they can attack any system having that (Xie & Yu, 2009).

Application Level: This level consists of session, presentation and application layers. In this level attacker scans the port and hence finds the unguarded part of application and use this mechanism to take down the mobile networks (Ahn, Blum & Langford, 2004).

The protocol level: the attacker takes great advantage of the feebleness of some of the features of protocol such as the acknowledgement from client by the server in TCP's three-way handshake (Li, Zhou, Li, Hai & Liu, 2011).

Now we classify the attacks based on the layers they affect:

1. **Physical Layer**
   a. **Node Tampering Attack:** Node of the network is damaged and tampered in this. Destroyed node because gaps among sensor hence communication is not effective.
   b. **Jamming Attack:** Jamming is interference with radio reception to deny the Authorized user of a communication channel. It renders the node which is jammed unable to communicate with others in the network (Khanna, Venkatesh, Fatemieh, Khan & Gunter, 2012).
2. **Link / MAC Layer**
   a. **Collision Attack:** In physical radio channel, an attacker can wilfully cause collisions or corruption at the link layer. Attacker can disrupt key elements of packets, such as fields that contribute to checksums or the checksums themselves (Dean, Franklin & Stubblefield, 2001).
   b. **Interrogation Attack:** Small messages (such as queries) may elicit larger responses. For example, an attacker may be able to replay a broadcast initialization command, causing nodes in network to time synchronization procedures. Such unauthenticated or stale messages provide an easy way for traffic amplification. It is known as solicitation of energy-draining responses interrogation (Dean, Franklin & Stubblefield, 2001).
3. **Network layer**
   a. **TCP Flooding:** Initializingcolossal number of TCP based connections (of spoofed IP address) with victim and not notifying the same that it has received the data by the server (known as TCP ACKNOWLEDGE attack). Many requests are left unanswered due to unavailability of connections for authorized clients (Because capacity is limited on a given server) (Dean, Franklin & Stubblefield, 2001).
   b. **ICMP Flooding:** Sending big amount of ICMP packets towards bandwidth of the victim. Network congestion is observed due to unavailability of bandwidth to true clients (Dean, Franklin & Stubblefield, 2001).
   c. **UDP Flood:** Sending large amount of UDP packets towards victim's bandwidth. Network is congested due to unavailability of bandwidth to true clients (Tian, Bi &Jiang, 2012).
4. **Transport layer**
   a. **Syn Flood:** Attacker sends many requests to a target's system to consume server resources to make the system unavailable to authorized traffic.

5. **Application layer**
   a. **HTTP Flooding:** Initiating colossal number of TCP connections with victim and sending heavy processing of requests through HTTP is also major problem. Unavailability of server's processing cycles for legitimate users because there are many unanswered requests from clients (All servers remains busy for answering attacker's requests of heavy data requests)
   b. **FTP Flooding:** Establishing heavily large number of TCP connections with victim and sending requests for bigger processing through FTP communication. Unanswered requests become pending because of unavailability of processing cycles of the server for true clients, server remains busy for answering attackers' requests of heavy processing (Li, Zhou, Li, Hai & Liu, 2011).

DDoS Attacks in Non-Wired Networks

Non-wired networks (Wireless networks) are vulnerable to many kinds of attacks which includes distributed denial of service attacks also. Their main vulnerability is shared medium because of which many attacks are possible to exploit wireless stations. It is possible in these ways: (Douceur, 1987)

1. Wireless sensor networks (WSN)
2. Mobile ad hoc networks (MANET)
3. Wireless local area networks (WLAN)

1. DDoS Attacks and IoT Devices

On 21st October 2016, Dyn, which is one company that controls much of internet's DNS infrastructure, was hit by the Mirai botnet in an attack which was considered as the biggest DDoS attack till date. The reason this attack was so effective was because this botnet consisted primarily of IoT devices that are categorically more vulnerable to getting infected by the "botnet" malware which transforms them into slave machines which then participate in the attack.

This incident has shifted the focus of the research community on securing the IoT devices to prevent such attacks in the future. This survey is a step towards that direction in which we aim to compare the various attack strategies that are used to exploit computers and IoT devices, compare them and also compare the underlying structures that leave these devices vulnerable to such attacks.

2. Wireless Sensor Networks: A Technology that Connecting IoT Devices

Wireless sensor networks are sensor networks that consist of low-power, low-cost, multifunctional sensor nodes that are small in size and communicate untethered across short distances.

In these, sensor nodes are densely deployed in large numbers either inside a phenomenon or close to it and are tasked with gathering and processing data before transmitting it (Weilian, Sankarasubramaniam & Cayirci, 2002).

Two interesting features of such networks are:

1. The position on these nodes can be random if the situation warrants, whereby they become versatile for deployment in areas where the terrain isn't easily accessible or during disaster relief efforts. This is made possible by the network protocols and algorithms used in these sensors that are self-organising in nature.
2. These nodes do not transmit raw data because of the presence on a processor on board which allows them to so simple processing and transmit only necessary partially processed data to the sink, hence reducing the computation effort for a single device.

These sensor nodes usually consist of the following hardware components:

1. Sensor module
2. Processing module
3. Memory chip
4. Transceiver module
5. Power unit

In WSNs, sensors are linked through a wireless medium like radio, infrared or optical media. Data is collected in the sensor fields through collaboration between various sensor nodes. Then the data is transmitted back to the sink using a multi-hop infrastructure less architecture after which the sink then communicates with the manager node using internet connectivity. The factors that affect these networks include but are not limited to, fault tolerance, scalability, production costs, operating environment, sensor network topology, hardware constraints, transmission media and power consumption (Weilian, Sankarasubramaniam & Cayirci, 2002)

3. Security Issues with WSNs

Wireless sensor networks provide us with a viable alternative to be used in situations where traditional network architectures can't be used and thus are used byte military, health care systems, disaster relief efforts etc. In such cases, it is critical for these sensors to be secure and resistant to exploitation, but the underlying communication technologies that these sensors apply are vulnerable to exploitation and in need of serious security protocols. Thus, exploitation of these networks can be categorised in three categories: (Shi & Perrig, 2004)

1. **Attacks on Service Integrity Constraints:** These include making the sensor pass false data values to the sink which are then sent to the user thereby compromising the data integrity of the system.
2. **Attacks on Privacy and Authentication:** These can be solved by using standard cryptographic techniques which prevent outsider attacks.
3. **Attacks on Network Availability:** These usually constitute of DoS attacks that prevent the user from accessing the collected data because the network resources are being consumed by an army of infected bots that attack different layers of the network. This area will be further expanded upon in the following paragraphs.

1. **DoS Attack on the Physical Layer in WSNs:** The physical layer in WSNs is responsible for representation bits, data rate synchronisation, providing an interface between the devices and the medium, line configuration and transmission modes. This layer is vulnerable to the following types of attacks: (Akyildiz, 2002)
    a. **Jamming:** In this type of attack, the nodes are prevented from communicating with each other because the medium is flooded with packets from the attacker. This is a problem here because the nodes are randomly distributed and rely on each other for transfer of data to the sink, so even if a small portion of the network is affected, the entire network can be brought down. Typical defences against this include spread spectrum communications variations and code spreading.
    b. **Node Tampering:** This can happen when the attacker has access to the nodes physically and can extract sensitive information from them by accessing them physically. One solution to this involves tamper-proofing the physical structure of the node and putting fail-safes in place in case the physical package is tampered with.

2. **DoS Attack on the Link Layer:** The link layer makes sure that there are reliable point-to-point and multi-point connections in the network by ensuring that multiplexing of data streams, medium access, data frame detection, and error control is taken care of. This layer is susceptible to the following attacks: (Akyildiz, 2002)

    a. **Collisions:** Here an attacker can plan a collision in between packets leading to a change occurring in the data section of these packets which then causes a checksum mismatch at the receiving end leading to the packet being sent again. This consumes extra network recourse and can lead to costly exponential back-off in certain media access control protocols. Typical defence against this includes traditional error-correcting protocols like Hamming code being used.

    b. **Exhaustion:** The attacker here can cause repeated collisions, which causes repeated attempts to retransmit the corrupted packets, which then lead to resource exhaustion of the network resources. A viable workaround to this is application of rate limits to the MAC admission control so that the network can ignore excessive requests, thus preventing resource exhaustion. Another technique that can be used is time-division multiplexing where each node is given a time slot in which they can transmit the data.

    c. **Unfairness:** An attacker can cause unfair distribution of resources by using the above-mentioned attacking techniques. Here the attacker doesn't outright cut off access to the network resources but degrades them to an extent where the network becomes practically unusable for the other nodes. This can be prevented by using smaller frames which don't allow the attacker to occupy the communication channel effectively but at the same time this then affects the efficiency of the data delivery of the packets.

3. **DoS Attacks on Network layer:** This layer is primarily tasked with maintaining the power efficiency of the nodes while transmitting data, maintaining the data-centricity of the nodes, and ensure attribute based addressing and location awareness in the nodes. The technologies usually used in this layer are usually Bluetooth, IrDA, Wi-Fi, ZigBee, RFID, NUWB, NFC, Wireless Hart etc. The attacks this layer is vulnerable to are:

    a. **Spoofed, Altered, or Replayed Routing Information:** This is achieved by altering or spoofing the routing information in order to disrupt the traffic by creation of routing loops, attracting or repelling network traffic from select nodes, extending and shortening source routes, generating fake error messages, partitioning the network, and increasing end-to-end latency. Possible solutions include appending a message authentication code in the end of the message or adding time stamps and counters in messages (Karlof & Wagner, 2003) (Perrig, 2002).

b. **Selective Forwarding:** This exploits the assumption that all nodes accurately forward the received messages because of which an attacker can create a malicious node that selectively forwards some messages while drops all others. This can be dealt with by using multiple paths to send the data or finding the malicious node and treating it as failed node until it can be recovered so that an alternative path can be formed (Karlof & Wagner, 2003).

c. **Sinkhole:** In here the attacker makes a compromised node more attractive to the surrounding nodes by manipulating the routing table values of that node because of which all the traffic is routed through that node and selective forwarding as an attack becomes more potent (Karlof & Wagner, 2003).

d. **Sybil:** Here the compromised node will represent more than one value to the other nodes which severely affects protocols and algorithms like fault-tolerant schemes, distributed storage, and network-topology maintenance (Karlof & Wagner, 2003) (Newsome, 2004).

e. **Wormholes:** Here data packets can be relocated from their original position in the network by tunnelling the bits of the data over a wormhole in the network. Packet leashes have proven to be an effective mechanism against this type of attack (Karlof & Wagner, 2003) (Hu, Perrig & Johnson, 2003).

f. **Acknowledgment Spoofing:** In this a compromised node can spoof the acknowledgments of the packets being routed through it to provide false information to the nearby nodes. (Karlof & Wagner, 2003)

g. **Homing:** Here the attacker will search for cluster heads and key managers that have capabilities to shut down the entire network.

h. **Hello Flood Attacks:** In many protocol if a node receives a hello packet then there is an assumption that the sender in within in range. This can be exploited by using a high-powered transmitter to trick a large number of nodes that they are neighbours with the sender node and if this is combined with broadcasting of a superior route to the base station, all these nodes will attempt transmission to these attacking nodes, despite it being actually out of their ranges (Karlof & Wagner, 2003).

      i.   **Protocol Exploitation Flooding Attacks:** Here the attacker exploits some specific features of the victim's protocols to deplete the resources of the networks.

4.   **DoS Attacks on the Transport Layer:** The transport layer in WSNs provides end to end reliability of data transmission and congestion control. The possible attacks in this layer are: (Akyildiz, 2002)

    a.   **Flooding:** This involves flooding of the communication channels using unnecessary messages and high traffic.

    b.   **De-Synchronisation:** Here fake messages will be created on one or both the endpoints requesting retransmissions for correction of an error that doesn't exists. This results in loss of network resources.

5.   **DoS Attack on the Application Layer:** The application layer in WSNs carries out traffic management in the network and also provides software for different applications to access the data in a particular form and execute queries. Here a DoS attack is carried by making the sensor nodes generate a lot of traffic towards the base station/sink (Alkhatib, & Baicher, 2012; Pathan, 2010). Some other DoS attacks are as follows: (Saxena, 2007) (Sen, 2009) (Padmavathi & Shanmugapriya, 2009)

    a.   Neglect and Greed Attack

    b.   Interrogation

    c.   Black Holes

    d.   Node Subversion

    e.   Node malfunction

    f.   Node Outage

    g.   Passive Information Gathering

    h.   False Node

    i.   Message Corruption

4. RFID Tags: The Technology that Connects IoT Devices

RFID, in the context of IoT, primarily consist of information tags which can interact with each other automatically. This technology allows a reader to activate a transponder on a radio frequency tag attached to, or embedded in, an item, allowing the reader to remotely read and/or write data on the RFID tag (Das, 2002; ITAA, 2004; Want, 2004). These tags use radio waves for cooperating and transferring information between each other without the need for the arrangement to be in the same observable pathway or in physical contact. It is uses Automatic Identification and Data Catch (AIDC) to do this.

Figure 1. RFID components

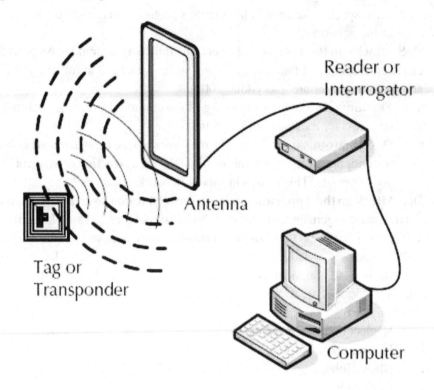

A RFID is made up of the following components:

1. **RFID tags (Transponders):** In a tag, the microchip has a radio wire embedded inside it. A RFID tag consists of memory units which contains an identifier called Electronic Product Code (EPC). A RFID tag works along with a RFID reader, where the EPC of the former is used to identify it when the latter is scanning for tags. As per the classification provided in (Mirkovic & Reiher, 2002), the types of RFID tags are:

2. **Active Tag:** These contain their own transmitters and a power source to maintain data integrity and the capability to transmit data on their memory chips through a broadcast. These usually operate in the ultra-high frequency band (300 MHz – 3 GHz) because of which they can offer a data transmitting range of 100 meters. Two categories of Active tags are:

    a.   **Transponders:** These are activated on receiving a radio signal from the reader, upon which the power up and respond with a signal. Since they don't actively transmit radio waves, they conserve battery life.

    b.   **Beacons:** These are used in more real time scenarios, where data needs to be transmitted continuously or at continuous intervals. These, unlike transponders, emit signals at a pre-set interval.

3.   **Semi-Passive Tag:** These are also called Battery-Assisted RFID tags which include a crucial feature of active tags. These use a power source to maintain data integrity while use the reader's signal to generate power to transmit the response and the data subsequently.

4.   **Passive Tag:** These tags do not contain an internal battery but instead use the electromagnetic signal sent by the reader to generate power to respond and transfer data. These are also activated only on receiving a signal from the reader, upon which they perform data transfer of their EPC when in the range of the reader.

5.   **RFID readers (Transceivers):** This works as a detector to identify a tag based on it's interaction with the EPC of the tag once it responds back.

5. Security Issues in RFID

RFID as a technology was developed with the intention of optimizing performance over resilience and security, because of which it suffers from various security vulnerabilities, and these gaps become an issue when RFID tags find their use in critical applications across various industries. In the subsequent paragraphs these vulnerabilities will be explained and various proposed security mechanisms will also be looked upon.

The four most common security vulnerabilities that are found in RFID chips are the following: (Burmester, Mike & Medeiros, 2007) (Xiao, Qinghan, Gibbons & Lebrun, 2009)

1.   **Unauthorized Tag Disabling:** Here the attacker can cause the RFID tags to move into a state in which they are no longer functional which results in these tags become temporarily or permanently disabled or malfunction on be-ing read by a reader by giving incorrect information. This problem is further aggravated by the fact that these tags are mobile in nature because of which they can manipulated by readers from a distance, thereby avoiding detection.

A possible response to this problem could be each tag having a permanent private identifying key which will be shared with the backend servers, which then use this key to decode the response generated by the tag upon a scan, which again has been encoded with the same private key.

2. **Unauthorized Tag Cloning:** Here the tag's integrity is attacked upon by which the attacker can capture the tag identification information using a reader from a distance. Using this information, exact same tags can be created which can be easily passed under scanners, leaving the counterfeit security measures unusable. These can be prevented by making the identification data of a tag private.

3. **Unauthorized Tag Tracking:** Here the attack is on the privacy and security of the customer using the RFID tag where the tag can be tracked using a reader which can then be used to extract confidential information of the customer. Thus, a user isn't guaranteed protection against attacks on his privacy and confidentiality while using these tags and hence it's a problem in this respect. This can be prevented by making sure that the values of a response appear to the attacker as randomly and uniformly distributed.

4. **Replay Attacks:** These attacks are on the integrity of the tags where the attacker uses the response generated by the tag against a rogue reader trying to get the identification information of that tag. The response here is intercepted, recorded and replayed when required against a scanner thereby the availability of the tag can be faked to gain access to sites where these tags are being used as access tokens. To deal with these the tag's responses to every server challenge must be unique, this can be achieved by making server challenges and tag responses should be unpredictable.

5. **Killing Tag Approach:** Here the attacker tries to permanently disable the tag. This can be done by using the kill command on the tag. To prevent against this, upon manufacturing, each tag is given a password but due to limited memory and processing capabilities, this password can be easily cracked using a brute force method.

6. **De-Synchronisation Approach:** Here the attacker uses a jamming technique to permanently destroy the authentication capability of a RFID tag by preventing synchronisation between the tag and the reader.

Other than these, some other security gaps in RFID tags are: (Saxena, 2007) (Sen, 2009) (Singla & Sachdeva, 2013)

- Reverse Engineering
- Power Analysis
- Eavesdropping
- Man-in-the-middle attack
- Spoofing
- Viruses
- Tracking

CONCLUSION

Preventive measures that are present to protect these structures against various attacks and their viability in various scenarios were analysed. The aim for this chapter was to provide a researcher interested in the field of DDoS attacks, a starting point from where they can delve into any specific field of this vast, complex problem that affects all of us today. Also focussed on the IoT device vulnerabilities that make them a ripe target for attackers to employ them as DDoS bots or attack them using a DDoS attacks, at the same time critically analysing the various methods in place to secure these devices against these very attacks. In conclusion, we would like to suggest that more effort should be diverted towards securing these security gaps in the network infrastructure that exist before going for further development of networking capabilities because the future devices can be proofed against exploitation but the old insecure devices and protocols in use pose the real threat.

REFERENCES

Ahmad, A. A. A., & Baicher, G. S. (2012). Wireless sensor network architecture. *IPCSIT, 35*, 11-15.

Ahn, L. V., Blum, M., & Langford, J. (2004). Telling humans and computers apart automatically. *Communications of the ACM, 47*(2), 56–60. doi:10.1145/966389.966390

Akyildiz, I. F., Weilian Su, , Sankarasubramaniam, Y., & Cayirci, E. (2002, August). A Survey on Sensor Setworks. *IEEE Communications Magazine, 40*(8), 102–114. doi:10.1109/MCOM.2002.1024422

Burmester, M., & De Medeiros, B. (2007). RFID security: attacks, countermeasures and challenges. *The 5th RFID Academic Convocation, The RFID Journal Conference*.

Cisco. (2008). *Strategies to protect against Distributed Denial of Service Attacks*. Document ID:13634. Cisco.

Crosby & Wallach. (2003). Denial of service via algorithmic complexity attacks. *Proceedings of USENIX Security 2003*.

DDoS Attack Types and Mitigation. (n.d.). Retrieved from https://www.incapsula.com/ddos/ddos-attacks

Dean, D., Franklin, M., & Stubblefield, A. (2001). An algebraic approach to IP traceback.*Proceedings of Network and Distributed Systems Security Symposium (NDSS)*, 3–12.

Defending Against Denial of Web Services Using Sessions. (2006). NEC Europe Ltd.

Douceur. (2002). The sybil attack. *IPTPS*, 251–260.

Ganesan, Govindan, Shenker, & Estrin. (2001). Highly-resilient, energy-efficient multipath routing in wireless sensor networks. *Mobile Computing and Communications Review, 4*(5).

Gligor, Blaze, & Ioannidis. (2000). Denial of service - panel discussion. *Security Protocols Workshop*.

Houle, K.J., & Weaver, G.M. (2001). *Trends in Denial of Service Attack Technology*. CERT Coordination Center.

Hu, Y.-C., Perrig, A., & Johnson, D. B. (2003, April). Packet Leashes: A Defense Against Wormhole Attacks in Wireless Networks. *Proceedings - IEEE INFOCOM*.

Karlof, C., & Wagner, D. (2003). Secure Routing in Wireless Sensor Networks: Attacks and Countermeasures. *Proc. First IEEE Int'l. Wksp. Sensor Network Protocols and Applications*, 113–27. doi:10.1109/SNPA.2003.1203362

Khanna, S., Venkatesh, S. S., Fatemieh, O., Khan, F., & Gunter, C. A. (2012). Adaptive Selective Verification: An Efficient Adaptive Countermeasure to Thwart DoS Attacks. *IEEE/ACM Transactions on Networking*, *20*(3), 715–728. doi:10.1109/TNET.2011.2171057

Li, K., Zhou, W., Li, P., Hai, J., & Liu, J. (2009). Distinguishing DDoS Attacks from Flash Crowds Using Probability Metrics. In *Proceedings of 3rd Intl Conference on Network and System Security* (NSS 09). IEEE.

Meena & Jadon. (2014). Distributed Denial of Service Attacks and Their Suggested Defense Remedial Approaches. *International Journal of Advance Research in Computer Science and Management Studies, 2*(4).

Mirkovic, J., Prier, G., & Reiher, P. (2002). Attacking DDoS at the Source.*Proceedings of the ICNP 2002.*

Mirkovic, J., & Reiher, P. (2002). A Taxonomy of DDoS Attack and DDoS Defense mechanisms. *Proceedings of the 2nd ACM SIGCOMM Internet Measurement Workshop.*

Newsome, J. (2004). The Sybil Attack in Sensor Networks: Analysis and Defenses. *Proc. IEEE Int'l. Conf. Info. Processing in Sensor Networks.* doi:10.1145/984622.984660

Padmavathi, G., & Shanmugapriya, D. (2009). *A survey of attacks, security mechanisms and challenges in wireless sensor networks.* arXiv preprint arXiv: 0909.0576

Pathan. (2010). Denial of Service in Wireless Sensor Networks: Issues and Challenges. In A. V. Stavros (Ed.), *Advances in Communications and Media Research* (Vol. 6). Nova Science Publishers, Inc.

Paxson, V., & Weaver, N. (2003). *DDoS protection strategies.* Stanford.

Perrig, A., Szewczyk, R., Tygar, J. D., Wen, V., & Culler, D. E. (2002, September). SPINS: Security Protocols for Sensor Networks. *Wireless Networks*, *8*(5), 521–534. doi:10.1023/A:1016598314198

Saxena, M. (2007). *Security in Wireless Sensor Networks-A Layer based classification.* Technical Report. Centre for Education and Research in Information Assurance & Security-CERIAS, Purdue University. Retrieved from pages.cs.wisc.edu/~msaxena/papers/2007-04-cerias.pdf

Seltzer. (2014, June). Brute and protocol attacks. *Zero Day*.

Sen. (2009). A Survey on Wireless Sensor Network Security. *International Journal of Communications Network and Information Security, 1*(2), 59-82.

Shi, E., & Perrig, A. (2004, December). Designing Secure Sensor Networks. *Wireless Commun. Mag., 11*(6), 38–43. doi:10.1109/MWC.2004.1368895

Singla, A., & Sachdeva, R. (2013). Review on Security Issues and Attacks in Wireless Sensor Networks. *International Journal of Advanced Research in Computer Science and Software Engineering, 3*(4). Retrieved from www.ijarcsse.com

Thatte, G., Mitra, U., & Heidemann, J. (2011). Parametric Methods for Anomaly Detection in Aggregate Traffic. *IEEE/ACM Transactions on Networking, 19*(2), 512–525. doi:10.1109/TNET.2010.2070845

Tian, H., Bi, J., & Jiang, X. (2012). An adaptive probabilistic marking scheme for fast and secure traceback. *Networking Science*. DOI: 10.1007/s13119-012-0007-x

Xiao, Gibbons, & Lebrun. (2009). RFID Technology, Security Vulnerabilities, and Countermeasures. In *Supply Chain the Way to Flat Organization*. Intech.

Xie, Y., & Yu, S. Z. (2009). Monitoring the Application-Layer DDoS Attacks for Popular Websites. *IEEE/ACM Transactions on Networking, 17*(1), 15–25. doi:10.1109/TNET.2008.925628

Chapter 6
Security Threats in Autonomous Vehicles

R. Thandeeswaran
VIT University, India

Rajat Pawar
VIT University, India

Mallika Rai
VIT University, India

ABSTRACT

The automotive industry has reached a stage categorisation of the degree of the automation has become crucial. According to the levels of automation defined by SAE, the automotive industry is already past the first four and development is now being heavily concentrated on level 5, that is, driving independent of human control. This obviously requires an array of sensors, microcontrollers and visual feedback systems like cameras, LiDAR (Light Detection and Ranging) to be present in the vehicle. With security concerns omnipresent among these devices, they are now ported to the realm of vehicles and must be tackled so that unsafe driving conditions are never experienced. In this paper, Section 3 elaborates upon the technologies that have shaped autonomous cars into the form known today and Section 4 explains the network architecture and network security amongst these cars. Section 5 describes the rippling effect of this evolution in the automotive industry on other supportive industries, Section 6 talks about the challenges posed to the development of AVs and finally, Section 7 discusses the future of autonomous vehicles in India.

DOI: 10.4018/978-1-5225-2296-6.ch006

INTRODUCTION

Automated autonomous vehicles (AVs) are no longer scientific fiction. With the evolution of AVs, the automobile industry seems to have come to life. Engendered from the need for intelligent systems in fields of military and agriculture, the cars have driven themselves a long way since then and are slowly but steadily making way into the near-production market that focuses on everyday driving on public roads. Google, Mercedes-Benz, Delphi Automotive, Audi and General Motors are a few to name of the many firms that have efficaciously set the wheels rolling. So far countries such as Germany, U.S, UK, Japan, South Korea, China, etc have successfully implemented AVs. But as this technology continues to amaze the masses and inspire these firms, there is still much speculation concerning autonomous vehicle impacts- accidents, attacks, trepidations and hence acceptance in the market still remains a challenge.

TECHNOLOGY APPLICATIONS

Autonomous cars need to be able to detect and avoid obstacles and distinguish objects on the road as a curb, a pedestrian or cyclist. For the purpose, they rely on a set of technologies referred to as the 'circle of safety' comprising of lane departure warning and lane keep assist, adaptive cruise control, blind spot detection, parallel and rear parking assist, driver monitoring system, traffic sign recognition, night view assist system, collision avoidance system, antilock braking system, airbags, navigation system and adaptive headlights (Howard, 2013; Sanchez, 2015)

Lane Departure Warning and Lane Keep Assist

Engendered from the need for lane driving to minimize crashes, the lane departure warning (LDW) system has been formulated to alert the driver when the vehicle begins drift away from its lane unless a turn signal is on in that direction on freeways and arterial roads. As the car approaches the lane marking, the system generates a warning in the form of a visual alert, and audible tone or a vibration in the steering wheel or seat. In response to these warnings, the driver steers back the vehicle into the lane. Figure 1 presents an autonomous car's perspective of the road ahead of it.

Figure 1. Lane Departure Warning System
Source: Howard, 2013

Most commonly, the system consists of a camera mounted at the top of the windshield, as a part of the rear-view mirror mounting block that captures the view of the road ahead and parses it for lane markings (Howard, 2013). This technology particularly addresses human-inflicted causes of collision such as driver error, distractions and drowsiness (Wikipedia, n.d).

Keeping in mind the above causes, the LDW system has been evolved into the lane keep assist system that automatically reacts when the vehicle goes astray, thus reducing dependency on human intervention for corrective measures. The vehicle is autonomously pivoted back into the lane by braking the opposite front wheel or simply turning the steering wheel (Howard, 2013). Since the reactions are subtle, the driver can always overcome the effect with minimal effort.

Alternatively, a very accurate GPS or magnetic markers in the roads may be used in addition to on board sensors (radar, LIDAR, ultrasonic range finders) to assist the systems (Sanchez, 2015).

Autonomous Cruise Control System

Autonomous (or adaptive) cruise control (ACC) system enables vehicles to adjust their speed to maintain a safe distance from the vehicles ahead of them and prevent collision (Jiang, Iyer, Tolani & Hussain, 2015). Ideal for stop-and-go-traffic and rush hour commuting, this technology allows the driver to pre-set the maximum speed. While the lane keep assist system locks the vehicle to the lane, the radar system monitors other vehicles on the road and instructs the container vehicle to maintain a certain safe distance. Commonly also known as assistive system, ACC is often combined with the forward collision warning system that operates even when ACC is not active. When engaged, ACC system sends a signal to its digital signal processor from its radar system that calculates the distance to the nearest car or object on the road. Following this, a longitudinal controller determines a safe following distance, which is usually 2 to 4 seconds behind the vehicle in front. If the vehicle's distance tends to be lesser than that distance, the system alerts the engine, brakes and slows the vehicle down. Once the way is clear again, the system accelerates the vehicle to the driver's predetermined maximum speed.

The chosen radar frequency band in ACC is such that it does not compete with the police radars or trigger radar detectors. For full range, depending on the discretion of automakers, two radars may be embedded in the system- one for short range (up to 100 feet) and the other for a longer range (up to 600 feet) (Howard, 2013).

Another two types of emerging ACC systems are under development, namely multi-sensor systems that use external systems (GPS and satellites) to provide additional information to the vehicle to enable it to make intelligent decisions, and Cooperative systems that allow vehicles to communicate amongst one another and respond to stimuli (Logan, 2015).

ACC technology has evolved into the form known today through a series of iterations. In 1992, Mitsubishi rolled out the precursor to ACC which was a LIDAR-based distance warning system capable of only warning the driver of any obstacles ahead, without influencing throttle, brakes or gear shifting. Later in 1995, it also released a laser-based Preview Distance Control which uses throttle control and downshifting to control the speed of the vehicle. Further research showed that radars could perform better than laser even in bad weather conditions and bring down the cost of ACCs considerably. Hence in 1999, radar-assisted ACCs started taking shape with Mercedes' release, Distronic. However, the efficiency of radars may be compromised in heavy rain or snow if the sensor gets caked with snow or dirt. The next challenge for automakers was to achieve speed control. So in 2006, Toyota introduced radar –assisted ACC systems that could operate across a wide range of speeds, designed to improve performance in situations such as highway traffic congestion. In 2010, Audi augmented the radar-based ACC system with a GPS. (Howard, 2013; Logan, 2015; Wikpedia, n.d)

Traffic Lights and Road Sign Recognition

The increase in the number of accidents, attributed to absence of road sense in drivers and the ever increasing traffic on roads, has become a serious problem for the society. Installing road signs such as "NO U TURN" or "ONE WAY AHEAD" was thought of as a solution to counteract road accidents, especially those common at entrances to one way streets, sharp turns and intersections, but a driver may not notice or pay heed to a road sign, leading to fatalities. (Hechri & Mtibaa, 2011) Hence, to tackle driver inattentiveness and misinterpretation of road signs, research is being pursued to device automated road sign recognition (RSR) systems that will extricate road signs captured in the images of the outside environment of a vehicle. But along with being accurate in detecting shape and colour, the system also has to be expeditious. How much information available in an image should be extracted in real-time is a limiting factor. (Springer, n.d)

The apparatus required for road sign detection and recognition in its simplest form consists of one or two powerful video cameras mounted at the front of the vehicle. RSR systems have 3 main functions:

1. Spotting probable regions containing road signs against a chaotic background using colour information.
2. Confirming the actual presence of a road sign by analysing the shape (equilateral triangle or circle).
3. Classification and identification of the captured road sign. The road signs are accurately identified using colour and shape detection techniques together.

The first step involves identification of the regions containing the standard traffic colours (red, blue, yellow, white and black). Studies have shown that the RGB colour system is least affected by outdoor illumination (Hossain & Hyder, 2015). Figure 2 represents the colour threshold.

Figure 2. Colour threshold expression
Source: Korosec, 2016

$$g(x,y) - k_1 \begin{cases} R_a \leq f_r(x,y) \leq G_b \\ G_a \leq f_g(x,y) \leq G_b \\ B_a \leq f_b(x,y) \leq G_b \end{cases}$$

$g(x,y) = k_2$ in any other case

Once the region of interest has been limited using colour information, triangular or circular shapes are sought for using one or more of Hough transform, fast radial transform, corner and edge detection,genetic algorithms and pattern matching. Genetic algorithm based techniques are used for indentificaton of circular signs while Hough tranform identifies lines or circles corresponding to a sign. (Springer, n.d)

In the classification stage, the class of the identified sign is determined by a neural network or template-based matching using distance tranforms. (Springer, n.d; Hossain & Hyder, 2015) Road signs may be classified into the following categories:

1. **Warning:** Usually upturned equilateral triangles with white background and red border
2. **Prohibition:** Circular signs with white/blue base and red border.
3. **Obligation:** Circles with blue background.
4. **Information:** Square signs having blue background

In areas of public works, warning and prohibition signs are likely to have yellow backgrounds. Two exceptional signs are- a) yield sign (inverted triangle) and b) stop sign (hexagon). (Korosec, 2016)

Another giant leap in the field has been made by Google self-driving cars which are capacitated to recognise cyclists on the roads and interpret their hand signals. After intense observation of cyclists on road and private test tracks, the gumdrop-shaped vehicles have finally learned to recognise patterns in behaviour and remember previous gestures to fortell a rider's turn or shift over. The vehicle perceives each rider differently and can even recognise different types of bikes. The use of LIDAR in addtion to sensors is what keeps these vehicles aware and sound around riders. (Newcomb, 2016)

In the years to come, as proposed by MIT Senseable City Lab, the traffic lights can be rendered obsolete with the advent of driverless technology. As quoted by Carlo Ratti, director of Sensable City Lab, the suggested "slot-based" navigation and intersection system will enable the sensor-laden vehicles to communicate their presence and keep at a safe distance from one another. According to the information received from other vehicles, a particular vehicle will be able to automatically adjust its speed to arrive at a crossing when the way is clear and hence move without stopping. This will considerably reduce fuel emissions at traffic signals in addtion to saving time, and hence benefit the environment in a huge way. (LidarUK, n.d). Figure 3 depicts this proposal at a glance.

Figure 3. Slot-based intersection system
Source: Wikipedia, n.d.

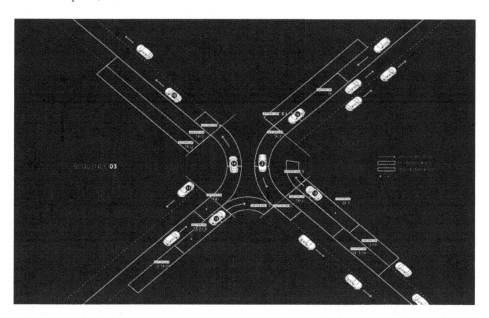

NETWORK ARCHITECHTURE

Vehicle to vehicle (V2V) communication uses wireless communication devices known as 'Dedicated Short Range Communication' (DSRC) devices to communicate, in 5.9GHz band with bandwidth of 75MHz. (Liang et al., 2014) Autonomous vehicles use an intricate network of sensors and Electronic Control Units (ECUs) to accumulate data pertaining to the vehicle and its environment, information regarding other vehicles, Road Side Units (RSUs) personal devices and servicecenter systems around it, and accordingly stimulate its functionalities. ECUs of a vehicle together comprise what is known as an in-vehicle network or on-board network. This network makes use of four protocols namely Controller Area Network (CAN), Local Interconnect Network (LIN), Media Oriented System Transport (MOST) and FlexRay, each working independently from the other (Wikipedia, n.d; CrankIT, 2015), ad summarised in Figure 4.

A key component of Intelligent Transportation System (ITS), Vehicular Ad Hoc Networks (VANETs) or inter vehicle networks are networks consisting of vehicles and RSUs that share information (directly or indirectly through nodes) such as location, speed and heading of the vehicle, to determine the traffic conditions on

Figure 4. Architecture of in-vehicle network
Source: Wikipedia, n.d.

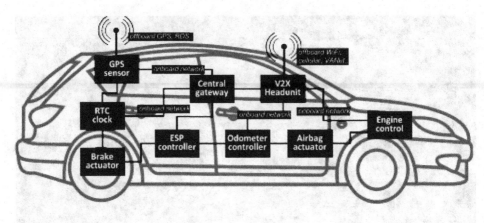

the road. It is a subclass of Mobile Ad Hoc Networks (MANETs). (Wikipedia, n.d
) Further, in VANETs, there are four types of communication:

1. **In-Vehicle:** The interconnected systems communicate amongst themselves
    to determine the state of the driver and the road ahead and alert accordingly.
    Particularly useful in technologies such as Lane keep assist, adaptive cruise
    control, airbag deployment, etc.
2. **Vehicle-to-Vehicle:** It enables vehicles to exchange information and warning
    messages about their speed and location. The slot-based intersection system
    proposed by MIT Senseable City Lab would heavily depend on this.
3. **Vehicle-to-Road Infrastructure:** This enables vehicles and hence drivers to
    obtain real-time updates on the weather, road and environmental conditions
    around. Road sign recognition system demonstrates this concept.
4. **Vehicle-to-Broadband Cloud:** This type of communication enables the drivers
    to procure useful traffic information from the cloud, which is a vast source of
    data and infotainment, and plan its course and make decisions. It also enables
    service centers and owners to stay connected with their vehicles.

While the IEEE standards support safety applications (that prevent accidents)
in VANETs, IPv6, TCP and UDP are used to provide network layer and transport
layer services in nonsafety applications (that provide convenience and efficiency
information).

Predominently VANET consists of four models:

1. **Driver and Vehicle Model:** Designed to focus on the behaviour of a single vehicle,which depends on the driver's driving style and vehicle's characteristics.
2. **Traffic Flow Model:** This model highlights the exchanges between drivers, vehicles, infrastruture and accordingly formulates an optimum road network.
3. **Communication Model:** It studies limiting factors such as communication layers, communication environment and routing stategies.
4. **Application Model:** It helps provide a visual model of all the cooperating sytems, thus helping developers analyse and make decisions regarding prioritisation of information and warnings. (Liang et al., 2015)

The network of comunictions of and with a vehicle has been extended to include personal devices as well. A Wireless Personal Area Network (WPAN) is a network for interconnecting devices in an individual's personal workspace (Chang & Chen, 2010; Wikipedia, n.d.). This network supports communication through short range wireless technologies namely Near Field Communication (NFC), Bluetooth, and Infrared (IR). The WPAN gateway of AVs helps personal devices communicate with ECUs of the vehicle and control features such as air flow, lights, wind shield wiper, etc.

Figure 5. A model Intelligent Transportation System (ITS)
Source: Wikipedia, n.d.

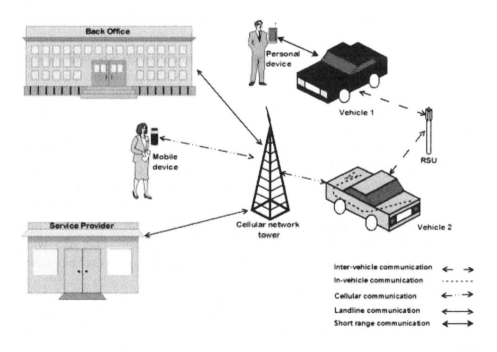

Vehicles provide data about their location, behavior and environment to nearby service centers over a cellular network using mobile devices enabled to do so. The service centers in turn process the received data and accordingly provide service to drivers, vehicle owners or general public. (Wikipedia, n.d)

BUSINESS IMPLICATIONS

Autonomous vehicles have invited tremendous speculations from business executives around the world. While truly independent of human intervention, these vehicles require to be fully tested for security and safety before they can be deployed. The cost inferred remains tremendous as the industries dig for profits. Autonomous vehicles will benefit the economy in a rippling manner as vehicles are the backbone of almost all businesses around the globe. Be it product delivery or transportation services, the impact of AVs will be large enough to require all businesses to change their existing business models.

The industry is currently divided into two categories, both aimed at ultimately achieving the goal of building these vehicles. Those looking to make the transition iteratively and those looking to jump into the age of AVs directly (Bertoncello & Wee, 2015). Some developers and manufacturers are incrementally adding features that eventually will render a car autonomous over the years, while some developers are making the transition directly with the direct conceptualization of an autonomous vehicle. Organizations like BMW, Audi and Tesla fall into the former while Google falls into the latter with development of it's completely 'Self-Driving Car'. According to the McKinsey report, (Bertoncello & Wee, 2015) the former category is known as '*Premium incumbents*' – established manufacturers who will use their largely luxury based clientele, and supplement vehicles with semi-autonomous features. The latter, known as the '*attackers*', directly will try to barge in with a fully functional AV and gain a strong market portion, position and gain volume – which is what Google aims to do.

In the next part of this section, scrutinizes and offers an insight into how AVs will be rolled out by the industry keeping in mind various factors, such as consumer trust, affordability, safety and guaranteed security, feasibility and acceptance. It will also focus on regulatory issues, insurance issues, consumer acceptance, and possible scenarios for companies and strategies to handle them. It will throw light upon the current scenario, profitability and the general consensus about AVs, while contemplating the pros and cons of machine controlled driving versus human controlled driving.

Roadmap

The roadmap is currently visualized as a division of three *eras* in which the unveiling and eventual acceptance of AVs will happen (Bertoncello & Wee, 2015). The first era coincides with the 2020s, where the first AVs will be released and consumer oriented development will take place. Autonomous vehicles will already be realities in industrial fleets. As of 2016, this is a reality. Uber has rolled out its first fleet of self-driving taxis (Uber, 2016) and plans to expand in the future. This era will bring about a decline in labour costs and diminishing CO_2 emissions through steady and optimized driving and reducing workplace accidents. Another integrant of this era is the continuous development of AVs as previously discussed. Businesses will alter models to fit innovation like Automated taxi sharing.

The present is the first era, and hence with certainty only this much can be said. The rate of market penetration, deployment scenarios and release of *safe* autonomous vehicles will all but determine the profitability of the AV ecosystem. As stated quite accurately in (Godsmark, 2016), the success of this ecosystem is some ways dependent on regulatory authorities and public acceptance, but mainly on the flows of money that will propel this product on to its feet.

Figure 6.
Source: Anthony & Uber, 2016

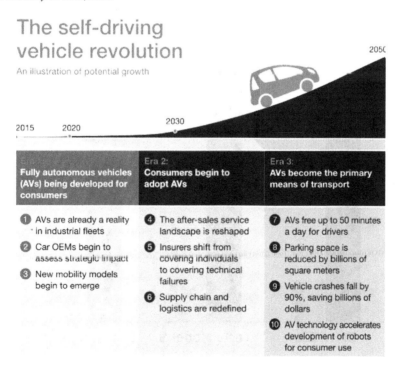

Assuming AVs will be generally accepted, era 2 will be ushered in with companies reshaping their logistics. Organizations like Amazon already are looking into autonomous product delivery through drones, while other companies like DHL are researching into automating warehousing operations, last-mile deliveries and transport operations (Amazon, n.d; DHL, n.d). However, the ushering in of this will be done with regards to various factors. Human factors, ethics, consumer satisfaction, logistic efficiency & fulfilment of required technologies are some to be considered.

Insurance is one sector that will be by large very vulnerable to change if AVs are to become the norm. Car insurance companies will have to largely change their guidelines for what acceptable scenarios and circumstances are valid claims. If two autonomous vehicles collide, who is to be blamed? Who will be penalized, the automotive company or the owner, and if the owner, which one of them? Insurance companies will be the biggest losers as accident rates will drop to almost nil. According to calculations done in (Bertoncello & Wee, 2015), the insurance industry can drop to $20B from $200B, essentially killing it. The below chart shows the estimated insurance costs, where self-driving cars are represented by red versus normal driven.

Figure 7. Ferenstein Wire
Source: KnowIndia, n.d

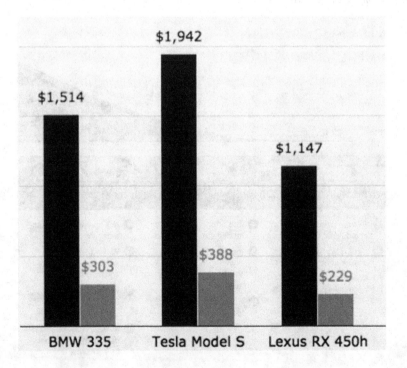

Era 3 will be the ideal scenario that most manufacturers aim to push today's world to. Diminished rates of accidents will be an obvious effect of this as human error will be eliminated. Approximately $180B will be saved just due to a decrease in accidents (FoxBusiness, 2016). Freed up roads, component manufacturers and miniaturization of current technology will some side-effects as well. This three-era division is mostly idealistic and needs to be taken lightly because such a smooth roll-out of AVs is hardly possible thanks to the large employment displacement it will cause in some sectors. However, if played right, the introduction of AVs can cause roads to be freed up to the extent of 90% traffic being reduced compared to today. (Pacific Standard, 2015) One positive side effect of this will be reduced pollution due to reduced personal vehicle usage.

Consumer Acceptance

The crux of the matter is that the public must accept it. For years, we have been groomed to ensure that absolutely undivided attention be given to the road while driving. The advent of AVs challenge this upbringing and the assumption is that many people will prematurely declare the vehicle as unsafe and untrustworthy. This has happened with many technologies that today we take for granted – escalators, elevators or aircrafts. Consumer and public acceptance will only come with time when it is proven that safety is in fact, pronounced when in an AV. Google's self-driving car experienced its first accident in one million miles according to the company (McGoogan, 2016) which is much lower what current driving statistics.

Affected Sectors

1. **City Municipalities:** These organizations gain a sizeable amount of money through human error, that is, tickets and fines handed out to drivers.
2. **Component & Sensor Manufacturers:** These companies will profit immensely due to an increase demand in the heavily specialized components that are required by AVs.
3. **Taxi Services:** This is a service that will be devastated. Already negatively affected by companies like Uber, taxi drivers in the past (Tovey, 2016) have conducted rallies and protests to show their displeasure regarding the same.
4. **Automotive Industry:** Companies which reject the AV technology risk being branded with the image of making 'inferior' cars which are to be driven manually.

5. **Insurance Companies:** As discussed in the previous section, this industry faces the most challenges as its value can depreciate from a kingly $200B to a measly $20B thanks to elimination of human error.
6. **Traffic Management Systems:** Start-ups which focus on this technology stand to gain and benefit greatly (Todd Litman, 2016).
7. **Logistics Companies:** Product delivery by hand will be rendered obsolete as AVs can replace workers, saving companies millions and reducing labour costs but also leaving a large amount of people unemployed.
8. **Military & Defence Sector:** AVs can be used to test out dangerous waters and risking of human life can be brought down to a minimum. The US military is (Fox Business, 2016) already using drones which eliminate the need of having a military driver.
9. **Private Contractors:** Private contractors will rent out vehicles, which can still transport goods and people irrespective of time and place, unlike normal vehicles.

Public transport could become obsolete thanks to ride sharing. Manufacturers may eliminate middlemen through legal contracts and levy charges for commercial vehicular use. The scenarios are endless, and which one may become the reality remains to be seen and is unpredictable as of now.

Costs Associated

Affordability is the usually the most important when estimating success of a product. Self-driving taxis are likely to be around $0.60-$1.00 a mile due to car sharing, while taxis are generally $2.00 - $3.00 per mile (Greg Ferenstein, 2015). This makes AVs much more cost efficient, not only to the public but also to the service providers as well. Costs of labour (drivers) is cut. However, there might be mark-up applied by owners, because AVs are more than likely to be very expensive. Google's Self Driving Car ranges from anywhere between $50,000 - $200,000 to build, and is a very hefty investment upfront. However, a decline is expected as sale increases, technology matures and more units are sold. As for the component and sensor manufacturers, a market of $8.7B to $13B is expected. The cost of the electronics and software for AVs is also expected to drop by 50% in the next 15 years (Bertoncello and Wee, 2015).

CHALLENGES FACED: A GLOBAL PERSPECTIVE

A plethora of problems is faced by autonomous cars.. We will be elaborating and majorly dividing these problems into three categories. The first category is developmental challenges. The second category is environmental challenges. The third category is security challenges. The first category relates to barriers that retard the progress of AVs. The second category relates to the challenges that are faced by AVs due to the environment and its surroundings. These challenges are not in the control of autonomous vehicles or their makers. The third category relates to the challenges faced while making the AVs secure, safe and completely reliable. Security against malicious, intended or unintended attempts, must be the highest priority as human lives are at stake. We will in this section elaborate and take a look at these problems individually.

Developmental Challenges

Technology is still one of the biggest obstacles that is barring AVs from entering the market. The technology required to map and look up billions of data points, thousands of maps which are highly detailed right down to the height of (The Guardian, 2016) is still in its infantile stages. The enormous detail that such mapping contains when scaled to the world renders an enormous and unimaginable set of data. AVs must not only store this data, but also look up and make split second decisions based on this data. The technology to perform operations on such huge sets of data in sub millisecond times is still not present. For example, Google (The Guardian, 2016). has only mapped 2000 miles out of 4 million miles available in the US and yet faces huge challenges regarding this data.

Other technology related problems are sensor issues. Sensory input to the vehicle must be a full hundred percent accurate and valid to ensure its safe working. Perfect accuracy is rarely guaranteed in cases of sensors and any misdirection may cause mishaps. Hence, this is another worry that we must deal with. Such a mishap was caused by a Tesla AV, which resulted in a death of a person. In the incident, the AV attempted to drive under a trailer at full speed. This can only be attributed to faulty sensory inputs (Brad Plumer, 2016). To deal with technological thresholds, different companies are using different approaches. Google believes in mapping the area to be driven ahead of time, so that it may free up the vehicle for more important decisions, while Tesla believes more in imaging and sensor processing. Google has come across difficulties like constantly changing environments, but that is to be seen.

Another issue is the lack of regulations. There hasn't been enough testing done to prove if an AV is safer or not. Regulators may have to come up with alternative ways to decide that, such as modelling or virtualizing procedures. Decisions to adopt AVs or not will have to be made under uncertainty.

Environmental Challenges

Another addition to the already growing list of complications is the challenge of unpredictability – Earth. There can be never a surety of weather, and hence bad weather will always remain a challenge. We might not be able to find a permanent solution to this challenge, but we may be able to circumvent it. Bad weather like extreme snowfall, rain, heat or windy situations can jeopardize the lives of passengers because these conditions jeopardize the stability of sensors. The stress that the surroundings put on the delicate components of an AV can cause it to malfunction. AVs are coming to places where the weather is mostly moderate all around the year. Once successful, then they can be moved up and tested in harsher conditions (Petit, Feiri, Kargl, Stottelaar, n.d.). Another complication is the constantly changing environment. A place and its topography cannot be expected to remain unchanged. Natural factors and human activity generally lead to a change in the places. This problem can be solved by constantly updated mapping, which again brings us full circle to developmental problems.

Security Challenges

The most important and critical to solve, security must be ensured a full hundred percent. As AVs get connected to each other through V2V connections, we must ensure that security is optimum. Malicious attacks can easy take advantage of lax security and force the vehicle to perform actions it might not have realistically, and cause damage financially or in the form of human life. Attacks can be done unknowingly as well and need not be malicious. A simple example of a security issue is an unconnected autonomous vehicle. Imagine a connected network of nodes which are communicating at a roundabout to decide the dispatching of vehicles. If an unconnected vehicle comes in and simply barrages in, it can cause unprecedented damage.

Malicious attacks can be demonstrated with equipment worth sixty dollars and can cause the vehicle to malfunction. Blinding of the sensors with white light, or acting as a fake node are examples of security issues. A fake node can be built at home (Othmane, Weffers, Mohd. Mohmad, Wolf, n.d.) and can fool the vehicle into thinking that there is a vehicle behind/ahead and that it must react accordingly. This can be quite dangerous if used with negative intentions. Cybersecurity is a worry that is ported to the field of AVs from the Internet. Since AVs will be connected to the Internet or at least some form of network, they will always be vulnerable to attacks like MitM, DDoS or message dropping.

We can also further classify these attacks as *Threats to the communication links, Threats to data validity, Threats to access control, Threats to privacy, Threats to devices and Threats to identity of vehicles* (Liang, Li, Zhang, Wang, Bie, 2014). The first threat is the vulnerability of communication links between two entities. (vehicles or devices) The second refers to the passing of *bogus* data to the vehicle to alter its behaviour in an undesirable way. The third defines the vulnerability of data and code, where attackers can illegally access and change certain things for personal benefit. Privacy threats are the most critical. With the intent of being malicious, a person with access to vehicular information could track a person, his/her driving habits, favourite locations and any other activity done inside the vehicle through browsers, etc. The last type of attack defines a situation where a person uses information from another vehicle to impersonate it and use it for negative applications.

Lastly, we look at some network specific challenges. Routing protocols, maintaining continuous connectivity, backward compatibility between various protocols as innovations come through, (Othmane, Weffers, Mohd. Mohmad, Wolf, n.d.) validation and encryption of messages are a few areas that must be looked into. Message passing must be made secure so that dropping and tampering is not possible. Routing protocols like GyTAR are being suggested recently. Maintaining latencies of very low magnitude is a must. This problem could be diminished with the ongoing development of 5G. There is as of now, a lot of debate regarding which strategy to use for vehicular networks.

IS THERE A FUTURE IN INDIA?

The Indian subcontinent boasts of a population of almost 1.3 billion (Aparajita Ray, 2012) with an expected population of 1.6 billion by 2050. India harbours over 182 million vehicles (May 2013) and this growth is expected to only increase in the coming years. Most of these vehicles are manual transmission vehicles as automatic transmission vehicles have not picked up in India due to reasons like fuel efficiency, and the pitching of automatic transmission as a *luxury* option. The figure of 182 million vehicles is largely disproportionate. When compared against the population – it comes down to a measly 18 vehicles per 1000 people (Wikipedia, n.d) It is very important to look at the car market in India before we discuss about the feasibility of AVs in India. India is a different ball game altogether because of various factors.

Autonomous vehicles are built and programmed to detect obstacles, move accordingly, and make decisions about lane changing, cruise control and traffic signals. This programming and development is done keeping in mind a few assumptions. We will elaborate on these expectations. Following traffic rules in a reasonable fashion, predictable pedestrian mannerisms, decent road conditions and a moderately favourable environment are some assumptions that are made in the testing phases of an AV. The stress the environment of a product can put on it is directly connected to its success.

Taking a look at the traffic mannerisms in India (TNN, 2003), we can roughly calculate daily traffic violations in India to a whopping 1,00,000 plus incidents which are taken note of. A horrifying 375 deaths occur in India daily per day due to road accidents (Corpuz, 2016). This statistic comes from 2012, hence we can definitely believe the number to have increased, as the number of vehicles on road also has gone up. The whopping number has been attributed to a lazy and improper driver licensing system. This is one of the biggest contributors to rash driving that occurs on Indian roads.

This only adds to the mix – the underdeveloped condition of roads mixed with a lack of proper traffic policing makes Indian roads a bad market to enter into. We cannot safely assume the factors that are usually assumed when building an autonomous vehicle. If pedestrians cannot be expected to adhere to certain behaviour, then the scenarios for which the vehicle must be programmed are infinitely many, and very difficult or almost impossible to accommodate.

The lack of traffic signals, symbols and the state of them also pose a problem in India. Flyers, banners and other material is usually stuck on top of traffic signs which barely are legible due to said vandalizing. Some autonomous vehicles may need to judge speeds of other vehicles based on speed limit signs, but if it does not know, then the chances of collisions simply increase because of unpredictability. Another issue is poor penetration of advanced technologies in India (USDOT, 2016). A preliminary and yet incomplete study by the market research firm Markets and Markets shows that technologies like advanced brake assist, parking assist have only penetrated the Indian vehicle markets in the single digit percentages, which is a poor result.

To roll out a product like an autonomous vehicle, clear regulations are required. Departments like the USDOT – United States Department of Transportation have already released guidelines (Wikipedia, n.d) regarding autonomous vehicles. This virtually sealed any doubts about the advent of AVs and confirmed that the US government considers US roads as feasible for a working autonomous vehicle.

Considering that the Indian counterpart – RTO has not even looked into autonomous vehicles as of now, we can safely say that AVs are at the least a few decades away from Indian roads. Road accessibility information in India is not published and is not generally available publicly. This hampers development of software that enables an AV to manoeuvre through roads. The only innovations that are being done in India are currently in private campuses, where the strictly controlled environment provides a reasonable surrounding to test AVs (USDOT, 2016). However, when Indian roads are ready for autonomous vehicles, it will be an extremely beneficial situation for consumers and manufacturers because of India's weather. Future AVs from Tesla will be incorporating solar power as a method of power generation. (Corpuz, 2016) (India receives a surplus of solar energy throughout the year) While partial automation is a realistic concept to dream about in the country, a plethora of problems stand in the way of completely automated vehicles in India.

CONCLUSION

While evolution of autonomous cars is a giant leap forward for science and technology and many other industries depending on this innovation, acceptance by public still remains a challenge. As attackers will always be a step ahead of developers, it is difficult to quote when the technology will be proficient enough to convince humans to let go off the steering and read a book, eat or even sleep. If allowed to take over, this technology will also help improve the environmental health by substantially reducing the fuel emissions due to optimum speed adherence and other factors. Also with its advent, this technology may also make the concept of owning and maintaining a vehicle archaic as each vehicle in the network will be able serve as a cab and could be summoned at will.

As much as this technology is dreaded, it has the potential to save lives. In desperate times, a patient would not need to drive himself to the hospital and AVs will lift the weight of incapacity to drive from the heads of family members and relatives.

However, as each coin has two sides, this technology also has its cons. If the entire network was to consist of only self-driving cars and no human intervention, failure of one component in a car under inevitable conditions could lead to nothing short of death for the passenger. Not only will one vehicle get affected by the accident, but all vehicles in the network, all of them being interconnected will be adversely affected. As all vehicles would communicate and depend on one another for signals and warnings, one vehicle rolling out of the web will disturb the entire network and may result in causalities elsewhere. Moreover, lives of children under the driving age will also be put to stake as they would feel empowered to take control of the car since it would require absolutely no driving experience.

Solving these issues is what everyone is aiming for and breakthroughs are being made quickly in this competitive industry. However, autonomous vehicles have a long way to go and a lot of groundwork needs to be done before humans can trust it more than themselves.

REFERENCES

Amazon. (n.d.). *Amazon Prime Air*. Retrieved from: https://www.amazon.com/b?node=8037720011

Anthony & Uber. (2016). *Uber rolls out Self Driving cars in Pittsburgh*. Retrieved from: https://newsroom.uber.com/pittsburgh-self-driving-uber/

Background on traffic sign detection and recognition. (n.d.). Retrieved from: http://www.springer.com/cda/content/document/cda_downloaddocument/9781447122449-c2.pdf?SGWID=0-0-45-1246851-p174192870

Ben Othmane, L., & Weffers, H. (n.d.). *A survey of security and privacy in connected vehicles*. Retrieved from: https://www.informatik.tu-darmstadt.de/fileadmin/user_upload/Group_CASED/Publikationen/2010/TUD-CS-2015-1208.pdf

Bertoncello, M., & Wee, D. (2015). *10 ways autonomous driving could redefine the automotive world*. Retrieved from: http://www.mckinsey.com/industries/automotive-and-assembly/our-insights/ten-ways-autonomous-driving-could-redefine-the-automotive-world

Broggi, A., Buzzoni, M., Debattisti, S., Grisleri, P., Laghi, M. C., Medici, P., & Versari, P. (2013). Extensive tests of autonomous driving technologies. *IEEE Transactions on Intelligent Transportation Systems*, *14*(3), 1403–1415. doi:10.1109/TITS.2013.2262331

Business, F. (2016). *How self-driving cars will change the economy*. Retrieved from: http://www.foxbusiness.com/features/2016/01/20/how-self-driving-cars-will-change-economy.html

Chen, M.-C., & Chang, T.-W. (2010). *Introduction of vehicular network architectures*. Retrieved from: http://www.igi-global.com/chapter/introduction-vehicular-network-architectures/39516

Clark, B. (2015). *How self-driving cars work*. Retrieved from: http://www.makeuseof.com/tag/how-self-driving-cars-work-the-nuts-and-bolts-behind-googles-autonomous-car-program/

Corpuz, E. (2016). *The Tesla Model 3 will incorporate Tesla's solar roof technology*. Retrieved from: http://futurism.com/elon-musk-the-model-3-will-incorporate-teslas-solar-roof-technology/

Crank, I. T. (2015). *Vehicle to vehicle communication*. Retrieved from: https://crankit.in/vehicle-to-vehicle-v2v-communication/

DHL. (n.d.). *Self-driving cars*. Retrieved from: http://www.dhl.com/en/about_us/logistics_insights/dhl_trend_research/self_driving_vehicles.html

Ferenstein, G. (2015). *How much will the self-driving version of your car save on insurance*. Retrieved from: https://medium.com/the-ferenstein-wire/how-much-the-self-driving-version-of-your-car-will-save-on-insurance-in-1-graph-16ebcc27f26e#.sp2n267c3

Godsmark, P. (2016). *Autonomous vehicles- the compelling business cases*. Retrieved from: https://avimpacts.com/2016/08/11/autonomous-vehicles-compelling-business-cases/

Gummadi, V. (2015). *Driverless cars – What's their future in India?* Retrieved from: https://www.linkedin.com/pulse/driverless-cars-boon-bane-india-its-future-vijay-gummadi

Hechri, A., & Mtibaa, A. (2011). Lanes and Road signs recognition. *International Journal of Computer Science Issues, 8*(6). Retrieved from: http://www.ijcsi.org/papers/IJCSI-8-6-1-402-408.pdf

Hossain & Hyder. (2015). Traffic road sign detection and recognition for automotive vehicles. *International Journal of Computer Applications, 120*(24). Retrieved from: http://research.ijcaonline.org/volume120/number24/pxc3904265.pdf

How Lidar Works. (n.d.). Retrieved from: http://www.lidar-uk.com/how-lidar-works/

Howard, B. (2013). *What is lane departure warning, and how does it work?* Retrieved from: https://www.extremetech.com/g00/extreme/165320-what-is-lane-departure-warning-and-how-does-it-work

Howard, B. (2013). *What is adaptive cruise control and how does it work?* Retrieved from: http://www.extremetech.com/extreme/157172-what-is-adaptive-cruise-control-and-how-does-it-work

IANS. (2015). *Traffic violations to attract steeper fines*. Retrieved from: http://www.indiatvnews.com/news/india/traffic-violations-to-attract-steeper-fines-half-baked-49591.html

Jiang, T., Iyer, U., Tolani, A., & Hussain, S. (2015). *Self-driving cars: disruptive or incremental?* Retrieved from: http://cet.berkeley.edu/wp-content/uploads/Self-Driving-Cars.pdf

KnowIndia. (n.d.). *Indian auto industry*. Retrieved from: http://www.knowindia.net/auto.html

Korosec, K. (2016). Google self-driving cars have learnt how to interpret cyclists' hand signals. *Fortune 500*. Retrieved from: http://fortune.com/2016/07/06/google-self-driving-cars-cyclist/

Krambeck, D. (2016). *Tesla vs Google. Do Lidar sensors belong in AVs?* Retrieved from: http://www.allaboutcircuits.com/news/tesla-vs-google-do-lidar-sensors-belong-in-autonomous-vehicles/

Liang, W., Li, Z., Zhang, H., Wang, S., & Bie, R. (2014). *Vehicular Ad Hoc Networks*. Retrieved from: http://dsn.sagepub.com/content/11/8/745303.full

Litman, T. (2016). *Autonomous Vehicle Implementation predictions*. Retrieved from: http://www.vtpi.org/avip.pdf

Logan, A. (2015). *How does adaptive cruise control work?* Retrieved from: http://www.proctorcars.com/how-does-adaptive-cruise-control-work/

McGoogan, C. (2016). *Google self-driving car involved in serious crash*. Retrieved from: http://www.telegraph.co.uk/technology/2016/09/26/googles-self-driving-car-involved-in-serious-crash-after-van-jum/

Miyata, S., Yanou, A., Nakamura, H., & Takehara, S. (2009). Feature extraction and recognition of road signs using dynamic image processing. *Image Processing*. Retrieved from: http://www.intechopen.com/books/image-processing/feature-extraction-and-recognition-of-road-sign-using-dynamic-image-processing

National tyres and autocare. (n.d.). *10 astonishing technologies that power Google self-driving cars*. Retrieved from: https://www.national.co.uk/tech-powers-google-car/

Newcomb, D. (2016). *Can self-driving cars kill traffic lights?* Retrieved from: http://in.pcmag.com/cars/102032/opinion/can-self-driving-cars-kill-traffic-lights

Petit, J., Feiri, M., Kargl, F., & Stottelaar, B. (n.d.). *Remote attacks on automated vehicle sensors*. Retrieved from: https://www.blackhat.com/docs/eu-15/materials/eu-15-Petit-Self-Driving-And-Connected-Cars-Fooling-Sensors-And-Tracking-Drivers-wp1.pdf

Pirzada, U. (2015). *The Tesla autopilot*. Retrieved from: http://wccftech.com/tesla-autopilot-story-in-depth-technology/2/

Plumer, B. (2016). *Five big challenges that self-driving cars still have to overcome*. Retrieved from: http://www.vox.com/2016/4/21/11447838/self-driving-cars-challenges-obstacles

Pulakkat, H. (2016). *Why Indian roads will take decades*. Retrieved from: http://economictimes.indiatimes.com/industry/auto/news/why-indian-roads-will-take-decades-to-be-ready-for-self-driving-cars/articleshow/52018034.cms

Rao, V. (2012). *Which industries will be disrupted by AVs*. Retrieved from: https://www.quora.com/Which-industries-and-jobs-will-self-driving-cars-and-trucks-disrupt-or-destroy/

Ray, A. (2012). *Bangalore sees 16,000 traffic violations daily*. Retrieved from:http://timesofindia.indiatimes.com/city/bengaluru/Bangalore-sees-16000-traffic-violations-daily/articleshow/15332697.cms

Sanchez, D. (2015). Collective technologies- autonomous vehicles. *Securing Australia's Future (SAF) Project 05*. Retrieved from: http://www.acola.org.au/PDF/SAF05/2Collective%20technologies.pdf

Santo, D. (2016). *Autonomous cars' pick: camera, Lidar, radar?* Retrieved from: http://www.eetimes.com/author.asp?section_id=36&doc_id=1330069

SaveTheDemocracy. (n.d.). *Reality of one of the RTOs in India*. Retrieved from: http://www.savethedemocracy.org/reality-check/reality-of-one-of-the-rtos-of-india/

Schweber, B. (n.d.). *The Autonomous Car: A Diverse Array of Sensors Drives Navigation, Driving, and Performance*. Retrieved from: http://www.mouser.in/applications/autonomous-car-sensors-drive-performance/

Standard, P. (2015). *The many impacts of AVs*. Retrieved from: https://psmag.com/the-many-impacts-of-autonomous-vehicles-9149b31c4f7d#.g7dx0ulns

Stewart, J. (2016). *Tesla's self-driving car plan seems insane but it might just work*. Retrieved from: https://www.wired.com/2016/10/teslas-self-driving-car-plan-seems-insane-just-might-work/

The Economist. (2012). *Self-driving cars in the military*. Retrieved from: http://www.businessinsider.com/the-military-is-getting-into-self-driving-vehicles-too-2012-12?IR=T

The Guardian. (2016). *Tesla driver dies in first fatal crash*. Retrieved from: https://www.theguardian.com/technology/2016/jun/30/tesla-autopilot-death-self-driving-car-elon-musk

TNN. (2003). *Caught red-handed. Cops taking bribes*. Retrieved from: http://timesofindia.indiatimes.com/delhi-times/Caught-red-handed-Cops-taking-bribes/articleshow/63371.cms

Tovey, A. (2016). *The end of the cabbie?* Retrieved from: http://www.telegraph.co.uk/business/2016/05/19/the-end-of-the-cabbie-uber-tests-driverless-taxis/

USDOT. (2016). *Federal Automated Vehicles Policy.* Retrieved from: https://www.transportation.gov/AV

Wikipedia. (n.d.). *Lane Departure Warning System.* Retrieved from: https://en.wikipedia.org/wiki/Lane_departure_warning_system

Wikipedia. (n.d.). *Autonomous cruise control system.* Retrieved from: https://en.wikipedia.org/wiki/Autonomous_cruise_control_system#Timeline

Wikipedia. (n.d.). *Lidar.* Retrieved from: https://en.wikipedia.org/wiki/Lidar#Design

Wikipedia. (n.d.). *Sonar.* Retrieved from: https://en.wikipedia.org/wiki/Sonar

Wikipedia. (n.d.). *Vehicular Ad Hoc Network.* Retrieved from: https://en.wikipedia.org/wiki/Vehicular_ad_hoc_network

Wikipedia. (n.d.). *Personal Area Network.* Retrieved from: https://en.wikipedia.org/wiki/Personal_area_network#Wireless_personal_area_network

Wikipedia. (n.d.). *Demographics of India.* Retrieved from: https://en.wikipedia.org/wiki/Demographics_of_India

Wikipedia. (n.d.). *Google Self-Driving Car.* Retrieved from: https://en.wikipedia.org/wiki/Google_self-driving_car

Chapter 7
Mechanisms to Secure Communications in the IoT

Azeddine Bilami
Batna 2 University, Algeria

Somia Sahraoui
Batna 2 University, Algeria

ABSTRACT

The maturity of the IoT depends on the security of communications and the protection of end-user's privacy. However, technological and material heterogeneities, and the asymmetric nature of communications between sensor nodes and ordinary Internet hosts, make the security in this case more problematic. Major problem facing the large deployment of IoT is the absence of a unified architecture and a lack of common agreement in defining protocols and standards for IoT parts. Many solutions have been proposed for the standardization of security concepts and protocols in IoT at different layers. Even though many advances and proposals were made for IoT adaptation as IPv6 for Low Power Wireless Personal Area Network (6LoWPAN), and at application layer with protocols such as XMPP, MQTT, CoAP, etc., security of the IoT remains a very challenging task and an open research topic. This chapter focuses on existing protocols and different proposed mechanisms in literature to secure communications in the IoT.

DOI: 10.4018/978-1-5225-2296-6.ch007

INTRODUCTION

We are already seeing the launch of a new connected world through the Internet of Things (Atzori et al., 2013) where digitization is not restricted to telecommunication and official management tasks, and Internet connectivity is not the feature of regular Internet hosts (computers, laptops, tablets and smart phones) alone. Rather, digitization will span any of the daily activities (e.g. driving, manufacturing, healthcare …) and Internet connection will invade a huge set of everyday objects (such as vehicles, TV, refrigerator, buildings, etc.), urban and even isolated rural environments. The emergence of that new generation of the Internet is made possible through the convergence between several successful wireless embedded technologies and the advances in networking engineering.

Indeed, wireless senor networks (Akyildiz et al., 2002) are a key technology in the enabling of everything connected paradigm of the future Internet. A wireless sensor network consists of several tiny sensor nodes that collect data of various types from the target field. The collected data help the users to monitor activities, predict events or enhance efficiency in numerous application fields. In the context of the IoT, sensed data representing either behavioral or environmental status are accessed from anywhere and at anytime for ubiquitous monitoring. Tagging, radio identification and contactless technologies (Gubbi et al., 2013) are also considered as important technological bloc that identifies IoT objects and stores different information related to their static features, such as manufacturer name, manufacturing date, expiration date of a product and many other useful information for object tracking purposes. Another important technology is recently joining the Internet of things for new perspectives and optimized efficiency. So, we talk about the drones (Loke, 2015) which brings flying terminal objects or relay points.

Furthermore, it is predicted that more than fifty billions of smart things will be connected via widespread Internet connection by 2020 (Atzori et al., 2010). At this stage, it is worth mentioning that huge storage and processing capabilities will be required to deal with the big data generated by the IoT and injected in the Internet.

The main goal of the Internet of things is to bring high levels of smartness to the world by providing smart and useful services. The IoT offers many advantages that can be described briefly as follows:

- Ubiquitous access to information for a sophisticated and comfortable lifestyle.
- Gain of time: unnecessary trips are therefore replaced by a simple web browsing to order products, check the status of connected objects and/or locations.
- Improved quality of services and remote monitoring in various application fields such as industrial applications, smart cities, smart healthcare, etc.

- Improved productivity and customer experience: the connected objects may send reports to their manufacturer indicating the preferences and habits of customers helping more companies to act proactively in an adapted way to meet the requirements of the customers.
- In some applications, IoT might help us to rationalize our spending and savings because we should consume only as needed, be it for shopping or energy consumption (required for lighting or air conditioning) for example.
- Possibility of leveraging Internet resources for storing and processing IoT's data.

Many architectures of the IoT are presented in the literature with minor differences between them. Basically a generic IoT architecture consists of three principal layers (Gubbi et al., 2013): perception layer, networking layer and application or service layer as illustrated in Figure 1. The scheme indicates how data are collected from the physical world by sensor nodes, communicated and processed throughout the Internet backbone to be finally used by different smart applications.

Depending upon the way smart things are integrating the IoT, data can be either directly extracted from the Internet-connected objects or indirectly from a front-end gateway. In fact, the direct incorporation via the adoption of IP (Internet Protocol) standards is generally much more advantageous as it fulfills the IoT requirements in terms of pervasiveness, interoperability and flexibility. Thus, smart objects interact with each other and with other Internet hosts directly according to several

Figure 1. General model of the Internet of Things

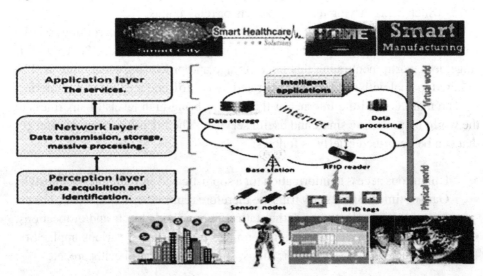

communication models, with different protocols. The main concern in that is to make possible such interactions while enabling efficient end-to-end security and/ or good quality of service.

Security is a key part in any IoT deployment, service and for the preservation of user's personal life. Surely, the success of IoT's project depends on its ability to secure end-to-end communications and to protect the end devices against different attacks. That is considered as tremendous issue due to many patterns such as the scarce resources and the heterogeneity at different levels (involved devices, adopted communication technologies, and proprietary communication protocols) which make difficult the development of unified, robust and constraints-aware security mechanisms. Two possible directions are theoretically possible to develop such solutions. To bring security to the IoT, realistic solutions should avoid the definition of innovative approaches whilst adopting the well-known mechanisms that are already used by the standard communication systems, but with the inevitability to optimize and adapt their implementation to the constraints of the deployed devices

This chapter is intended to provide in-depth study of proposed mechanisms to guarantee security for the different communication styles in the IoT. The chapter is structured as follows: the second section points out generalities on IPv6-based Internet of things and the third section presents the communication models in such environment. The fourth section highlights the communication protocols in the IPv6 Internet of things. The fifth and the sixth sections present the security vulnerabilities and the principal threats, respectively. Then, the seventh section gives a brief review on the security building blocks in the IoT. the eighth section deals with the raised challenges with the security of communications in the IoT while the ninth section gives the basic communications security-related requirements. A state-of-the-art on the proposed solutions that treat the security of the communications in the context of the IoT is given in the tenth section. Finally, we conclude the chapter and underline the open research issues.

OVERVIEW OF IPv6-ENABLED INTERNET OF THINGS

The Internet of Things tends to integrate all things surrounding us. IPv6-based communication technologies are expected to integrate everything into the already existing and well-approved IP infrastructure. This trend identified as IPv6 Internet of Things (6IoT), is also known as all-IP or ubiquitous IP. These nominations are all referring to the extension of TCP/IP standards to the real world's physical objects and environments. This integration approach is stack based; it considers that each sensor node must implement the TCP/IP protocol stack to ensure direct communication between the internet hosts and this sensor without any translation. In this case, the integration of sensor networks into the Internet is done in a seamless, unified and standardized fashion which promotes the interoperability in the future Internet. As IPv6 provides a huge set of available IP addresses, each connected sensor obtains its own public IPv6 address. Also, sensors can by now act as web hosts (clients and servers) requesting and serving relevant services in several smart applications. From technical base, the adoption of IP protocols by highly constrained networks, like WSNs, sounds a bold step. This is due to the fact that TCP/IP standards were tailored for unconstrained networks and are consequently onerous both in communication overhead and processing costs. So, they cannot be directly projected on resources-limited networks such as WSNs. Following this way, IETF has brought many useful and standardized IPv6-compliant solutions that are more likely suitable for sensor networks integrating the Internet. The basic standard is the 6LoWPAN (IPv6 Low power Wireless Personal Area Networks) (Montenegro et al., 2007) that stands for an adaptation layer that renders possible the communication of huge IPv6 datagrams (1280 bytes of minimal Maximum Transmission Unit: MTU) over wireless sensor networks. The basic adaptation techniques are message compression and fragmentation. Hence, the communication costs (energy consumption and network overhead) of the IPv6 datagrams decrease sensibly. Note that 6LoWPAN standard recommends that the IPv6-anabled WSNs adopt IEEE 80.15.4 as an underlying transmission technology. Such technology is known for being WSNs-friendly and energy-efficient but this is not the only reason why it is suggested for IoT. In fact, IEEE 802.15.4 helps the 6LoWPAN mechanism to optimize the compression rates (it is possible in some cases to replace 128-bit IPv6 addresses by 16-bit IEEE 80.15.4 short addresses). Thereby, the 6LoWPAN-enabled sensor network is henceforth called 6LoWPAN network and its border router is thus named 6BR (6LoWPAN Border Router).

Many other standardization efforts have been carried out by several IETF working groups. We cite namely the RPL (Winter et al., 2012) that is an efficient IPv6 distance vector routing protocol for 6IoT, developed by RoLL (Routing over Low power and Lossy networks) group. Also, many applicative protocols have been standardized in order to support the interactions among smart objects in the IoT and/or between external hosts end IoT hosts. These protocols will be discussed in deeply in the continuation of the chapter. The Figure 2 illustrates the architectural design of the 6IoT.

The 6IoT approach may be the most important integration solution of WSNs to Internet, but it is not the single one. Actually, there are other approaches, mainly the front-end and gateway approaches where the WSN is completely independent from the internet network, i.e. there is no direct communication between the internet hosts and sensors nodes because they implement different protocols and services. So, a device must be installed for enabling the interactions and exchanges

Figure 2. Simple architecture of 6IoT

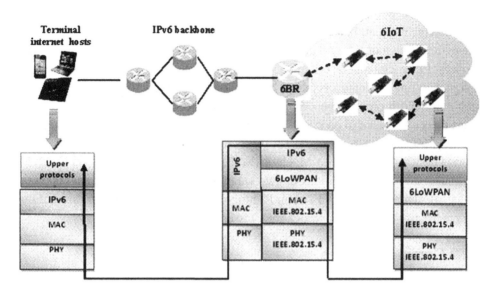

between the external internet hosts and sensor nodes. In front-end approach, the device can be a base station which implements protocols to save incoming data from any network and forward them to the destination network using the service interface. The gateway approach uses a gateway as a centralized device which acts as an application layer gateway for data stream translating and routing. In this approach, the internet hosts or the WSN nodes can be able to address each other for exchanging data without setting a direct connection; in fact a gateway device is still needed to allow the good exchange of information. As stated, the best and most realistic integration approach possibly will the TCP/IP solution, but it is not usable in all cases because many WSN networks cannot support the implementation of this approach. Generally, the selection of an integration approach depends on the sensor network characteristics and the end user's needs. Some situations recommend a more suitable approach to satisfy WSN constraints by adopting for example a hybrid solution while combining the TCP/IP and the gateway approaches. Another possible approach is the middleware for providing the necessary services. The middleware aims to address and solve many problems like the security, the standardization, the heterogeneity and others issues by hiding the complexity and the technical details of both hardware and software. It enables the application developers to improve their applications and making them more efficiency, extensible, flexible, reusable and simple to use (Nam et al., 2014).

COMMUNICATION MODELS IN 6IoT

In nowadays Internet, human-to-human (H2H) communications are the dominant interaction style, not to say that it is the only one. All web applications, tools and services, like social media, e-mail ... are human-centric which means that they are designed to link human users across the web, allowing them to communicate with each other. With the emergence of the Internet of things, the Internet-connected smart things will need to interact with each other and eventually with other regular Internet hosts. Hence, two big classes of interactions appear with the advent of the internet of things: Machine-to-Machine (M2M) and Human-to-Thing (H2T). M2M communication class encompasses two subclasses of automatic communications in the IoT: Thing-to-Thing (T2T) and Thing-to-Human (T2H). The figure bellow depicts the IoT-related communication classes.

M2M Communications

Machine-to-Machine communications (Gen et al., 2011) stand for the automatic and autonomous interactions between machines that are never initiated by human and do not need for its later intervention. This kind of transactions fosters pervasive-

Figure 3. Communication patterns in the IoT

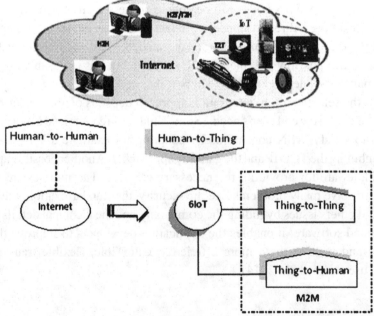

ness and automation in many potential applications of the IoT, namely smart cities, industries, e-healthcare, e-shopping, etc. where for example connected things can send automatically commands to the market, reports to their manufacturer, health status to the doctor, etc.

As already illustrated in Figure 3, there are two types of M2M communications in the Internet of things: T2T and T2H. Thing-to-thing communications happen among sensor nodes belonging to the same 6LoWPAN network or to separate Internet-integrated WSNs. This style of M2M communications is homogenous since the interacting things (sensors) are submitted to similar constraints and almost have the same capabilities. Contrary to thing-to-thing communications, thing-to-human (and even human-to-thing) transactions are qualified of being highly hardware and software heterogeneous. Human hosts in the internet use powerful devices (laptops, desktops, tablets, smartphones…) that are incomparable with resource-limited sensor nodes in the IoT side. The homogeneity and the heterogeneity features of M2M communications in the IoT depend not only upon material-based similarities, but it depends also on other considerations, such as the adopted communication standards and networks-related specificities (transmission support, MTU …).

Human-to-Thing Communications

The direct interactions between human users and the surrounding or remote smart things are likely in many applications. Such as smart home, smart cities and e-healthcare. One user needs to change remotely (e.g. via its smartphone) the settings of its smart home or to ask it if his children are at home. We can also imagine smart buildings that respond to the user's requests helping him to know exactly where everything (colleagues, workplaces, devices and assets) is, in real time. Thus, a doctor may query the patient's body sensors to know about his health status. These are just some few examples of application scenarios where human-to-thing transactions (Garcia-Morchon et al., 2012) are expected.

Like thing-to-human communications, human-to-thing communications are heterogeneous. The major difference between both communication styles resides in the fact that T2H are automatic whereas H2T are always initiated by the human.

Group Communications

Group communications (or multicast communications) in the Internet are very interesting in many applications. In the context of the IoT, group communications (Rahmani et al., 2015) cover thing-to-things (T2Ts) as well as human-to-things (H2Ts) communications. Indeed, it is anticipated that the connected sensors will cooperate to perform shared missions. In addition, users can instruct a group of sensor nodes to achieve simultaneously the same task for example; we order the lights in a room to switch on.

COMMUNICATION PROTOCOLS IN THE 6IoT

There is a large pool of promising protocols designed to deal with the different communication styles in the IoT. The operational mode of those protocols is based either on request/response paradigm or publish/subscribe paradigm. Certain communication protocols may support both paradigms. With a request/response communication protocol, a client sends a request to a server. This last reacts by sending the required response or an error message if something goes wrong with the received request. By this, the transaction may either get ended if it is qualified by short lived. Otherwise, in a long-lived transaction, the client keeps listening to the server for receiving any updated data about the already requested resource.

In publish/subscribe communication pattern, a sender does not send the messages directly to the destination node(s). It rather publishes them in an intermediary domain and the interested destination nodes, the subscribers to a given message category, obtain the right messages.

In this section, we are intended to describe briefly the most popular communication protocols in the Internet of things.

CoAP(Constrained Application Protocol)

The CoRE working group at the IETF has defined CoAP (Shelby et al., 2012), a leader web transfer protocol that is destined to work over constrained devices in the 6IoT. For this reason, CoAP is invited to be simple and extremely lightweight. CoAP is a request/response protocol that is especially tailored to support M2M communications in the Web of Things (WoT). Human-to-thing communications can be also supported among CoAP-discussing sensors in the 6LoWPAN network and the external HTTP hosts. At this stage, it is worth mentioning that CoAP is similar to HTTP but both protocols are not compatible with each other. So, to efficiently support CoAP-HTTP interactions, a proxy should intervene to ensure transparently the required protocol translations between the two protocols. The proxy may provide additional services like resource local caching. In addition to unicast communications, CoAP protocol supports also multicast communications, which presents a major advantage.Contrary to HTTP that is based on a reliable transporting protocol, CoAP is based on UDP that is constraints-friendly and consequently, more suitable for WSN deployments. It defines four messages: CON, ACK, NON and RST. The requests sent in CON (confirmable) messages have to be acknowledged by a response encapsulated in ACK message. This is a shifted reliability management for critical communications at the application layer instead of the transport level. Otherwise, if the communication between CoAP devices does not need for reliability, requests have just to be communicated in NON messages. In the case when anomaly happens during the communication, a node may send the message RST to reset the session between the CoAP client and server. The figure bellow illustrates a M2M communication with CoAP, where a CoAP client sends a confirmable request to the CoAP server. This last responds by a response message containing the most recent temperature reading.

MQTT(Message Queuing Telemetry Transport)

MQTT (Oasis-Standard, 2014) is an example of a messaging application protocol on the web that was invented by IBM. Its effectiveness is increasingly approved in many successful applications such as Facebook messenger. Now its adoption for M2M applications in the IoT is highly investigated. MQTT's operational mode is generally concentrated around publish/subscribe model. Moreover, the protocol operates over TCP with an acceptable level of simplicity to effectively meet the strong constraints of sensor networks connected to the Internet.

From an architectural standpoint, MQTT clients (sensor nodes in our case) should connect to a central MQTT server said broker. Each message is published at the broker in a given topic corresponding to a type of data (e.g. temperature, light ...) carried by the message. Clients can subscribe to multiple topics and receive every message posted in the topic they are interested in. In the figure below (Figure 5), we illustrate an example of M2M communication with MQTT. The model consists

Figure 4. Simple CoAP communication model

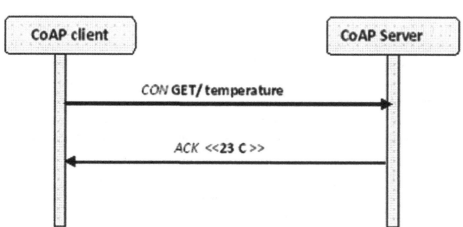

Figure 5. Exemplification of MQTT's communication architecture

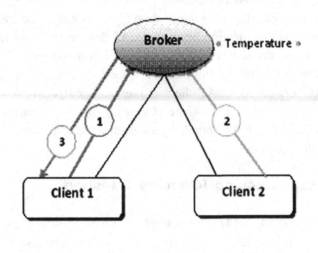

1. Subscription

2. Publication of a new message (e.g. temperature = 24)

3. Reception of the published message (temperature = 24)

of two customers who create TCP connections with the broker (server). The client 1 subscribes to the topic temperature then, client 2 publishes a new message in this topic. The server starts immediately, to transmit a copy of the message to the client 1.

XMPP(EXtensible Messaging and Presence Protocol)

XMPP (Andre, 2011) is a leader standard that allows the exchange of instant messages on the web. It works according to publish/subscribe architecture quite like MQTT. Nevertheless, it can also operate under request/response model. The XMPP servers can be either centralized or distributed (network of servers). Moreover, we can find public XMPP servers or private ones (intranet). XMPP is also based on TCP protocol. The client and the server establish TCP connection before exchanging their messages in XML format. For the internet of things, XMPP protocol is an adapted candidate for M2M communications in many applications, particularly the industrial applications.

We have briefly described CoAP, MQTT and XMPP protocols which are among the most popular communication protocols in the IoT. This does not mean that they are the only protocols we can use in that context (Schneider, 2013). Being based on TCP that is considered as a heavy transporting protocol, MQTT and XMPP protocols are not really well suited for LLNs (Low power and Lossy Networks) such as 6LoWPAN networks in the 6IoT. For this reason, CoAP is more preferred. However, if publish/subscribe technique is required MQTT or XMPP should be adopted. In this last case, research works have to be directed in this way to make possible the support of both protocols by constrained IPv6 networks in the future Internet.

IoT SECURITY AND VULNERABILITIES

Security concerns in IoT exist at different levels (IoT devices, communication networks) since threats can be launched against both hardware and software IoT systems. Thus, the security should be maintained throughout the whole network. To secure communications and to enable devices to ensure the authenticity of their pairs, encryption and authentication techniques are used with an optimization of cryptography techniques such as lightweight asymmetric key cryptosystems and elliptic curve cryptography to offer appropriate solutions for constrained devices.

To ensure protection to end devices against any attack on the embedded operating systems and to avoid possible alteration of the operating code, security solutions should be developed at the same time as the devices. Moreover, any access to the device must be checked before being authorized using access control techniques.

As we are interested in 6IoT architecture and TCP/IP as Integration approach, we focus in the remaining of the chapter on vulnerabilities and solutions related to IPv6-based Internet of Things.

In this context, IoT is vulnerable to several kinds of threats that can be categorized in three main classes: network-related vulnerabilities, connection-related vulnerabilities, protocols-originated vulnerabilities and application-related vulnerabilities.

Network-Related Vulnerabilities

In fact, wireless sensor networks which are the most dominant technology in the Internet of things are inherently vulnerable to a large set of attacks. This is due to many factors like wireless nature of the medium. Scarce resources are among the most severe vulnerabilities of WSNs; the limited energy reserve of the battery-powered sensor nodes, as well as the insufficient memory space that is limited to some tens of kilobytes, and the weak computational capabilities. Another important factor making WSNs exposed to susceptible attacks is the short radio communication ranges of the sensor nodes. Thus, two disjoint communicating sensor nodes are obliged to opt for multi-hop communication and pass their messages through intermediary nodes. Consequently, there will be a high probability that the exchanged messages get (maliciously) altered, dropped or diverted.

A WSN may undergo the risk of nodes compromising acts that lead to the modification of the program of the targeted sensor nodes so that they behave in a malicious way. Thereafter, the compromised sensor nodes become insider intruders that benefit from the fact that it is considered as a trusted node in the networks and causesserious security problems.

Connection-Related Vulnerabilities

The connection between constrained sensor networks and the Internet is challenging enough. The none-equivalent capabilities of the involved hosts in the future Internet create a deep hole that can be exploited by adversaries to disrupt the communications in the IoT. Indeed, the communication between ordinary Internet hosts and sensors connected to the IoT is characterized by strong material and technological heterogeneities. Regular hosts are more powerful, have no energy restriction, belong to more reliable networks providing very high communication throughputs, unlike tiny sensor nodes which are provided with limited resources and are part of unreliable networks allowing communications with slight throughputs. These heterogeneities help substantially the attackers to harm the 6IoT-connected sensor nodes, as well as their services.

Moreover, packet fragmentation technique that is required to deal with the big difference between the maximum sizes of data units that can be communicated inside a sensor network and the Internet (the minimum MTU is about1280 bytes with IPv6 networks, compared to only 127 bytes of maximum MTU in a IEEE 802.15.4-enabled 6LoWPAN network) is among the most attractive vulnerabilities related to internet connection scaling. If it is illegally managed, the fragmentation can turn from a useful function to a harmful practice since the maliciously accelerated packets fragmentation rates at the edge router in the sensor network side lead to huge problems, like for example network flooding and services subverting.

According to 6IoT scenarios, attackers do not have to be physically closer to the connected WSN so that they could threaten it. They can rather do it in much easier way, remotely, from anywhere, at anytime and using any internet-connected device. In other words, attacks targeting connected sensor nodes in the 6IoT are generally launched in a ubiquitous manner. This amplifies sensibly the security issues in the 6IoT and hence, crucifies the researcher's mission in finding out efficient security solutions in this situation.

In addition to all the cited vulnerabilities in this class, sensor networks integrated into the 6IoT are also likely to inherit the vulnerability to the classic threats that are already known in the today's Internet with deeper effects onto the 6LoWPAN networks.

Protocol-Originated Vulnerabilities

Besides the network and connection-specific vulnerabilities, we distinguish also the protocol-originated vulnerabilities that can arise from gaps in protocol conception and/or implementation phases. For example, IP (v4 and v6) protocol that identifies the communicating hosts in the Internet by the (public) IP addresses is vulnerable to identity spoofing threats. Besides that, a recent research (Hummen et al., 2013) has been carried out in order to give in-depth study of datagram fragmentation vulnerabilities in 6LoWPAN standard. It was found out through the realized study that the fragmentation functionality in 6LoWPAN is highly vulnerable. Furthermore, transport level's standards (UDP and TCP) are also concerned by many well-known security breaches (Schaffer, 2006).

Regarding application standards in the IoT, attackers can exploit some features related to the protocol operation. The necessity of the interposition of a cross-proxy in case of human-to-thing communications between HTTP and CoAP hosts can be vulnerable if the security of the proxy is omitted. Indeed, a bad-intentioned proxy can take advantage from the fact that it is the only entity that holds the control over the final format and content of all incoming and outgoing messages to and from the 6LoWPAN network to launch several attacks (e.g., malicious proxy may drop messages or alter them). Moreover, resource-caching functionality according to which the CoAP server tells the proxy to save temporarily a certain resource's reading whose value does not change frequently. This allows the proxy to respond quickly to the future requests. Once again, the HTTP-CoAP proxy can misbehave while responding to external requests by sending CoAP responses including contradictory resource values. Thus, MQTT and XMPP protocols are also criticized for security weakness issues (Sicari et al., 2015), notably access control and authentication issues. In this case, identity validation with all involved devices (clients and servers) has to be performed and a set of authorization rules has to be defined according to user's preferences and requirements (Smimov et al., 2013).

Application Scenario-Related Vulnerabilities

In some cases, the specification of the application scenario can include implicit vulnerabilities that if detected by intruders may cause serious security problems to the physical and logical IoT users. For example in smart home application the connected sensors and cameras that are integrated everywhere in the home in order to guarantee comfort and smartness should not be aware of all about the home and persons who live inside. A hacker that succeeds in holding the control on home's smart things can retrieve highly sensitive and private information. Another example where such kind of vulnerabilities may raise with is military applications. Although the internet-connected sensors are mandatory for an efficient accomplishment of the military missions, they may have a negative effect on the secrecy of the infrastructures, the critical operations and the agents in such sensitive IoT application field. So, as a simple security measure, soldiers can be outlawed from wearing all kinds of smart things (smart watch, glasses, etc.) in barracks to avoid the situation when hacked smart things spy, without the knowledge of their users, on highly sensitive places and missions.

POTENTIAL THREATS

Communications in the IoT are subject to many harmful threats. In each type of attack, the intruder tries to exploit vulnerabilities or features related to network or device natures to disturb the communications inside the IoT and between external Internet hosts and IoT's devices. In this section, we identify the most dangerous attacks that threaten the communications in the IoT.

Denial of Service Attacks

DoS attacks represent an enormous danger threatening sensor networks opened to the Internet (Kasinathan et al., 2013). They have different shapes and generally occur when the adversary (usually an external host) simply takes advantage from the constraints of sensor nodes (especially scarce resources) and the heterogeneity of the communications between powerful devices and sensor nodes in human-to-thing communications, to exhaust sensor node's capabilities (and the entire WSN). This by the concentration of continuous flows on the connected sensors, causing memory overflow, processing resources overloading and excessive energy consumption. The affected services on the targeted sensors will get weighed down or completely blocked. At this stage it is important to notice that in the case of machine-to-machine communications, the impact of DoS attacks become much more reduced because the attack is in this case initiated by sensor nodes that are already constrained so, they cannot cause enormous damage to other devices (sensors or other connected entities).

Attackers experiencing DoS attacks can also infiltrate by exploiting certain vulnerabilities to cause problems at the terminal connected sensor nodes in the 6IoT

Figure 6. Illustration of DoS risks on connected sensor networks in the IoT

leading to their crash or to the destabilization of their functioning. The figure below illustrates the risk of DoS attacks in 6IoT

Another type of DoS attacks, where the related impact on the 6IoT-connected sensor networks is even more severe, are said DDoS attacks for distributed denial of service. A DDoS attack is performed by a network of attackers, called Botnet, which all address the same target. Attackers (also called zombies) in a Botnet are often themselves victim nodes that the main attacker employs unknowingly to attack other victims connected to the Internet. The distributive quality of the attack is advantageous enough for the attacker because it would be practically difficult to discover his identity and location as it hides behind several compromised devices. In the context of the Internet of things, an external attacker which is supposed to be strong enough does not have to resort to other machines to assist him in subverting the connected sensor nodes. Instead, it uses huge sets of connected sensors in the IoT. The resulting Botnet in this case is called Thingbot (Botnet of Smart Objects) (Paganini, 2014) (see Figure 6). Corrupted sensor nodes are configured to generate a very large mass of spam messages on the Internet. So we imagine car, refrigerator, connected TV ... that become web attackers without their owner's knowledge.

Attacks on Packet Fragmentation

The fragmentation process within the IoT-integrated WSNs is sensitive to a variety of attacks (Hummen et al., 2013), as messages amplification attack. The main principle of such attack is to generate messages of very large sizes and direct them to the connected sensor networks in the Internet of Things (6LoWPAN networks). Upon the reception of the huge IPv6 messages, the border router splits them into several and smaller messages that will be injected in the sensor network. This last gets flooded with the plenty of messages it receives.

Figure 7. Thingbot in the IoT

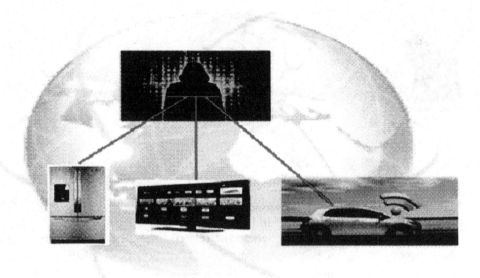

An external attacker sending huge messages or small ones at high frequency can collaborate with an internal adversary (sensor node) which itself aims to disrupt the process of fragmentation/reassembly of the communicated messages within the 6LoWPAN network. For example: an intruder can drop randomly a fragment and after receipt of all other fragments by the final sensor node, it detects the missing fragment, ignores the incomplete message and reports the error. A compromised sensor node has also the ability to forge a fragment and send it to the targeted ultimate sensor node (the victim) making it believe that a new message is being communicated to it. The corrupted sensor node reserves the buffer for this new fake message and waits the remaining fragments that the attacker will never send just to prevent the victim from receiving the right message. This attack is called attack by buffer reservation.

Threats Targeting IoT's Data on the Cloud

Some IoT applications (particularly medical applications and smart cities) generate massive sensory data (often sensitive) that need to be stored and processed in the cloud data centers. The risk that IoT data in the cloud get altered, analyzed and unlawfully disclosed by a malicious third party or by corrupt cloud services is very likely (Nguyen et al., 2015).

Attacks Threatening Users Privacy

The sensors connected to the Internet and integrated into our environment (our bodies, our homes, our objects, etc.) collect information that is private enough, for example: health status, geographic location, etc. These sensors are learning about the behavior, the preferences and habits of their users over time. Consequently, it will be required that the users can protect their privacy against leakage of information that they consider critical on the Internet. Thus, by ensuring confidentiality service for the critical data and allowing the users to identify the parties who handle their proper information, privacy issues could be mitigated. It is worth noticing at this stage that the IoT users may be asked whether to allow the use of their data by third parties (e.g. to employ them in statistical studies) or simply refuse it (Sicari et al., 2015).

The figure below shows the risks that IoT data collected as part of smart home and smart health care applications are disclosed by malicious third party in social networks, on the Internet.

Identity Spoofing Attacks

As the underlying communication architectures in the 6IoT and the future Internet of everything are identity-centric, (applications identify the Internet hosts basing on public and easy-to-forge identifiers such as IP addresses) attackers infiltrate by faking several identities and make the attacked entities think that the identities correspond to several legitimate devices. In our context, if the forged identities are IP addresses the attack is said IP spoofing. Else, if the systems adopt none-IP identi-

Figure 8. IoT user privacy issues in the IoT

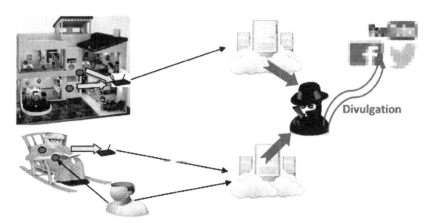

fiers, the attack is rather called Sybil attack. Identity spoofing attacks are ranked among the most sever attacks menacing communications in the IoT (Zhang et al., 2014) and (Cowan, 2015).

SECURITY BUILDING BLOCKS IN THE IoT

Classic communication security services are kept in the IoT. Hence, data confidentiality and integrity, messages and user's authentication, data freshness, secure localization, non-repudiation and service availability are always highly recommended. Additionally, other security services have to be ensured in the context of the Internet of things such as:

Key Management

The elaboration of efficient mechanisms for key exchange among explosive sets of Internet-connected stations, including sensor nodes in the IoT, throughout a platform recognized by its insecurity (the Internet) is a major challenge facing the current and future Internet. To match this end, scalable and seamless key management schemes have to be developed to allow IoT sensors to exchange safely the cryptographic keys with the other devices connected to the Internet. However, the proposed solutions in this context must present good constraints-awareness and low levels of energy dissipation.

Identity Management, Authentication and Access Control

These three concepts are tightly linked to each other and are all mandatory for the security of the Internet of things. As the services of sensor networks are often highly critical, it is recommended to define rules for access control to the services. This means that only authorized entities whose identities are well authenticated will have the right to access IoT resources directly from one connected sensor, a collection of connected sensors or from the cloud. There are several techniques that can be used for access control and authorizations, taking into account certain considerations related to the intention behind each access. Accordingly, we distinguish role-based and policy-based access control rules. Nevertheless, the induced techniques are often expensive enough both in memory space and computational resources. So, tailoring lightweight and effective solutions is highly encouraged.

Privacy Protection and Trust Management

Users of sensors connected to the IoT should know how their privacy is protected and they must have the right to authorize or prohibit the manipulation of data reported by the sensors surrounding them. Thus, the evaluation of trust is more than necessary between sensor networks and data storage services provided on the cloud. At this stage, it is necessary to note that in the context of IoT, trust management is also running over interactive smart objects but more importantly, it should take place between the users and that smart objects. In this last case, trust evaluation is bidirectional; sensor nodes need to communicate their data only to the trusted users and conversely, IoT users want to use and to be surrounded by safe and trusted smart objects.

Intrusion Detection

Intrusion detection is mandatory in the security of sensor networks. In the context of the Internetof Things, logical intrusions introduced via the Internet connection are very dangerous. So, it is henceforth necessary to develop robust mechanisms that will be able to prevent intrusions, and filter malicious flows that are destined to create intrusion holes within the Internet-connected WSNs.

RAISED CHALLENGES WITH COMMUNICATIONS SECURITY IN THE IoT

Internet of things is an emerging evolution in which security is expected to be a dominant problem. It is evident that the fusion of Internet connection with the real world will deepen the security risks and will provide a large fertile space for attackers to produce new generation cyber attacks. Till now, security problematic and challenges in IoT domain are not well-defined. In other words, it is actually not clear if security issues will arise from the application scenarios themselves or from the underlying communication infrastructures along with the involved devices, or from other aspects not yet discovered. In this section, we underline the current and the most important challenges facing security in the context of the Internet of things.

- Internet connection expandability.
- High degrees of material and technological heterogeneities.

- Distributive nature.
- Mobility of users and smart devices.
- Lack of trust on Internet.

BASIC REQUIREMENTS

Each security mechanism developed for the IoT has to fulfill the following requirements:

- Robustness (security efficiency with end-to-end protection of the communications).
- Scalability.
- Good constraints-awareness.
- QoS preservation.
- Support of mobility.
- Fault tolerance.

TAXONOMY OF PROPOSED MECHANISMS FOR SECURE COMMUNICATIONS IN THE 6IoT

This section presents a review of the most recent security solutions aiming to protect all styles of communications in the IoT. According to the communication pattern, the studied solutions are organized in three categories: M2M communications security, H2T communications security and finally group communications security. As we are interested in this work to the IPv6-enabled IoT, we will highlight only the proposed security solutions in this context that are generally based on TCP/IP model.

Security of Machine-to-Machine Interactions

The autonomy that characterizes M2M communications running over unattended networks in the IoT may be a source of numerous vulnerabilities. In order to address the problem of M2M communications security in the IoT many security solutions have been proposed. DTLS (Datagram Transport Layer Security) (Rescorda et al., 2006) is proposed in many research works for the security of CoAP-based M2M communications at the transport layer. DTLS is onerous both in communication and computations because its key agreement process requires the exchange of many big-sized signaling messages and the computation of expensive asymmetric cryptographic operations. In order to make such security protocol it applicable for constrained environments, some optimizations have been conducted. Authors in (Kothmayr et al., 2011) propose to use DTLS over materially-assisted sensor nodes so that to accelerate the computations of the security primitives. For the mitigation of communication overhead and energetic-related costs during the establishment of DTLS security session among M2M devices in the IoT, authors propose in (Raza et al., 2012) to extend the 6LoWPAN compression model to compress DTLS messages. On the other side, a solution (Wang et al., 2013) proposes to abandon locally the DTLS security within the 6LoWPAN network if we make sure that internal communications will go safely without any security accompaniment or if we entrust the lower layer security. In this case DTLS security is guarded only between the edge-proxy and the external host. Otherwise, if the 6LoWPAN network's local security is threatened, or the internal CoAP host does not trust the underlying security, DTLS security association is in this case set up from end-to-end. Since asymmetric security solutions are not well adapted with scalability perspective, a recent research work addresses this issue and proposes symmetric-based security for DTLS (Raza et al., 2016).

Regarding publish/subscribe M2M communications where MQTT or XMPP protocols are generally adopted, security consists mainly in the adoption of TLS protocol (Dierks & Allen, 1999); the popular variant of DTLS protocol destined to secure reliable communications from end-to-end. Although TLS was the subject of some efforts (SariKaya et al., 2012) and (Ben-Saied et al., 2014) aiming to adapt it for WSNs incorporated in the IoT. It remains despite of all a bad and expensive choice for highly constrained networks, quite like 6LoWPAN networks. We recall that the heaviness of reliability management functions in TCP protocol is preventing the adoption of MQTT and XMPP protocols by the low power and lossy networks in the IoT.

IPsec (IP security) (Frankel & Kishnan, 2011) protocol can also be used for M2M security especially, for thing-to-human (T2H) interactions where the involved devices are heterogeneous (from resources availability and used communication point of view) and do not use the similar upper layer protocols (TCP/HTTP against UDP/CoAP). IPsec ensures confidentiality and authentication of IPv6 datagrams. In order to adapt such protocol to 6LoWPAN constraints in the IoT, an efficient compression model of IPsec messages headers is proposed in (Raza et al., 2011). For key agreement, IPsec uses either IKE (Internet Key Exchange) (Frankel & Kishnan, 2011) or

HIP (Host Identity Protocol) (Moskowitz et al., 2015) protocols. Like all IP-based security standards, IKE is not appropriate to run directly across 6IoT. For this reason, the protocol received many alleviation proposals through message compression, keys pre-distribution or the delegation of the most expensive asymmetric security operations if the automatic session key establishment is preferred (Ben-Saied et al., 2014) and (Bonetto et al., 2012). Regarding HIP protocol that is more advantageous for IoT applications because it defines cryptographic identifiers rather than using IP addresses which facilitates end-users mobility and promotes location transparency. HIP is also communication and computationally-expensive. Authors propose Diet HIP (Moskowitz, 2016) a lightweight alternative of the standard HIP that makes use of economic asymmetric cryptography (elliptic curve cryptography (Batina et al., 2006)), and its compression model in (Hummen et al., 2013). In (Ben-Saied et al., 2012) a distributed fashion of the security load induced in the standard HIP is proposed. The presented system can be especially advantageous with M2M thing-to-human communications because it suggests that the constrained host (the sensor node) is the part which initiates the security establishment routine.

In case of thing-to-thing communication that are characterized by their homogeneity; involved devices have similar constraints and use identical communication protocols. It will be more efficient if the M2M communication security is concentrated on application level. This is exactly what authors envisaged in (Yegin et al., 2011) where they proposed to define new option in CoAP protocol to negotiate and set up security. If the interacting smart things belong to the same segment (6LoWPAN network) link layer security mechanisms can be useful. For example, it is possible to use MAC security mechanism defined in the IEEE 802.15.4 standard and that focuses on a network pre-shared and renewable key along with AES (Advanced Encryption Standard) ciphering algorithm (Khambre et al., 2012).

Security of Human-to-Thing Interactions

Human-to-thing communications are very similar to thing-to-human ones in terms of the none-equivalent capacities of the implicated devices. However, H2T transactions are the most interesting from security point of view. Indeed, H2T communications are always initiated by a powerful internet host that when it acts maliciously risks damaging the sensor nodes he is interacting with and even the whole Internet-connected WSNs. Although its importance, the security of H2T communications has not received the interest it deserves in the research works.

Appling security at the application layer is not practical as the communicating devices use different applicative protocols (HTTP from human side and CoAP or

MQTT... in the IoT). Authors of the work (Trabalza et al., 2013) propose a security solution of H2T communications. The solution assumes the support of CoAP by smartphones powered on Android OS and suggests DTLS protocol for end-to-end protection of the communications. The proposed solution treats the smartphone in the internet side as a sensor node. Besides, most of the successful web applications in the Internet are based on HTTP and CoAP is not yet well supported by the web browsers (web clients). Though CoAP is considered as the most popular applicative protocol in the IoT, many other IoT-dedicated applicative protocols can be used (as we have already seen in this chapter). Thus, the interposition of an adapted proxy is required.

In (Kothmayr et al., 2013) authors propose to adopt transport-layer security and use TLS protocol in the Internet part and DTLS protocol in IoT's segment. The solution presents a translation algorithm between both security protocols, in addition to the translation between HTTP and CoAP, at the front-end proxy. HIP protocol can also be used to establish security association among human and smart things in the future Internet. We have proposed in (Sahraoui & Bilami, 2014) and (Sahraoui & Bilami, 2015) an efficient HIP-based solution (named CD-HIP) to set up end-to-end security in H2T communications. The solution relies on the combination of the first 6LoWPAN compression model of HIP header and a suitable security distribution scheme operating over a powerful assisting node and terminal (constrained) sensor node. The solution presents optimized security costs both on communications and computations of HIP when it is running on the 6LoWPAN network's side. Note that IKE-based security adaptations cited in the previous sub-section are also viable for H2T communications.

We have stated that IPsec protocol appears the best choice to secure the interactions between heterogeneous devices adopting different protocols. This allows the avoidance of the employment of different security protocols at the transport layer (TLS and DTLS) but the proxy has always to break the end-to-end security of the messages to perform the translation between the application protocols (HTTP and CoAP). To guarantee end-to-end security of H2T transactions while considering the asymmetric nature of such communication style, we have proposed in (Sahraoui & Bilami, 2016) an asymmetric security system based on IPsec protocol. The proposed model concentrates the security only on the communication sense that carries the most sensitive messages, which is sensor-to-human direction. Besides, end-to-end security is preserved by shifting CoAP-to-HTTP translation to the HTTP host that is assumed to be sufficiently powerful. The evaluation results showed that the proposed security model contributes in decreasing the security overhead on the CoAP servers, which helps substantially to mitigate the impact of DoS attacks.

Group Communication Security

There are really few solutions that deal with multicast communications security in the IoT. This is due to the fact that group communications are application-specific and therefore may not be needed in all IoT application scenarios. Also, each scenario has its proper security requirements that should be carefully considered.

In (Veltri et al., 2013) a new centralized batch-based group key distribution protocol is tailored. The proposed protocol allows a server that has to send the same data to a set of destinations, to distribute a group key to all members in a multicast group in seamless way dealing with dynamic (predictable and unpredictable) joins and leaves of the group members. In order to minimize the amount of exchanged messages required for handling group memberships and rekeying, time is split into several intervals. According to batch method, a key distribution center manages all membership changes that happen within the same time interval. For each time interval, all active members generate together a new key. Key generation is in this case done automatically without any interaction the central entity, which is benefic enough for the management of join and pre-determined leave actions. Explicit communication between the central key distribution entity and group members is required only in case of key revocation events. The centralized fashion featured in the presented solution is feasible and even advantageous in some potential applications in the IoT, such as smart cities. Nevertheless, in some other IoT applications a distributed design can be much more preferred. Following this direction a distributed and also batch-based key management is proposed in (Abdmeziem et al., 2015) the solution supports end-nodes mobility which is a great advantage.

In (Porambage et al., 2015) authors propose two key management protocols to ensure secure multicast communications in the Internet of things that ensure authentication, secrecy and integrity properties while generating the secret group key. Authors claim that their solutions respond well to scalability constraint as the solutions introduce only slight amount of messages.

The table 1 compares analytically the relevant security solutions according to several performance criteria.

CONCLUSION

Throughout this chapter, we have highlighted the context of communications security in the Internet of things. Our study has been concentrated on IPv6-enabled Internet of things (6IoT) which presents an attractive trend allowing the achievement of pervasiveness and interoperability aspirations in the future Internet. However, the advent of the 6IoT will certainly widen the space of security issues in the future

Table 1. General comparison between security solutions proposed for protecting communications in the IoT

Solution	Comm. Style	Robustness	Constraints Awareness	Scalability	QoS	Mobility Support	Fault Tolerance
(Kothmayr et al., 2011)	H2T/ T2T/ T2H	Good	Fair	Bad	Low compt delay	No	
(Raza et al., 2012)	T2T	Good	Fair	Bad	Low comm delay	No	
(Wang et al., 2013)	T2T/ T2H	Medium	Fair	Bad	Fair	No	Fair
(Raza et al., 2016)	T2T/ T2H/ H2T	Very good	Good	Good	Good	No	Good
(Sarikaya et al., 2012)	H2T	Medium	Fair	Fair	Low compt delay	No	Fair
(Ben-Saied et al., 2014)	H2T	Medium	Fair	Fair	Low compt delay	No	Good
(Raza et al., 2011)	T2H/H2T	Good	Good	Bad	Low comm. delay	No	
(Bonetto et al., 2012)	H2T	Fair	Fair	Fair	Low compt delay	No	Fair
(Moskowitz et al., 2016)	T2T	Medium	Fair	Fair	Bad	Yes	
(Hummen et al., 2013)	T2T	Good	Good	Fair	Low comm delay	Yes	
(Ben-Saied et al., 2012)	T2H	Good	Fair	Fair	Low compt delay	Yes	Good
(Yegin et al., 2011)	T2T	Good	Good	Fair	Fair	No	
(Trabalza et al., 2013)	H2T	Medium	Fair	Fair	Fair	No	
(Kothmayr et al., 2013)	H2T/T2H	Good	Fair	Fair	Low compt delay	No	Fair
(Sahraoui & Bilami, 2015)	H2T/T2H	Good	Good	Fair	Good	Yes	Fair
(Sahraoui & Bilami, 2016)	H2T	Good	Good	Fair	Good		Fair
(Veltri et al., 2013)	Group comm	Good	Medium	Fair	Good	No	Fair
(Abdmeziem et al., 2015)	Group comm	Good	Good	Good	Good	Yes	Good
(Porambage et al., 2015)	Group comm	Good	Good	Good	Good	No	

Internet due to many aspects, mainly the direct reaching of the connected sensors from everywhere at anytime. Thus, we have identified the major threats as well as the major security challenges. Then, a review of the proposed security mechanisms for the security of the different communication styles in the IoT is presented.

The Internet of things is just in its beginnings and the security-related problems in such domain are not yet well determined. We think that application scenarios will play an important role in the enhancement or the degradation of security. The communication technologies and protocols are also concerned. In one hand, the standardization of the communication protocols promotes the interoperability but it affects the security. In the other hand, the diversification enhances security but it damages strongly the interoperability. So, research works have to be conducted to find out efficient solutions that will be able of balancing security with interoperability in the next generation Internet.

REFERENCES

Abdmeziem, M. R., Tandjaoui, D., & Romdhani, I. (2015, October). A Decentralized Batch-based Group Key Management Protocol for Mobile Internet of Things (DBGK).*Proceedings of the 14th IEEE International Conference on Ubiquitous Computing and Communications (IUCC-2015)*. doi:10.1109/CIT/IUCC/DASC/PICOM.2015.166

Akyildiz, I. F., Su, W., Sankarasubramaniam, Y., & Cayirci, E. (2002). Wireless sensor networks: A survey. *Computer Networks*, *38*(4), 393–422. doi:10.1016/S1389-1286(01)00302-4

Andre, P.S. (2011). Extensible Messaging and Presence Protocol (XMPP): Core. *Request for Comments*, 6120.

Atzori, L., Lera, A., & Morabioto, G. (2010). The internet of things: A survey. *Computer Networks*, *54*(15), 2787–2805. doi:10.1016/j.comnet.2010.05.010

Batina, L., Mentens, N., Sakiyama, K., Preneel, B., & Verbauwhede, I. (2006, September). Low-Cost Elliptic Curve Cryptography for Wireless Sensor Networks. *Proceedings of the Third European Workshop ESAS*, 6-17.

Bcn Saicd, Y., & Olivereau, A. (2012, June). D-HIP: A Distributed Kkey Exchange Scheme for HIP-Based Internet of Things.*Proceedings of the IEEE International Symposium on World of Wireless Mobile and Multimedia Networks (WoWMoM)*, 1-7. doi:10.1109/WoWMoM.2012.6263785

Ben-Saied, Y., Olivereau, A., Zeghlache, D., & Laurent, M. (2014). Lightweight collaborative kcy cstablishmcnt scheme for the Internet of Things. *Computer Networks*, *64*, 273–295. doi:10.1016/j.comnet.2014.02.001

Bonetto, R., Bui, N., Lakkundi, V., & Olivereau, A. (2012, June). Secure communication for smart IoT objects: Protocol stacks, use cases and practical examples. *Proceedings of the World of Wireless, Mobile and Multimedia Networks (WoWMoM) IEEE International Symposium*, 1-7.

Cowan, J. (2015). *Article*. Retrieved May 1, 2016, from http://www.iot-now.com/2015/03/26/31426-securing-the-identity-of-things-idot-for-the-internet-of-things/

Dierks, T., & Allen, C. (1999). The TLS protocol. *Request for Comments*, 2246.

Frankel, S., Kishnan, S. (2011). IP Security (IPsec) and Internet Key Exchange (IKE) document roadmap. *Request for Comments*, 6071.

Garcia-Morchon, O., Keoh, S., Kumar, S., Hummen, R., & Struik, R. (2012). Security Considerations in the IP-based Internet of Things. *draft-garcia-core-security-04*.

Geng, W., Talwar, S., Johnsson, K., Himayat, N., & Johnson, K. D. (2011). M2M: From mobile to embedded internet. *IEEE Communications Magazine*, *49*(4), 36–43. doi:10.1109/MCOM.2011.5741144

Gubbi, J., Buyya, R., Marusic, S., & Palniswami, M. (2013). Internet of things (IoT): A vision, architectural elements, and future directions. *Future Generation Computer Systems*, *29*(7), 1645–1660. doi:10.1016/j.future.2013.01.010

Hummen, R., Hiller, J., Henze, M., & Wehrle, K. (2013, October). Slimfit – A HIP DEX Compression Layer for the IP-based Internet of Things.*Proceedings of the IEEE WiMob 2013 Workshop IoT*, 259-266. doi:10.1109/WiMOB.2013.6673370

Hummen, R., Hiller, J., Wirtz, H., Henze, M., Shafagh, H., & Wehrle, K. (2013, June). 6LoWPAN fragmentation attacks and mitigation mechanisms.*Proceedings of the sixth ACM conference on Security and privacy in wireless and mobile networks*, 55-66. doi:10.1145/2462096.2462107

Kasinathan, P., Pastrone, C., Spirito, M. A., & Vinkovits, M. (2013, October). Denial-of-Service detection in 6LoWPAN based Internet of Things. *Proceedings of IEEE 9th International Conference on Wireless and Mobile Computing, Networking and Communications (WiMob)*, 600-607.

Khambre, P. D., Simbhare, S. S., & Chavan, P. S. (2012). Secure Data in Wireless Sensor Network via AES (Advanced Encryption Standard). *International Journal of Computer Science and Information Technologies*, *3*(2), 3588–3592.

Kothmayr, T., Hu, W., Schmitt, C., Brunig, M., & Carle, G. (2011, November). Poster: Securing the Internet of Things with DTLS.*Proceedings of the 9th ACM Conference on Embedded Networked Sensor Systems*, 345-346.

Kothmayr, T., Schmitt, C., Hu, W., Brunig, M., & Carle, G. (2013). DTLS based Security and Two-Way Authentication for the Internet of Things. *Ad Hoc Networks*, *11*(8), 2710–2723. doi:10.1016/j.adhoc.2013.05.003

Loke, S.W. (2015). The internet of flying-things: opportunities and challenges with airborne fog computing and mobile cloud in the clouds. *IEEE Internet of Things Journal*, 1-5.

Montenegro, G., Kushalnagar, N., Hui, J., & Culler, D. (2007). Transmission of IPv6 packets over IEEE 802.15.4 networks. *Request for Comments*, 4944.

Moskowitz, R. (2016). HIP Diet EXchange (DEX). *draftmoskowitz-hip-rg-dex-05*.

Moskowitz, R., Heer, T., Jokela, P., & Henderson, T. (2015). Host Identity Protocol Version 2 (HIPv2). *Request for Comments*, 7401.

Nam, C., & Kim, D. H. (2014). A study of open middleware for wireless sensor networks. Proceedings of Advanced Science and Technology Letters, 60, 105-109. doi:10.14257/astl.2014.60.26

Nguyen, K. T., Laurent, M., & Oualha, N. (2015). Survey on secure communication protocols for the Internet of Things. *Ad Hoc Networks, 32*, 17–31. doi:10.1016/j.adhoc.2015.01.006

Oasis-Standard. (2014). Retrieved May 1, 2016, from http://docs.oasis-open.org/mqtt/mqtt/v3.1.1/os/mqtt-v3.1.1-os.html

Paganini, P. (2014). Retrieved May 1, 2016, from http://securityaffairs.co/wordpress/21397/cyber-crime/iot-cyberattack-large-scale.html

Porambage, P., Braeken, A., Schmitt, C., Gurtov, C., Ylianttila, M., & Stiller, B. (2015). Group Key Establishment for Enabling Secure Multicast Communication in Wireless Sensor Networks Deployed for IoT Applications. *IEEE Access, 3*, 1503–1511. doi:10.1109/ACCESS.2015.2474705

Rahmani, R., & Kanter, T. (2015). Layering the internet-of-things with multicasting in flowsensors for internet-of-services. *International Journal of Multimedia and Ubiquitous Engineering, 10*(12), 37–52. doi:10.14257/ijmue.2015.10.12.05

Raza, S., Seitz, L., Sitenkov, D., & Selander, G. (2016). S3K: Scalable security with symmetric keys—DTLS key establishment for the Internet of Things. *IEEE Transactions on Automation Science and Engineering, 13*(3), 1270–1280. doi:10.1109/TASE.2015.2511301

Raza, S., Trabalza, D., & Voigt, T. (2012, May). 6LoWPAN compressed DTLS for CoAP.*Proceedings of the 8th IEEE International Conference on Distributed Computing in Sensor Systems*, 287 – 289.

Raza, S., Voigt, T., & Roedig, U. (2011). 6LoWPAN Extension for IPsec. *Proceedings of the Interconnecting Smart Objects with the Internet Workshop*, 1-3.

Rescorla, E., & Modadugu, N. (2006). Datagram Transport Layer Security. *Request for Comments*, 4347.

Sahraoui, S., & Bilami, A. (2014, May). Compressed and distributed host identity protocol for end-to-end security in the IoT.*Proceedings of the Fifth International Conference on Next Generation Networks and Services (NGNS)*, 295 – 301. doi:10.1109/NGNS.2014.6990267

Sahraoui, S., & Bilami, A. (2015). Efficient HIP-based approach to ensure light-weight end-to-end security in the internet of things. *Computer Networks, 91*, 26–45. doi:10.1016/j.comnet.2015.08.002

Sahraoui, S., & Bilami, A. (2016, May). Asymmetric End-to-End Security for Human-to-Thing Communications in the Internet of Things.*Proceedings of the 4th International Symposium on Modeling and Implementation of Complex Systems (MISC 2016)*, 249-260. doi:10.1007/978-3-319-33410-3_18

Sarikaya, B., Ohba, Y., Moskowitz, R., Cao, Z., & Cragie, R. (2012). Security Bootstrapping Solution for Resource-Constrained Devices. *Technical report IETF Internet Draft draft-sarikaya-coresbootstrapping-05*.

Schaffer, G. P. (2006). Worms and viruses and botnets, oh my!: Rational responses to emerging internet threats. *IEEE Security and Privacy, 4*(3), 52–58. doi:10.1109/MSP.2006.83

Schneider, S. (2013). Retrieved May 1, 2016, from http://electronicdesign.com/iot/understanding-protocols-behind-internet-things

Shelby, Z., Kartke, K., Bormann, C., & Frank, B. (2012). Constrained application protocol (CoAP). *draft-ietf-core-coap-12*.

Sicari, S., Rizzardi, A., Grieco, L. A., & Coen-Porisini, A. (2015). Security, privacy and trust in Internet of things: The road ahead. *Computer Networks, 76*, 146–164. doi:10.1016/j.comnet.2014.11.008

Smirnov, A., Kashevnik, A., Shilov, N., & Teslya, N. (2013, June). Context-based access control model for smart space. *Proceedings of the 5th International Conference on Cyber Conflict*, 1-15.

Trabalza, D., Raza, S., & Voigt, T. (2013, April). INDIGO: Secure CoAP for Smartphones Enabling E2E Secure Communication in the 6IoT. *Proceedings of the International Conference on Wireless Sensor Networks for Developing Countries (WSN4DC 2013)*.

Veltri, L., Cirani, S., Busanelli, S., & Ferrari, G. (2013). A novel batch-based group key management protocol applied to the Internet of Things. *Ad Hoc Networks, 11*(8), 2724–2737. doi:10.1016/j.adhoc.2013.05.009

Wang, L., Wang, W., Zhu, L., & Yu, F. (2013). CoAP option extensions: profile and sec-flag. *Internet draft*.

Winter, T., Thubert, P., Brandt, A., Hui, J., Kelseky, R., Levis, P., Pister, K., Struik, R., Vasseur J.P., &Alexander, R. (2012). RPL: IPv6 routing protocol for low-power and lossy networks. *Request for Comments, 6550.*

Yegin, A., & Shelby, Z. (2011). CoAP Security Options. *draft-yegin-coap-security-options-00.*

Zhang, K., & Lu, R. (2014). Sybil attacks and their defenses in the internet of things. *IEEE Internet of ThingsJournal, 1*(5), 372–383. doi:10.1109/JIOT.2014.2344013

Chapter 8
IoT in Healthcare:
Breaching Security Issues

Somasundaram R
VIT University, India

Mythili Thirugnanam
VIT University, India

ABSTRACT

The fields of computer science and electronics have merged to result into one of the most notable technological advances in the form of realization of the Internet of Things. The market for healthcare services has increased exponentially at the same time security flaws could pose serious threats to the health and safety of patients using wearable technologies and RFID. The volume and sensitivity of data traversing the IoT environment makes dangerous to messages and data could be intercepted and manipulated while in transit. This scenario must absolutely respect the confidentiality and privacy of patient's medical information. Therefore, this chapter presents various security issues or vulnerabilities with respect to attacks and various situations how information will be attacked by the attacker in healthcare IoT. The working principle of healthcare IoT also discussed. The chapter concludes the performance of various attacks based on the past work. In the future this work can be extended to introduce a novel mechanism to resolve various security issues in healthcare IoT.

DOI: 10.4018/978-1-5225-2296-6.ch008

INTRODUCTION

Internet of Things (IoT) is a set of technologies that consist of wide range of appliances, devices, and things to interact and communicate among themselves using networking technologies. IoT devices being used now to expose limitations that prevent their proper use in healthcare systems. Interoperability and security are especially impacted by such limitations. TJ McCue (McCue, 2015) reported that healthcare Internet of Things market segment is poised to hit $117 billion by 2020.

As the use of networked medical devices becomes prevalent in the healthcare world, security breaches are growing and if not addressed and mitigated they threaten to undermine technology development in the field and result in significant financial loses. A new report from the Atlantic Council and Intel Security says, The Healthcare Internet of Things: Rewards and Risks, there is marked growth in adoption of these devices, with 48 percent of healthcare providers polled saying that they had integrated consumer technologies such as wearable health-monitoring devices or operational technologies like automated pharmacy-dispensing systems with their IT ecosystems. But the question is how far this technology will be safe.

Five fundamental questions therefore need to be asked about connected devices in health care industries asked by William A (William A, 2015).

- Do the IoT devices store and transmit data security?
- Do they provide new path to unauthorized access of data?
- Do they accept software security updates to address new risk?
- Do they provide a new way to steal data?
- Are the APIs through which software and devices connect secure?

These flaws can be managed and even reduced with a handful of steps: With this intention this chapter focus on security by design: better collaboration among industry; manufacturers, regulators, and medical practitioners; a change in the regulatory approval paradigm, and encouraging feedback from patients and families who directly benefit from these devices. Santos, A (Santos, A et al, 2014) described that Healthcare IoT using Radio Frequency Identification (RFID) is an adaptable and user-friendly technology, where a radio signal is used to get data from transponders into the target application. Rajagopalan (Rajagopalan et al, 2010) explained possibility of reading information without physical contact is the biggest advantage of using RFID. One can implant it under the skin of a patient and read this information even if it is moving. Whenever using RFID enabled devices or tags, special security concern is needed to ensure the security of the device.

OVERVIEW OF HEALTHCARE IOT

The importance of healthcare IoT and various security issues in Healthcare Internet of Things are analyzed and summary of the same is discussed in the following section.

Importance of the Internet of Things

Ovidiu Vermesan (Ovidiu Vermesan et al) explained about enabling the sustainable Internet of Things network. The key issues like identification, privacy, security and semantic interoperability have to be tackled. The interaction with cloud technologies, big data and future networks like 5G have also to be taken into account. This will lead to better services, huge savings and a smarter use of resources. To achieve these promising results, it is vital to enhance users trust in the Internet of Things.

The following chapters will provide for interesting reading on the state-of-the-art of research in security issues in healthcare IoT and will expose to progress towards the bright future of the secured Internet of Things.

Introduction on Healthcare IoT

IoT applications are pushing the development of platforms for implementing ambient assisted living (AAL) systems that will offer services in the areas of assistance to carry out daily activities, health, activity monitoring, enhancing safety and security, getting access to medical and emergency systems, and facilitating rapid health support. These smart health monitoring applications are discussed by Santosa (Santosa et al, 2014).

A smart health applications in health monitoring are:

- Applications require gathering of data from sensors
- Applications must support user interfaces and displays
- Applications require network connectivity for accessing to infrastructural services
- Applications have in-use requirements such as low power, robustness, durability, accuracy and reliability.

The main objective is to enhance life quality for people who need permanent support or monitoring, to decrease barriers for monitoring important health parameters, to avoid unnecessary healthcare costs and efforts, and to provide the right medical support at the right time.

Challenges exist in the overall cyber-physical infrastructure (e.g., hardware connectivity, software development and communications), specialized processes at the intersection of control and sensing, sensor fusion and decision making, security, and the compositionality of cyber-physical systems. Proprietary medical devices in general were not designed for interoperation with other medical devices or computational systems, necessitating advancements in networking and distributed communication within cyber-physical architectures.

Architecture of Healthcare Internet of Things is depicted in the above Figure 1. Interoperability and closed loop systems appears to be the key for success. System security will be critical as communication of individual patient data is communicated over IoT networks.

REVIEW ON SECURITY ISSUES IN HEALTHCARE IOT

Several researchers have studied various faces of wearable sensors as they are relevant to the security in Healthcare IoT. Wang (Wang et al, 2006) discussed a very

Figure 1. Architecture of healthcare IoT

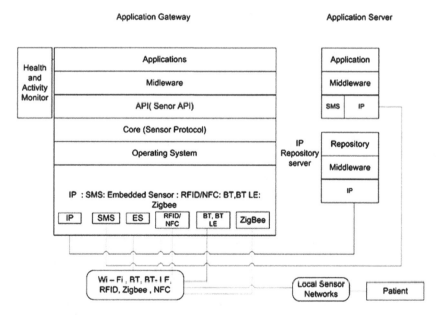

IP- Internet Protocol, SMS-Short Message Service, ES-Embedded Systems, RFID- Radio Frequency Identification,
BT-Bluetooth, BT LE – Bluetooth Low Energy, NFC-Near Field Communication.

detailed survey of security issues in wireless sensor networks, the constraints and the requirements based on the existing attacks against the IoT at different layers are mentioned. Atzori (Atzori et al, 2014) focused on authentication, data integrity and privacy issues in the IoT, particularly in RFID systems and sensor networks. Kumar (Kumar et al, 2010) explained overview of security and privacy issues in IoT. Different security threats and privacy concerns while processing, storing, and transmitting data are discussed. The main line of the existing surveys in relation with the IoT security is that they generally focus on identifying the challenges and the security threats present in the IoT. However, several security solutions and techniques have been proposed since the advent of the IoT. With this motivation, various aspects of security protocols and techniques in healthcare IoT are reviewed and discussed Table 1.

Table 1. Review of various healthcare IoT concepts

S.No	Author(s)	Observation	Identified Issues
1	(Santosa, A et al, 2014)	Author developed an Architecture that introduced for m-health Ambient to assisted living applications. Also presents the security context that has been defined, applied both to devices, users and software applications. The paper also argues that the broad development of RFID technology has the potential to increase patient safety in medical services and to reduce costs. As most health services can be enhanced with the location, tracking and monitoring, especially in mobile and ubiquitous environments, an IoT system for monitoring and position referral of any of health-related entities - people (such as patients, nurses, doctors visits, auxiliary) and goods (such as medicines, clinical analyzes, wheelchairs, beds, medical equipment) - has been presented and discussed.	AAL does not enable testing entities/ objects location in real scenarios, also testing the systems' usability by the elderly, personnel adherence to secure authentication mechanisms, encrypted communications and the other global security levels
2	(Pedro Maiaa et al., 2014)	Eco Health implemented to improve health monitoring and better diagnosis for the patients with real-time data control, visualization, processing, and storage functionalities. The eco-Health design is based on several well established Web technologies in order to standardize and simplify the development of applications in the IoT context, thus minimizing compatibility and interoperability issues between manufacturers, proprietary protocols, and data formats.	The proposed system not evaluated with real-world case studies, as well as quantitative and qualitative evaluations.
3	(Pedro Maiaa et al, 2014)	Ontology based frame work is introduced to reduce death rate to provide betterment of diagnosing diseases. For that, disease details such as symptoms, treatment, causes, effect are all constructed in ontology format and put into various databases. Doctor also provided the treatment process and what medicine does the patient to have.	Security is big concern Ontology technology helps us to understand the specific risks related to security and doesn't address security issues.

continued on following page

Table 1.Continued

S.No	Author(s)	Observation	Identified Issues
4	(FLAUZAC Olivier et al, 2015)	An architecture which is scalable with multiple SDN domains are introduced. In each domain networks with or without infrastructure and each controller is responsible only for its domain. The communications between domains is made with special controllers called Border Controllers. These edge Controllers have to work in a new distributed interaction in order to guarantee the independence of each domain in case of failure. Adopt an architecture to guarantee the security of the entire network with the concept of grid of security embedded in each controller to prevent attacks.	Less security mechanisms. Not addressed the possibilities of employing them in the context of SDN. Not introduced in the larger scale in order to optimize our system design.
5	(Antonio J. Jara et al, 2010)	The mobility issue requires developing a protocol over 6LoWPAN network to be carried out in sensor networks with high specification related with low power consumption and capacity. While in the RFID/NFC technologies need to support secure Communications.	Doesn't discuss about power consumption of the 6LoWPAN sensors to check whether the introduction of the mobility protocols maintains the principles of low power consumption from LoWPAN.
6.	(Anass RGHIOUI et al, 2014)	Author presented a security model based on symmetric model based cryptography in order to secure an IoT healthcare monitoring system. This model is based on the establishment of security pairwise keys in order to secure communication between the health center monitoring server and patient's WSN. This model ensures the confidentiality and nodes authentication as on integrate the network. The analysis showed that this scheme meets the measures that must be taken into adaption for network flexibility and scalability.	No proper defined specific cryptography algorithms or keys generation function to give the user the choice according to this need.
7.	(A. Dohr1, 2010)	This paper deals with personal communication between elderly people, their environment and relevant groups of care givers is an important aspect in AAL (Ambient Assisted Living). Through the combination of KIT (Keep In Touch) and Closed Loop Healthcare, a central AAL paradigm can be realized through the IoT, where the elderly live in their homes with smart objects, thus smart homes, communicating to the outside world in an intelligent and goal-orientated manner. The Internet of Things thereby enables communication between • people and things, • things and things and • people and people in a secure manner.	Closed loop healthcare is not feasible for all kind of health monitoring activity.

continued on following page

Table 1.Continued

S.No	Author(s)	Observation	Identified Issues
8	(Sara Amendola et al, 2014)	Author presented a survey on the state-of the-art of RFID for application to body centric systems and for gathering information (temperature, humidity, and other gases) about the user's living environment. Many available options are described up to the application level with some examples of RFID systems able to collect and process multichannel data about the human behavior in compliance with the power exposure and sanitary regulations. Open challenges and possible new research trends are finally discussed.	Implementation of processing human behavior data from RFID is complex one.
9	(Danilo F.S. Santos et al, 2015)	A system that enables Personal Health Devices to share information in home networks and with the Internet based on a new Internet of Things protocol, namely the Constrained Application Protocol (CoAP).Discussed how the CoAP communication model was adapted to the IEEE 11073 model network. Communication overhead is around 50% lighter when compared to other protocols	The work fails to give security assurance of light weight protocols.
10	(Xiao Ming Zhang et al, 2011)	This paper is proposing an open, secure and flexible platform based on IoT and Cloud computing, on which several mainstream short distant ambient communication protocols for medical purpose are discussed to addressing interoperability. Secure Sockets Layer (SSL), authentication n and auditing are taken into consideration to solve the security issue. An adaptive streaming QoS model is utilized to improve streaming quality in dynamic environment; and an open Cloud computing infrastructure is adopted to support elastic Electronic Health Record (EHR) archiving in the backend. Finally an integrated reference implementation is introduced to demonstrate feasibility.	No information about providing security to cloud data.

The general issues identified on various IoT Healthcare concepts are discussed in Table 1. It is observed that the AAL does not enable secure authentication mechanism, lack of security in Eco health monitoring system, security issue in ontology based framework, less feasibility in SDN, implementation problem in closed loop approach, complexness in RFID technology, security issues in Lightweight protocols and cloud computing. Which make the task of secured communication over IoT healthcare is difficult by the IoT stakeholders. At times this leads to several security attacks to the IoT network. As a conclusion of this review on security issues in healthcare IoT carried over on the concepts like Ambient to Assisted Living (AAL), Software defined Networking and cloud computing reveals that current scenario of Internet of Things healthcare is vulnerable to several types of security attacks. The Overview of Attacks in healthcare IoT is discussed in next section.

OVERVIEW OF ATTACKS IN HEALTHCARE IOT

An Attack is any kind of malicious activity that attempts to collect, disrupt, deny, degrade, or destroy patient's protected health information or the information itself .Attack can be classified into viutwo types namely Active Attack and Passive Attack. An "active attack" attempts to alter system resources or affect their operation. A "passive attack" attempts to learn or make use of information from the system but does not affect system resources. An attack can be executed by an insider or from outside of the health organization.

Threats to Medical Devices

In April 2014, Scott Erven and his team of security researchers released the results of a two-year study on the vulnerability of medical devices. The study revealed major security faults that could pose serious threats to the health and safety of patients. They found that they could remotely manipulate devices, including those that controlled dosage levels for drug infusion pumps.

Primary Targets for Security Attack

Potential attacks against the Internet of Things into three primary categories based on the target of the attack.

- Attacks against a device
- Attacks against the communication between devices and masters,
- Attacks against the masters.

Attack on IoT Medical Device

To a potential attacker, a device presents an interesting target for several reasons. First, many of the devices will have an inherent value by the simple nature of their function. For example, a connected security camera could provide valuable information about the security posture of a given location when compromised. As devices will be trusted with the ability to control and manage things, they also present a value for their ability to impact things. This could be something as simple as controlling the lights in a house or business, medical device in a way that could cause physical harm. Finally, devices have a value based on what is entrusted to those devices. The smart grid, for example, trusts connected meters to be true and accurate. Hackers could manipulate a single meter to reduce an energy bill or attempt to deny power to a home or business. However, if enough smart meters were manipulated it could lead to grid instability of a wider scale.

Attack on Medical Device Communication

A common method of attack involves monitoring and altering messages as they are communicated. The volume and sensitivity of data traversing the IoT environment makes these types of attacks especially dangerous, as messages and data could be intercepted, captured, or manipulated while in transit. All of these threats jeopardize the trust in the information and data being transmitted, and the ultimate confidence in the overall infrastructure. For instance, information regarding the energy consumption from your home or business to your utility provider opens itself up to a number of threats. A few examples include the following, a hacker could track your energy usage to see when had downtime or uptime at your home or business in order to plan an attack on your property; a hacker could manipulate the data being transmitted to the utility company and alter the information.

Attack on Master of Devices

Attacks against manufacturers, cloud service providers, and IoT solution providers have the potential to inflict the most amount of harm. These parties will be entrusted with large amounts of data, some of it highly sensitive in nature. This data also has value to the IoT providers because of the analytics, which represent a core, strategic business asset—and a significant competitive vulnerability if exposed. Disrupting services to devices also poses a threat as many of the devices will depend on the ability to communicate with the masters in order to function. Attacking a master also presents the opportunity to manipulate many devices at once, some of which may already be deployed in the field. For example, a provider who issues frequent firmware/ software could have that mechanism compromised to instead introduce malicious code into devices. Several types of security attacks are discussed in D. Martinset (Martinset, D et al, 2010), K. Sharma (Sharma, K, 2010), K. Xing (Xing, K, 2005). Various types of healthcare security attacks are described in Table 2.

Table 2. Table List for Healthcare IoT Security Attacks

Attacks	Description
Eavesdropping	It is a passive attack which only listen the network to intercept information, but does not modify data. That's why, it is very difficult to detect.
Radio Jamming	An attacker sends the radio waves at the same frequency that is used by other authorized sensor nodes of the network
Message Injection	It is an active attack, in which aim of the attacker is to send the false messages on the network to corrupt the records or to saturate the Network.
Message Replication	It is also an active attack, here attacker catches the transmitted packets over the network and sends those packets to wrong nodes of the network.
Node Destruction	It is a type of physical attack in which ne or many nodes of sensor network are destroyed, making network not to work to destroy a node the link two nodes. In this type of attack, the attacker can also reprogram the sensor nodes.
Denial of service	This is another active attack which makes the wireless sensor network out of order by sending large amounts of data to the sensors to be active and consumes their energy.
Hello Flooding	With an attack of Hello flooding, an attacker can use a device with large enough transmission power for compromising every node in its neighbor.
Black Hole Attack	In black hole attack, at first a malicious node is inserted into the network. This malicious node changes the routing tables of the network. The aim is to force a maximum of neighboring nodes to send data to it. Once it captures all sent data, it does not forward or replies back.
Gray Hole Attack	It is a variant of the black hole attack. In this attack the malicious node replays all information concerning the route and non-critical data. That's why this attack is more difficult to detect.
Wormhole Attack	Unlike the black hole attack, this attack needs to insert in the network at least two malicious nodes. These nodes are connected by powerful connection. This attack wrongs the other nodes of the network and proposes a quicker path. Nodes choose this shortest path to send their data, and in actual they send their data to malicious nodes.
Sinkhole Attack	In this attack the malicious node attacks directly the data, which circulate near the sink i.e. base station. To perform this attack, the Malicious node offers the quickest path to reach the sink. All nodes, which are near the malicious node, send data for the sink which may be captured by the attacker.
Sybil Attack	In Sybil attack, a malicious sensor which is masquerading as multiple sensors, modifies the routing table
Message Alteration	A malicious node catches a message and changes it, by adding wrong information or deleting some information
Slowdown	An attacker can make use of malicious nodes to slow down the network. This attack prevents a sensor to sleep in different ways, in order to consume its battery quickly

Analysis of Various Attacks

Various attacks in IoT are explained, these attacks happened mainly because of insecure web interface in Iot Application, weak physical security, lack of proper encryption and weak password credential. Attacker uses vulnerable IoT network services to attack the device itself. Attack could come from external or internal users. An insecure web interface present in IoT Application can result in data loss, lack of accountability, denial of access and can lead to complete device takeover.

Attackers uses weak credentials, captures plain text credentials or Massage tampering. Active attacks like message injection, in which aim of the attacker is to send the false messages on the network to corrupt the records or to saturate the Network. Lack of protection of that data can lead to compromise a user's personal health data.

Physical security weaknesses are present, when an attacker can disassemble a device to easily access the storage medium. Insufficient physical security could lead to compromise of the device itself and any data stored on that device. Attacker uses routes such as USB ports, SD cards or other storage means to access the Operating System and potentially any data stored on the device. Data could be stolen or modified and the device taken control of for purpose other than what was originally intended.

Out of all these attacks Denial of Service (DoS) is one of the most dangerous attack on IoT healthcare data. It is one type of active attack which makes the wireless sensor network out of order by sending large amounts of data to the sensors to be active and consumes their energy. Insecure IoT network services may be vulnerable to Denial of service attacks.

The main intention of the attack is takes place IoT medical devices is to steal patients PHI. Every year, data breaches expose millions of records that are used by cyber criminals for illegal activities. Particular attention is given to medical records like Electronic Health Record (HER), a specific type of data that is attracting the attention of the criminal ecosystem. The concept which disused in table concluded that DoS attack is more dangerous than any other attacks in the cyber physical network.

Case Study for Healthcare Record Breaches and DoS Attacks

Every day in healthcare industry and patients PHI are threatened by several types of attacks and devices are got hanged by DoS attack. A data breach in the healthcare industry not only has financial and reputational effects on the company targeted by the threat actors, but the effects could be dramatic for the patients due to the nature of the data disclosed. Individuals' identity could be stolen directly from hospitals, healthcare insurance companies, and from any system that manages medical records.

Figure 2 shows the number of protected health information breaches over last five years from the study of Dan Munro (Dan Munro, 2015). They estimate that data breaches could be costing the industry $6 billion. More than 90 percent of healthcare organizations represented in this study had a data breach, and 40 percent had more than five data breaches over the past two years. No healthcare organization, regardless of size, is immune from data breach.

The figures are not surprising when consider the migration process from paper based files to Electronic Health Records (EHR) that has occurred in recent years. A growing number of healthcare institutions have adopted health records systems, a move encouraged by the government and made attractive by several advantages for the adoption of such systems. The number of EHR systems has more than tripled in the last 5 years, but the growth of electronic health records systems was not supported by a similar evolution under the cyber security perspective. Based on this statistics the adoption of IOT concept in Healthcare industry will need more security to mitigate the attacks and securing patients PHI.

CONCLUSION

The study discussed working principle of IoT healthcare Applications, security issues in IoT and different types of attacks. Major security attacks in recent years

Figure 2. Number of Protected Health Information breaches over last five years

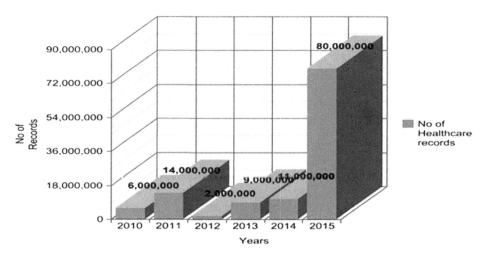

that could pose serious threats to the Healthcare Internet of Things. Once the device compromised with attacker then attacker can remotely manipulate devices, misusing medical records and controlling dosage levels of drug. The sensitivity of data traveling the IoT environment makes these types of attacks especially dangerous. With all kind of information there is a need to improve the security of IoT healthcare, in future a novel mechanism will be introduce to resolve various security issues in healthcare IoT.

REFERENCES

Amendola, S., Lodato, R., Manzari, S., Occhiuzzi, C., & Marrocco, G. (2014). RFID technology for IoT-based personal healthcare in smart spaces. *IEEE Internet of Things Journal, 1*(2), 144-152.

Atzori, L., Iera, A., & Morabito, G. (2010). The internet of things: A survey. *Computer Networks, 54*(15), 2787–2805. doi:10.1016/j.comnet.2010.05.010

Dan Munro. (2015). *Defenders Unite Against Cyber Threats In Healthcare.* Retrieved May 2015, from http://www.forbes.com/sites/danmunro/2015/05/10/

Dohr, A., Modre-Osprian, R., Drobics, M., Hayn, D., & Schreier, G. (2010). The Internet of Things for Ambient Assisted Living. *ITNG, 10*, 804–809.

Energetics Incorporated Columbia, Maryland, Foundations for Innovation in Cyber-Physical Systems, Workshop Report, NIST. (2013). Retrieved from http://www.nist.gov/el/upload/CPS-WorkshopReport-1-30-13-Final.pdf

Ervin. (2014). *Building a Trusted Foundation for the Internet of Things - Guidebook.* Recovered from http://www.safenet-inc.com/resources/

Kumar, J. S., & Patel, D. R. (2014). A survey on internet of things: Security and privacy issues. *International Journal of Computers and Applications, 90*(11).

Kumar, V. (2015). Ontology Based Public Healthcare System in Internet of Things (IoT). *Procedia Computer Science, 50*, 99–102. doi:10.1016/j.procs.2015.04.067

Maia, P., Batista, T., Cavalcante, E., Baffa, A., Delicato, F. C., Pires, P. F., & Zomaya, A. (2014). A web platform for interconnecting body sensors and improving health care. *Procedia Computer Science, 40*, 135–142. doi:10.1016/j.procs.2014.10.041

Martins, D., & Guyennet, H. (2010, September). Wireless sensor network attacks and security mechanisms: A short survey. In *Network-Based Information Systems (NBiS), 2010 13th International Conference on* (pp. 313-320). IEEE.

McCue, T. J. (2015). *Billion market for internet of things in healthcare by 2020.* Retrieved April 22, 2015, from www.forbes.com/sites/tjmccue/2015/04/22/117

Olivier, F., Carlos, G., & Florent, N. (2015). New Security Architecture for IoT Network. *Procedia Computer Science, 52*, 1028–1033. doi:10.1016/j.procs.2015.05.099

Rajagopalan, H., & Rahmat-Samii, Y. (2010, July). On-body RFID tag design for human monitoring applications. In *2010 IEEE Antennas and Propagation Society International Symposium* (pp. 1-4). IEEE.

Rghioui, A., L'aarje, A., Elouaai, F., & Bouhorma, M. (2014, October). The internet of things for healthcare monitoring: security review and proposed solution. In *2014 Third IEEE International Colloquium in Information Science and Technology (CIST)* (pp. 384-389). IEEE.

Santos, A., Macedo, J., Costa, A., & Nicolau, M. J. (2014). Internet of things and smart objects for M-health monitoring and control. *Procedia Technology, 16,* 1351–1360. doi:10.1016/j.protcy.2014.10.152

Santos, D. F., Almeida, H. O., & Perkusich, A. (2015). A personal connected health system for the Internet of Things based on the Constrained Application Protocol. *Computers & Electrical Engineering, 44,* 122–136. doi:10.1016/j.compeleceng.2015.02.020

Sharma, K., & Ghose, M. K. (2010). Wireless sensor networks: An overview on its security threats. *IJCA,* 42-45.

Valera, A. J. J., Zamora, M. A., & Skarmeta, A. F. (2010, January). An architecture based on internet of things to support mobility and security in medical environments. In *2010 7th IEEE Consumer Communications and Networking Conference* (pp. 1-5). IEEE.

Viret, J., Bindel, A., Conway, P., Justham, L., Lugo, H., & West, A. (2011, September). Embedded RFID TAG inside PCB board to improve supply chain management. In *Microelectronics and Packaging Conference (EMPC), 2011 18th European* (pp. 1-5). IEEE.

Wang, Y., Attebury, G., & Ramamurthy, B. (2006). A survey of security issues in wireless sensor networks. IEEE Commun. Surv. Tutorials, 8.

William, A. (2015). *Internet of Things and Security of Things*. Retrieved May 19, 2015, from http://www.healthcareitnews.com/author/william-tanenbaum

Xing, K., Srinivasan, S. S. R., Jose, M., Li, J., & Cheng, X. (2010). Attacks and countermeasures in sensor networks: A survey. *Network Security,* 251–272.

Zhang, X. M., & Zhang, N. (2011, May). An open, secure and flexible platform based on internet of things and cloud computing for ambient aiding living and telemedicine. In *Computer and Management (CAMAN), 2011 International Conference on* (pp. 1-4). IEEE.

Chapter 9
A Contemplator on Topical Image Encryption Measures

Jayanta Mondal
KIIT University, India

Debabala Swain
KIIT University, India

ABSTRACT

Images unduly assist digital communication in this aeon of multimedia. During times a person transmits confidential images over a flabby communication network, sheer protection is an accost contention to preserve the privacy of images. Encryption is one of the practice to clutch the reticence of images. Image encryption contributes a preeminent bite to charter security for secure sight data communication over the internet. Our work illustrates a survey on image encryption in different domains providing concise exordium to cryptography, moreover, furnishing the review of sundry image encryption techniques.

DOI: 10.4018/978-1-5225-2296-6.ch009

INTRODUCTION

Information technology in the web is proliferating without warning, causing massive users communicating via interactive media, especially; image, audio, and video. Images immerse the ample snippet of digital communication and play a consequential role in communication, for instance; military, medical agencies and diplomatic concerns (Shannon, 1949). Images, carrying significant private information, needs absolute protection during transportation or storage. In short, an image entails protection from diverse security attacks. The major motive to safeguard images is to ensure confidentiality, integrity and authenticity. Various techniques are at disposal for keeping images secure and encryption is one of them. Encryption does transform images into a cipher images mostly by assistance of a key. Later, an authorized user can recover the original image by decryption, the reverse process of encryption. This process is a part of the study called cryptology. Cryptology is the addition of cryptography; science of making ciphers, and cryptanalysis; science of breaking ciphers.

The field of modern cryptography provides a theoretical upheld focused around which a person can comprehend what indubitably these concerns are, the finest approach to assess practices that fancy to light up them and the means to gather conventions in whose safety one can have conviction (Kumar, Aggarwal, & Garg, 2014). Modern automated progresses have made private information by and large available. Security concerns over internet data made cryptography the field of interest for the researchers. The traditional and basic issue of cryptography is to provide secure communication over an untrusted channel. A has to send a secret message to B over an unsecured media, which can be hacked. The late forge ahead in technology, exceptionally in automation and information industry, allowed huge business for electronic interactive multimedia data through the Internet. This advancement made the web highly accessible with its contents, which encouraged obvious security problems. Digital security is maintained by some methods used to protect the sight and sound substance (Shannon, 1948). This whole picture acutely centered on cryptography.

PRELIMINARIES

Cryptography is the art or science encompassing the principles and methods of transforming an intelligible message into one that is unintelligible, and then retransforming that message back to its original form.

- **Plaintext:** Plaintext is the original intelligible message.
- **Ciphertext:** Ciphertext is the transformed message.
- **Encryption:** Encryption is the process (algorithm) for transforming a plaintext into a ciphertext.
- **Decryption:** Decryption is the reverse process of encryption, i.e. transforming the ciphertext back to plaintext.
- **Key:** Key is the most important data used by encryption algorithms, known to the both authorized parties. Encryption mechanisms relies on the key. Encryption algorithms are available for all, so, attacker's objective is to achieve the key.

Basic cryptography process for a text message at its simplest form can be described as:

Plaintext $P=[P_1, P_2, ..., P_X]$ of length X, where X belongs to finite alphabet set. The key $K=[K_1, K_2, ..., K_Y]$ of length Y. Ciphertext $C=[C_1, C_2, ..., C_Z]$ of length Z. With message P and key K the encryption algorithm creates the ciphertext $C=EK(P)$. The plaintext can be achieved by $P=DK(C)$. D being the decryption algorithm.

A cryptosystem thus can be formulated mathematically as a five tuple *(P, C, K, E, D)* where the following should satisfy:

1. P is a finite set of possible plaintext.
2. C is a finite set of possible ciphertext.
3. K, the key space, is the finite set of possible keys.
4. E is encryption rule, and, D is decryption rule.
5. $\forall k \in K, \exists e_k \in E, \exists d_k \in D$

Each $e_k: P \rightarrow C$ and $d_k: C \rightarrow P$ are functions,
Such that $\forall x \in P, d_k(e_k(x))=x$

CRYPTOGRAPHIC GOALS

The primary goals of cryptography are confidentiality, i.e. hiding information from unauthorized access, Integrity, i.e. preventing information from unauthorized modification, and, availability, i.e. information should be available to authorized users. International Telecommunication Union-Telecommunication standardization sector (ITU-T) includes authentication, nonrepudiation, and access-control as important objectives of cryptography. ITU-T provides standardized some security mechanisms to achieve security services, namely, encryption, data-integrity, digital-signature, authentication, traffic-padding, routing-control, notarization, and, access-control.

TYPES OF ENCRYPTION

Encryption is by far the best mechanism to achieve most of the security goals. Encryption algorithms are primarily classified into two categories—Symmetric key and Asymmetric key encryption.

Symmetric Encryption

In symmetric cryptography same key is used in encryption is and in decryption. Hence the key has to be distributed before sending the encrypted message. The key has the most significant role to play in symmetric cryptography as security depends straight on the essence of the key. For existing examples there are a number of symmetric key algorithms such as AES, DES (Shannon, 1949), TRIPLE DES, RC4, RC6, BLOWFISH (Shannon, 1949) available and frequently used. Symmetric algorithms can be classified into two categories; Block ciphers and Stream ciphers (Menezes, van Oorschot, & Vanstone, 1996).

In block cipher the process maps n bit blocks of plaintext to n bit blocks of ciphertext. Here the block length is denoted by n. The process can be parameterized by k (a randomly chosen key of n bits), where $k \in K$ (the key space), will transform into Vk (k bit vector). To avoid data expansion equal sized blocks of plaintext and ciphertext are used.

In stream ciphers each and every of the plaintext get encrypted one by one. The encryption transformation process changes with time. Stream ciphers are less complicated and time efficient. It can be more appropriate at times as they hardly have any error propagation. When the probability of transmission errors is high stream ciphers are proved to be more advantageous (Menezes, van Oorschot, & Vanstone, 1996). Stream ciphers are generally of two types based on the key distribution process namely, synchronous stream ciphers or self-synchronizing stream ciphers.

Asymmetric Encryption

In Asymmetric or public-key encryption the sender and the receiver uses different keys. For encryption public key is used, which is available for all, and for decryption a private key is used, which is confidential and resides with the receiver only (Menezes, Oorschot, and Vanstone, 1997). Examples of well-established public key include: ElGamal, Diffie-Hellman, Cramer-Shoup, RSA etc.

Public Key algorithms are relied on mathematical problems that presently give no accurate solution. Asymmetric encryption undoubtedly more secure but are complex and time consuming.

Properties of a Good Cryptosystem

There are two properties that a good cryptosystem must follow: diffusion and confusion (Schneier, 1996). Diffusion is the measure of change reflected on the plaintext for a slight change in the ciphertext, or vice-versa. An encryption algorithm must have a high diffusion rate. If a character of the cipher text is changed, then a significant number of characters of the plain text should change. Confusion refers to the complexity of relation of the key with the ciphertext, i.e. the key should not relate in a simple way.to be more specific, each bit/letter of the ciphertext should rely on different parts of the key.

This paper is further organized as follows in section 2 we present general guide lines about image encryption. In section 3 we survey on some recently proposed research papers, finally we conclude in section 4.

IMAGE ENCRYPTION

Challenges in Image Encryption

In the web open wide, several security issues exists with the processing and transmission of sight and sound data. Hence it is highly essential to affirm the privacy and security of the digital image being in the internet. During recent past, many image encryption techniques have been put forward. Image encryption algorithms varies from data encryption algorithms (Kaur & Singh, 2013). All existing data encryption algorithms cannot be applied straight to the multimedia contents mainly because of their large size. Encryption of digital images are different and difficult due to some inherent features of the images. Images have bulk information capability, high correlation between pixels, and data redundancy that square measure typically tough to handle like a text message. Moreover, an important feature of digital image is their less sensitivity as matched to text data, i.e. a small alteration in a single pixel value does not bother the entire original image (Khan & Shah, 2014). Therefore, efficient techniques are necessary for ultimate security of images.

Approaches Towards Image Encryption

Image encryption techniques transform the original image to encrypted image that is difficult to understand. A number of approaches exists relying on diverse features towards image encryption, each of them having different techniques, such as pixel value modification (Öztürk and Soukpinar, n.d.), chaos theory, visual image encryption (Naor and Shamir, 1995), or key less approach (Srivastava, 2012). Belonging to the image splitting or pixel modification method the image encryption techniques are classified into three main types: transposition (position permutation), substitution (value transformation) and combination of transposition and substitution techniques. The transposition techniques randomly rearranges the pixel position within the original image and generally have less safety as histogram of the encrypted image does not alter. In the value transformation algorithms, the pixel values of the original image are altered, making it more secure and efficient. Lastly, the combination carries out both substitution and transposition, and achieve high measure of security.

The other approach for protecting digital images is centered chaotic functions. Recently, various image encryption algorithms have been suggested focused on chaotic maps to deal with image encryption problems. Theoretically in technical aspect, chaos is described as when the current decides the future, but the rough present does not approximately decide the future (Matthew, 1989). Chaos theory was introduced in cryptography for its ergodicity, sensitivity-dependency on starting condition, random behavior, complex structure and control parameters. Chaotic techniques give excellent mixture of high security, lesser time and computational overheads (Pareek, Patidar and Sud, 2006). For multimedia content encryption those ciphers are only granted efficient, which takes less time and provides absolute security. Chaos theory based modern algorithms are such ciphers.

Visual Cryptography is the approach where encryption of visual information like images, is done in such a way that decryption can be performed by human visual systems without high computational efficiency. Simple algorithms are performed without the necessity of complex computations. Concerning security problems it provides good amount of certainty against mediocre level of cryptanalytic attacks. Images are encrypted to split the original image into a fixed number of shares using a simple algorithm. At the time of decryption all the shares are required. Without a single share the whole image cannot be recovered. In some specific areas, a number of authorities follow this approach for image security; most importantly military and security services (Rakhunde & Nikose, 2014).

In mixed approach an image is first split into random shares with the help of using some kind of encryption key then pixel distribution happens. It includes some traditional encryption technique and visual cryptography together. Generally a keyless approach is applied for image share distribution. This approach involves low computation cost and keyless management offers a fresh approach (Malik, Sardana, & Jaya, 2012).

Spatial and Frequency Domain

In spatial domain method, the pixel comprising of image specifics are acknowledged and different methods are put in application straight on these pixels (Khan & Shah, 2014). The image processing procedure in the spatial domain can be formulated as

$g(x,y) = T[f(x,y)],$

where, the input image is represented as $f(x,y)$, $g(x,y)$ represents the processed output image, and, T is the operation on f performed on a neighborhood of (x,y).

The operation (T) also can be performed on multiple images at a time. In spatial domain, an alteration in position in the image does reflect a straight change in the scene-position. Distances between the pixels in the image correspond to actual distances in the scene. The frequency that changes image values is defined as the number of pixels periodically repeating a cycle.

In frequency domain every image value at a given position stands for the variation of distances over that position. Here, the change of position gives the rate of change in spatial frequency in the spatial domain image. High frequency components correspond to edges where as low frequency components correlates with the smooth regions in an image (Khan & Shah, 2014).

Spatial domain trades in with images as it is, where, the pixel-values changes against scenes. Whereas the frequency domain reflects the rate of pixel-value change spatial domain.

In some recent techniques hybrid domain (frequency and time domain) system is proposed to achieve better security.

Full Encryption and Partial Encryption

Information privacy is an important factor of image encryption. Privacy of the encrypted data correctly balanced in computational time and resource of the encryption technique will be the hard challenge worth achieving in image encryption. These issues have been differentiated in some works extending across the spatial domain (Nien et al., 2009; Rhouma, Arroyo, and Belghith, 2009; Ahmad & Alam, 2009; Wei, Fen-lin, Xinl, and Yebin, 2010; Kamali, Hossein, Shakerian, and Hedayati, 2010; Z, L, and Z, 2010; Rodriguez-Sahagun, Mercado-Sanchez, Lopez-Mancilla, Jaimes-Reategui, and Garcia-Lopez, 2010; Mastan, Sathishkumar, and Bagan, 2014; Pareek, Narendra and Patidar, 2011; Abugharsa & Almangush, 2011; Yadav, Beg, and Tripathi, 2013), frequency domain (Sinha and Singh, 2013; Zhou, Wang, Gong, Chen, and Yang, 2012; Abuturab, 2012; He, Cao, and Lu, 2013; Chen, Du, Liu, and Yang, 2013) and the hybrid domain (Yu, Zhe, Haibing, Wenjie, and Yunpeng, 2010; El-Latif, Niu, and Amin, 2012) techniques in full encryption schemes, where the full image is encrypted for privacy preservation (Jawad1 and Sulong, 2013).

Generally multimedia content security schemes are called fully layered, the entire content is encrypted. Selective encryption or partial encryption is a process which only encrypts a part of a sight and sound data. It includes encryption of a subset of the data. With the ability of partial encryption, various targets could be achieved. The selective encryption scheme unlike the full encryption scheme, encrypts solely significant parts of the image. The fundamental worth of the partial encryption technique will be that it can offer the exact security and computational needs without tradeoffs. Huge research (Jawad1 and Sulong, 2013) has been carried out centered around selective encryption. Some of the work on varied domain; spatial (Rao, Mitra, and Prasanna, 2006; Wong & Bishop, 2007; Oh, Yang, & KH, 2010; Steffi & Sharma, 2011; Parameshachari and Soyjaudah, 2012; Kumar, 2012; Rodrigues, Puech, and Bors, 2006; Ou, Sur, and Rhee, 2007), frequency (Yekkala, Udupa, Bussa, and Madhavan, 2007; Brahimi, Bessalah, Tarabet, and Kholladi, 2008; Krishnamoorthi and Malarchelvi, 2008; Kulkarni, Raman, and Gupta, 2008; Younis, Abdalla, and Abdalla, 2009; M. and Agaian, 2010; Sasidharan and Philip, 2011; Kuppusamy and Thamodaran, 2012; Munir, 2012; Taneja, Raman, and Gupta, 2011; Parameshachari, Soyjaudah, and Devi, 2013), and, hybrid (Kumar, Aggarwal, & Garg, 2014; Shannon, 1949), noted for reference.

Evaluation Parameters for Image Encryption Schemes

1. **Correlation Coefficient:** The correlation coefficient assesses the level of equivalence in two images. Correlation within one image is termed as self-correlation. The self-correlation of neighboring pixel for a relevant image is consistently lofty as the value of neighboring pixel is near to each other. The correlation analysis calculated on two diagonally adjoining, horizontally adjoining and vertically adjoining pixels of encrypted image as well as original image (Ruisong, 2011). Correlation coefficient is again used to measure the quality of cryptosystem. An acceptable encryption algorithm conceals all features of the actual image transforming the image to uncorrelated. When correlation coefficient is one, then the original image and cipher-image are totally identical. If it is zero or nearing zero then they are completely different.

2. **Entropy:** Entropy of an image gives details about the image itself. It points out the degree of uncertainty of a communication system. It is the randomness feature of the image (Shannon, 1949). Mathematically entropy can be formulated as –

$$E\left(s\right) = \sum_{i=0}^{2N-1} p\left(s_i\right) \log\left(\frac{1}{p\left(s_i\right)}\right)$$

whenever the value of the entropy in a method gets closer to 8(ideal value), the predictability becomes less and the security improves (Kaleem and Ahmed, 2007).

3. **Compression Friendliness:** Image compression plays an important part in image security. Image compression lessens the need of transmission bandwidth and repository space. Diverse compression approaches are used, focused on the entropy theory. When the encryption does not influence the compression effectiveness largely nor does it instigate extra data then it can be called compression friendly (Lian, 2008).

4. **Encryption Quality:** The quality of encryption is measured by calculating three factors Maximum Deviation (zaid and El-Fishawy, 2009), Irregular Deviation (Noaman & Alla, 2008), and, Deviation from the Uniform Histogram (Ahmed & Ahmed, 2012).

High maximum deviation is the better for the quality of encryption. A good encryption technique must randomize the input pixels in a same way. Irregular deviation is relied on how much deviation causes irregularity on encrypted image. It calculates the irregular deviation of pixels from the basic position. A good encryption algorithm has irregular deviation and nears to uniform distribution. If the histogram of the encrypted image after encryption is uniform then the algorithm is regarded as a good encryption technique.

5. **Diffusion Characteristic:** A little alteration in original image should change cipher-text image significantly. This characteristics is known as avalanche effect. Number of Pixel Change Rate (NPCR) (Ahmed & Ahmed, 2012) and Unified Average Change Intensity (UACI) (Mohamed & Kachouri, 2011) are the means to measure Diffusion Characteristic. Higher the value of NPCR and UACI, better is the algorithm. Mathematically they can be formulated as –

$$NCPR = \frac{\sum_{i,j} D(i,j)}{M \times N} \times 100\%$$

$$UACI = \frac{1}{M \times N} \left[\sum_{i,j} \frac{C_1(i,j) - C_2(i,j)}{255} \right] \times 100\%$$

where M, N, $C_1(i,j)$ and $C_2(i,j)$ respectively represents width of the plain-text image, height of the plain-text image, gray scale value of encrypted image C_1 and the gray scale value of encrypted image C_2.

6. **Key Space Analysis:** Key is the primary need for all kind of cryptology. The ultimate security of the system at the end depends on the key (Forouzan, 2011; Alvarez & Li, 2006). Therefore, larger the key space, better the security. The algorithm should be sensitive on its key. If a small change happens in the initial key, the encryption/decryption should result in drastic difference.
7. **Mean Square Error:** The mean square error measures the difference between the cipher image and the original image. The MSE value should be higher for better image security. MSE can be mathematically defined (Alvarez & Li, 2006) by –

$$MSE = \frac{1}{s \times s} \sum \sum (X_{ij} - Y_{ij})^2$$

S, X_{ij}, and Y_{ij} respectively represents size of the image and parameter values, original image, and cipher-image. The difference between two images will be evident when MSE>30dB.

LITERATURE REVIEW

A First Approach on an RGB Image Encryption

In Kumar, Mishra, and Sharma (2014), M Kumar, D.C. Mishra, and R.K. Sharma proposed a foremost step towards a new image encryption centered on RGB un-scrambling using TSRMAC. For achieving high security during image transmission the random matrix affine cipher (RMAC) is being used in two steps combining with Discrete Wavelength Transformation (DWT). The new feature proposed is to introduce RMAC parameters in key distribution. This approach suits well foe large size images with a huge key space. Though affine cipher is highly regarded for text encryption but the proposed RMAC is specifically well suited for images in matrix format. The total number of choices for RMAC parameters get increased as it's done in two phases, makes the encryption stronger as well as decryption difficult for attackers. For decryption the correct number of RMAC parameters are essential with the right key. The proposed approach is highly sensitive on the key space. The security analysis proves this approach efficient with uniform histogram and low MSE value.

Multiple-Image Encryption Based on Optical Wavelet Transform and Multichannel Fractional Fourier Transform

In 2014, Kong et al, suggested a new image encryption strategy for multiple image encryption based on optical wavelet transform (OWT) and the multichannel fractional Fourier transform (Mfrft) is proposed in 2014. The technique enabled to fully utilize the multi-determination deterioration of wavelet transform (WT) and multichannel handling of Mfrft. The scheme makes use of the specified properties that can efficiently handle the encryption of multi-image and single image. Each and every image gets a unique autonomous key and their fractional request for transmission, after completion of the encryption process. Experimental testing of scrambled impacts has been found satisfactory. Furthermore, the exclusive effect of wavelet transformation and execution order of the multiple images are thoroughly examined with the application and examination of multichannel fractional Fourier transform proved to be proficient too. Numerical reenactment substantiates the applicability of the theory and proves that the complication of insufficient limit is better fathomed. Therefore, the flexibility of techniques increases. In the proposed plan the authors used a straightforward opto-electronic mixed device for better understanding of the strategy. The proposed work achieves high security, increasing key sensitivity and efficiently overcomes the challenge of real-time image security, reducing the encryption time using multiple images at a time.

Interference-Based Multiple-Image Encryption by Phase-Only Mask Multiplexing with High Quality Retrieved Images

In 2014, Y Qin, H Jiang, and Q Gong in 2014, proposed a manageable advanced method fundamentally rooted on optical intrusion concept for multiple-image encryption. The particulars of miscellaneous images can be numerically encoded into two phase-only masks multiplexing (POMs) unaccompanied by some iterative process, and the secure keys, essential for decryption are achieved logically. The prosed work can be seen as the extension of (Qin & Gong, 2011), where similar technique is used for multiple image encryption, but the cross-talk noise has gravely demeaned the standard of the recovered images. Even though some digital techniques, like filtering, may be used to subdue the cross-talk noise, the standard is still unsatisfactory. Hence, its use is narrowed to binary image encryption. Therefore, it is wise developing new techniques that can utterly remove the cross-talk noise. In a current work (Wang, Guo, Lei, & Zhou, 2013), also primarily based on the interference-based encryption scheme has been proposed with a little advancement on multiple-image encryption, although the encrypted images are complex images, making decryption process much complex. Moreover, the degree of security achieved using POMs is also compromised. In this proposed work under the IBE scheme centered on phase only mask multiplexing is resistant to cross-talk noise and the secret keys which are also POMs increases the security level. Hence, for real time multiple grayscale image encryption this proposed approach is well suited, providing higher security through POMs, time saving without any iterative algorithm, no cross-talk noise and silhouette problem, and, with a fast decryption mechanism.

Novel Image Compression–Encryption Hybrid Algorithm Based on Key-Controlled Measurement Matrix in Compressive Sensing

In 2014, Nanrun Zhoua, Aidi Zhang, Fen Zheng, and, Lihua Gong, in the year 2014, proposed a new hybrid technique combining image compression and image encryption. The proposed algorithm is rooted on compressive sensing and random pixel exchanging. Compressive sensing (CS) is a brand-new sampling and then reconstruction process that finishes sampling and compressing side by side at the same time. Severel researchers have worked on CS and implemented their proposals in recent past. But all the CS-based encryption algorithms so far has followed the full measurement matrix as the key that makes the key colossal for distribution and memorization. Both the compression and encryption techniques in a few proposed methods are unable to execute at the same time. The authors proposed the concept of constructing a circulant matrix where the key will control the measurement matrix to prevail over these issues. The proposed algorithm divides the original image into four blocks for compression and encryption. Further, the changed blocks go through a scrambling process. The scrambling process is performed based on random pixel exchanging process, which is supervised by the random matrices.

The proposed algorithm is well-suited for square-sized images. The whole encryption-decryption process goes through five steps. Firstly, the image is divided into four blocks. Then two measurement matrices are constructed with keys for two pairs of non-neighboring blocks. Thereafter, the adjoining blocks are scrambled, guided by two random matrices to get the cipher image. For decryption the inverse scrambling is carried out in the reverse order prior to the utilization of SL0 algorithm for decryption and decompression.

The measurement matrices in CS in this proposed work are created by using the circulant matrices and availing logistic maps to supervise the primary row vectors of the circulant matrices. Simulation outcomes show the efficacy of the work. By introducing the random pixel exchanging and binding the random matrices with the measurement matrices higher security is achieved and throughput is increased by its compression friendliness.

Image Scrambling Using Non Sinusoidal Transform and Key Based Scrambling Technique

In 2014, Kekre et al, proposed a hybrid image encryption scheme in the year 2014, based on image scrambling which includes an amalgamation of spatial domain and frequency domain. The authors have focused on creating a robust and versatile technique for image encryption which leads them to combine spatial domain and frequency domain as the factors in transform domain provide much robustness compared to spatial domain.

The work goes through a survey of different hybrid methods then proposes a new image scrambling scheme in the transform domain. A detailed implementation has been made utilizing four different non sinusoidal transformation techniques. The used transformation techniques are Walsh (Kekre & Patil, 2008), Slant (Pratt, Chen, & Welch, 1974), Haar (Kekre, Thepade, & Maloo, 2010), and Kekre (Kekre et al., 2010) transforms. Different mode of transformations such as row transforms, column transforms, and full transforms are tried on each of the four transforms. A diverse sequence generation algorithm is used for the scramble-process based on plaintext image-size. All existing scrambling methods can be applied on the proposed scheme, which makes it a different, versatile and effective technique for image security. The experimental results for all four non sinusoidal transformation schemes show efficiency and almost similar energy distribution. Among the four applied transforms, Kekre transform is proved to be the best in terms of security, robustness, and energy distribution.

Threshold Visual Cryptographic Scheme with Meaningful Shares

In 2014, Shyong Jian Shyu in 2014 has proposed an effective and advanced method for gray-scale image encryption on Visual Cryptography (VC) domain. In VC (Naor & Shamir, 1995) a number of participants shares a confidential image where a threshold exists, out of the number of Visual Cryptographic Schemes (VCS) should be able to part the original image into same number of shares (diverse transparencies) that are accordingly allotted to each members in a way that a group containing minimum threshold number of members can recover the image by superimposing their shares, however, any lesser number of shares than the threshold achieves no meaningful data justifying the purpose of encryption. The decryption method is totally centered on human visual recognition of the superimposition of the required number of transparencies. Therefore, no complex calculation or digital computing is necessary, which makes VC dissimilar from other mainstream cryptographic schemes.

A viable VCS encrypts each and every pixels in the plaintext image into sub pixels, this process is termed as pixel expansion, in all shares based on a random column permutation. This permutation process is conducted based on basis matrices in such a way that the superimposition of threshold number of shares or more than that gives the original image but less number of shares do not reveal any clue about the confidential image. The challenges in making a practical VCS are to minimize pixel expansion and to design applicable basis matrices with lesser complexity.

This proposed work concentrates on defining and constructing a threshold VCS where the pixel expansion can be minimum and the superimposed image of threshold shares gives the original image information. In Shyu and Jiang (2013) a successful technique is implemented based on threshold access structure utilizing Integer Linear Programming (ILP). The author has made some advancements on that work. This proposed work provides a better implementation of the ILP that can efficiently constructs the basis matrices, besides giving the formal definition of Visual Cryptographic Schemes with Meaningful Shares (VCS-MS).

An Image Encryption Algorithm Utilizing Julia Sets and Hilbert Curves

In Sun et al., (2014), a novel image encryption algorithm combining Julia sets and Hilbert curves is proposed by Yuanyuan Sun, Lina Chen, Rudan Xu, and Ruiqing Kong in 2014. The approach uses Julia sets' parameters to originate a unusual order as the primary keys and acquires the resulting encryption keys by clambering the beginning keys by the Hilbert curve. The encrypted image is acquired by modulo arithmetic and diffuse operation. In the proposed algorithm, the Julia set is clambered in bit-level through the Hilbert curve to amplify the key sensitivity. The diffusion process is instrumented to counter cryptanalytic attacks.

Along a thorough survey of the tested outcomes, the following deductions are achieved:

1. Plentiful Julia-like images lessens the key storage, which are easily generated by a few parameters. Security of the encryption algorithm can be enhanced by a large extent by the chaotic behavior of the Julia images, giving the key absolute sensitivity. The experimental research shows the key sensitivity achieves 10215.
2. Security against attacks is extraordinarily increases with highly sensitive immense key space provided by the diffusion process.
3. The algorithm succeeds to achieve the ideal value as per cipher image entropy is concerned, resulting in good security, uniform distribution, and randomization of the cipher-image.

A Block-Based Image Encryption Algorithm in Frequency Domain Using Chaotic Permutation

In 2014, Rinaldi Munir in 2014 proposed a new algorithm for Images encryption in frequency domain based on chaotic permutation for achieving robustness against any image processing attacks. For this purpose the original image is first transformed and encrypted in 8×8 blocks. After encryption some image processing based modifications were made on the cipher image to check the robustness of the image. The author has suggested encryption in favor of frequency domain to resist general image processing functions. Therefore, when a modification is targeted on the encrypted image, only the low frequency pixels get affected a little. Discrete Cosine Transform (DCT) is used for the image transformation process. Each block is encrypted using chaos based permutation technique.

The algorithm proposed is a small modification of an existing simple image transformation algorithm. A JPEG grey scale image of $N{\times}N$ pixels is considered for encryption. The original image is split into blocks of size 8×8 pixels and a DCT is applied for each bock. Then, DCT coefficients of each block are scrambled, except the upper leftmost element, by iterating Arnold Cat Map m times. The upper leftmost element coefficient is not encrypted because it carries significant visual information. Finally, IDCT is applied on each block to get the ciphertext image. Experimental results shows the cipher image is still recognizable, therefore the author randomized the pixels of plain-image before encryption using Arnold Cat Map twice, the first for scrambling the pixels of plain-image in spatial domain, and the second for scrambling the DCT coefficients of each block 8×8, to overcome the weakness of the simple algorithm.

A Novel Image Encryption Scheme Based on Hyper Chaotic Systems and Fuzzy Cellular Automata

In Wei, Fen-lin, Xinl, and Yebin (2010), a new image encryption scheme based on hyper chaotic system and Fuzzy Cellular Automata is proposed by Samaneh Zamani et.al, in 2014. Chaos theory has an immense impact on recent image encryption scenario. Hyper chaotic system has been suggested in this paper, as it has more complex dynamical characteristics than chaos systems. Therefore, it suits safe sight data encryption schemes. In this technique the authors have made a worthy research to enhance the computational efficiency besides providing high security by using four hyper chaotic systems. The first level of security is provided by the transposition of pixels, bit prior to that, the original image is parted in four pieces, each having its own hyper chaotic system. Two neighbor parted-images are considered first for the pixel transposition centered on the sequence numbers generated by the different hyper chaotic systems. Fuzzy logic is used in the encryption process. The algorithm is based on right neighbor theory. For this process five numbers if one dimensional non-uniform Fuzzy Cellular Automata is used. For different cell types (odd/even), two different encryption methods are used. The implementation results, on a few USC-SIPI database images, shows that the proposed method achieves great security level providing confusion, diffusion, and key sensitivity.

Image Encryption Using Chaotic Maps in Hybrid Domain

In 2014, S. Ramahrishnan, B. Elakkiya, R. Geetha, P. Vasuki, S. Mahalingam in 2014 proposed a new chaos based encryption in hybrid domain seeking more security. Pseudo random images are obtained utilizing chaotic maps for secure encryption. In the proposed system two transformation process are used for two domains. Discrete Wavelength Transformation (DWT), for time and frequency domain, and, Discrete Fourier Transform (DFT), for frequency domain. To compute different parts of time domain signal varied in different frequencies DWT is used. In encryption process the plain image is decomposed using DWT, then, divided into seven sub-bands, each of which are applied to DFT. Thus, encryption is performed in two steps: Transformation by DFT, using tent map, and, Substitution by DWT which uses Bernoulli map. The system is analyzed through rigorous performance test. The tests on the encrypted image shows that the proposed method produce a uniform histogram, a correlation coefficient of 0.024, MSE value around 17952, NCPR value of 100, and UACI is 46.88. With all these result this proposed technique should be granted as a good Image Encryption method.

CONCLUSION

In this paper, we made a theoretical survey over image encryption. We reviewed from the beginning, starting from the basic idea, we have gone through the several approaches to diverse existing image encryption techniques in different domain, lastly we reviewed some of the most recently proposed work on total and selective image encryption approaches under spatial, frequency and hybrid domains. In the route of this survey, a few remarks were made, such as, full encryption schemes, chaos based algorithms ensures high level of security of encrypted data, though less time is spent in selective encryption process.

Conclusively, from the literature review, by a thorough theoretical analysis we can conclude all the recent proposed techniques are efficient on their own goals, some providing ultimate security and some are made for enhance robustness. Almost every current method relies on the chaotic nature and the hybrid schemes for maximum security, efficiency, and, robustness.

REFERENCES

Abd El-Latif, A., Niu, X., & Amin, M. (2012, October). A new image cipher in time and frequency domains. *Optics Communications*, *285*(21–22), 4241–4251. doi:10.1016/j.optcom.2012.06.041

Abugharsa, A. B., & Almangush, H. (2011). A New Image Encryption Approach using Block-Based on Shifted Algorithm. *International Journal of Computer Science and Network Security*, *11*(12), 123–130.

Abuturab, M. R. (2012, May). Securing color information using Arnold transform in gyrator transform domain. *Optics and Lasers in Engineering*, *50*(5), 772–779. doi:10.1016/j.optlaseng.2011.12.006

Ahmad, M., & Alam, M. (2009). A New Algorithm of Encryption and Decryption of Images Using Chaotic Mapping. *International Journal on Computer Science and Engineering*, *2*(1), 46–50.

Ahmed & Ahmed. (2012). Efficency Analysis and Security Evaluation Parameters of Image Encryption schemes. *International Journal of Video & Image Processing And Network Security, 12*.

Alvarez & Li. (2006). Some Basic Cryptographic requirement for Chaos-Based Cryptosystems. *International Journal of Bifurcation and Chaos, 16*.

Bd, P., Sunjiv Soyjaudah, K., & Devi, K. A, S. (2013). Secure Transmission of an Image using Partial Encryption based Algorithm. *International Journal of Computers and Applications*, *63*(16), 33–36. doi:10.5120/10553-5746

Brahimi, Bessalah, Tarabet, & Kholladi. (2008). A new selective encryption technique of JPEG2000 code stream for medical images transmission. *5th International Multi-Conference on Systems, Signals and Devices*, 1–4.

Chen, H., Du, X., Liu, Z., & Yang, C. (2013, June). Color image encryption based on the affine transform and gyrator transform. *Optics and Lasers in Engineering*, *51*(6), 768–775. doi:10.1016/j.optlaseng.2013.01.016

Flayh, Parveen, & Ahson. (2009). Wavelet based partial image encryption. *International Multimedia, Signal Processing and Communication Technologies (IMSPCT)*, 32–35.

Forouzan. (2011). *Cryptography and Network Security*. McGraw Hill Education Private Limited.

He, Cao, & Lu. (2012). Color image encryption based on orthogonal composite grating and double random phase encoding technique. *Optik - International Journal for Light and Electron Optics, 123*(17), 1592–1596.

Jawad, & Sulong. (2013). A Review of Color Image Encryption Techniques. *International Journal of Computer Science Issues, 10*(6).

Jiang, Shyuand. (2013, May). General constructions for threshold multiple-secret visual cryptographic schemes. *IEEE Trans. Inf. Forensics Security, 8*(5), 733–743. doi:10.1109/TIFS.2013.2250432

Kaleem & Ahmed. (n.d.). Implementation of RC% block cipher algorithm for image cryptosystem. *International Journal of Information Technology, 3*.

Kamali, M. R. (2010). A New Modified Version of Advanced Encryption Standard Based Algorithm for Image Encryption. *International Conference on Electronics and Information Engineering (ICEIE), 1,* 141–145.

Kaur, R., & Singh, E. K. (2013). Image Encryption Techniques : A Selected Review. *Journal of Computer Engineering, 9*(6), 80–83.

Kekre, H. B. (2014). Image Scrambling Using Non Sinusoidal Transform And Key Based Scrambling Technique. *International Journal of Computers & Technology, 12*(8), 3809–3822.

Kekre, H. B., & Kavita, B. (2008). Walsh Transform over color distribution of Rows and Columns of Images for CBIR. *International Conference on Content Based Image Retrieval (ICCBIR).*PES Institute of Technology.

Kekre, Thepade, & Maloo. (2010). Query by Image Content using Color-Texture Features Extracted from Haar Wavelet Pyramid. *IJCA,* 52-60.

Kekre, Thepade, Athawale, Shah, Verlekar, & Shirke. (2010). Energy Compaction and Image Splitting for Image Retrieval using Kekre Transform over Row and Column Feature Vectors. *International Journal of Computer Science and Network Security, 10*(1).

Khan, M., & Shah, T. (n.d.). *A Literature Review on Image Encryption Techniques.* Springer. DOI .10.1007/s13319-014-0029-0

Kong, D., & Shen, X. (2014). Multiple-image encryption based on optical wavelet transform and multichannel fractional Fourier transform. *Optics & Laser Technology, 57,* 343–349. doi:10.1016/j.optlastec.2013.08.013

Krishnamoorthi, R., & Malarchelvi, P. D. S. K. (2008). Selective Combinational Encryption of Gray Scale Images using Orthogonal Polynomials based Transformation. *International Journal of Computer Science and Network Security*, 8(5), 195–204.

Kulkarni, N. S., Raman, B., & Gupta, I. (2008). Selective encryption of multimedia images. *32th National Systems Conference*, 467–470.

Kumar, M., Aggarwal, A., & Garg, A. (2014). A Review on Various Digital Image Encryption Techniques and Security Criteria. *International Journal of Computer Applications, 96*(13).

Kumar, M., Mishra, D. C., & Sharma, R. K. (2014). A first approach on an RGB image encryption. *Optics and Lasers in Engineering*, 52, 27–34. doi:10.1016/j.optlaseng.2013.07.015

Kumar, P. (2012). RC4 Enrichment Algorithm Approach for Selective Image Encryption. *International Journal of Computer Science & Communication Networks*, 2(2), 181–189.

Kuppusamy, K., & Thamodaran, K. (2012). Optimized partial image encryption scheme using PSO. *International Conference on Pattern Recognition, Informatics and Medical Engineering*, 236–241. doi:10.1109/ICPRIME.2012.6208350

Lian, S. (2008). *Multimedia content encryption: techniques and applications*. CRC Press.

Mastan, J. M. K., Sathishkumar, G. A., & Bagan, K. B. (2011). A Color Image Encryption Technique Based on a Substitution Permutation Network. *Advances in Computing and Communications*, 4, 524–533. doi:10.1007/978-3-642-22726-4_54

Matthew, R. (1989). On the derivation of a chaotic encryption algorithm. *Cryptologia*, 8(1), 29–42. doi:10.1080/0161-118991863745

Menezes, A., van Oorschot, P., & Vanstone, S. (1996). *Applied cryptography*. Boca Raton, FL: CRC. doi:10.1201/9781439821916

Menezes, A. J., Oorschot, P. C. V., & Vanstone, S. A. (1997). *Handbook of applied cryptography*. Boca Raton, FL: CRC Press.

Mohamed, Zaibi, & Kachouri. (2011). Implementation of RC5 and RC6 block ciphers on digital images. *8th International Multi-Conference*. IEEE.

Munir. (2014). *A Block-based Image Encryption Algorithm in Frequency Domain using Chaotic Permutation*. IEEE.

Munir, R. (2012). Robustness Analysis of Selective Image Encryption Algorithm Based on Arnold Cat Map Permutation. *Proceedings of 3rd Makassar International Conference on Electrical Engineering and Informatics*, 1–5.

Naor, M., & Shamir, A. (1995). Visual cryptography. *Advances in Cryptography: Eurocrypt'94*.

Naor, M., & Shamir, A. (1995). Visual cryptography. *Proc. EUROCRYPT'94, 50,* 1–12.

Nien, H. H., Huang, W. T., Hung, C. M., Chen, S. C., Wu, S. Y., Huang, C. K., & Hsu, Y. H. (2009). Hybrid image encryption using multi-chaos-system. *7th International Conference on Information, Communications and Signal Processing (ICICS)*, 1–5.

Noaman & Alla. (2008). Encryption Quality Analysis of the RCBC Block Cipher Compared with RC6 and RC5 Algorithms. *International Journal of Imaging, 10.*

Oh, Yang, & Chon. (2010). A Selective Encryption Algorithm Based on AES for Medical Information. *Healthcare Informatics Research, 16*(1), 22–9.

Ou, Y., Sur, C., & Rhee, K. H. (2007). Region-Based Selective Encryption for Medical Imaging. *1st Annual International Workshop*, 4427(4613), 62–73.

Parameshachari, B. D., & Soyjaudah, K. M. S. (2012). Analysis and Comparison of Fully Layered Image Encryption Techniques and Partial Image Encryption Techniques. *Communications in Computer and Information Science, 292,* 599–604. doi:10.1007/978-3-642-31686-9_70

Pareek, Narendra, & Patidar. (2011). A Symmetric Encryption Scheme for Colour BMP Images. *International Journal of Computer Applications in Special Issue on Network Security and Cryptography*, 42–46.

Pareek, N. K., Patidar, V., & Sud, K. K. (2006). Image encryption using chaotic logistic map. *Image and Vision Computing, 24*(9), 926–934. doi:10.1016/j.imavis.2006.02.021

Pratt, Chen, & Welch. (1974). Slant Transform Image Coding. *IEEE Trans. Comm., 22.*

Qin, Y., & Gong, Q. (2013). Interference-based multiple-image encryption with silhouette removal by position multiplexing. *Applied Optics, 52*(17), 3987–3992. doi:10.1364/AO.52.003987 PMID:23759846

Qin, Y., Jiang, H., & Gong, Q. (2014). Interference-based multiple-image encryption by phase-only mask multiplexing with high quality retrieved images. *Optics and Lasers in Engineering, 62,* 95–102. doi:10.1016/j.optlaseng.2014.05.010

Rakhunde, S. M., & Nikose, A. A. (2014). New Approach for Reversible Data Hiding Using Visual Cryptography.*Sixth International Conference on Computational Intelligence and Communication Networks*. doi:10.1109/CICN.2014.180

Ramahrishnan, S., Elakkiya, B., Geetha, R., Vasuki, P., & Mahalingam, S. (2014). Image encryption using chaotic maps in hybrid domain. *International Journal of Communication and Computer Technologies*, 2(5), 44–48.

Rao, Y. V. S., Mitra, A., & Prasanna, S. R. M. (2006). A Partial Image Encryption Method with Pseudo Random Sequences. Lecture Notes in Computer Science: vol. 4332. International Commission on Intervention and State Sovereignty (ICISS), (pp. 315–325). Berlin: Springer.

Rhouma, Arroyo, & Belghith. (2009). A new color image cryptosystem based on a piecewise linear chaotic map. *6th International Multi-Conference on Systems, Signals and Devices*, 1–6.

Rodrigues, J. M., Puech, W., & Bors, A. G. (2006). A Selective Encryption for Heterogeneous Color JPEG Images Based on VLC and AES Stream Cipher. *3rd European Conference on Colour in Graphics, Imaging and Vision (CGIV'06)*, 1, 34–39.

Rodriguez-Sahagun, M. T., Mercado-Sanchez, J. B., Lopez-Mancilla, D., Jaimes-Reategui, R., & Garcia-Lopez, J. H. (2010). Image Encryption Based on Logistic Chaotic Map for Secure Communications. *IEEE Electronics,Robotics and Automotive Mechanics Conference*, 319–324. doi:10.1109/CERMA.2010.44

Ruisong, Ye. (2011). *An Image Encryption Scheme with Efficient Permutation and Diffusion Processes*. SpringerVerlag Berlin Heidelberg.

Sasidharan, S., & Philip, D. S. (2011). A Fast Partial Encryption Scheme with Wavelet Transform and RC4. *International Journal of Advances in Engineering & Technology*, 1(4), 322–331.

Schneier, B. (1996). *Applied cryptography: protocols algorithms and source code in C*. New York: Wiley.

Shannon, C. E. (1948). The mathematical theory of communication. *The Bell System Technical Journal*, 27(3), 379–423. doi:10.1002/j.1538-7305.1948.tb01338.x

Shannon, C. E. (1949). Communication theory of secrecy systems. *The Bell System Technical Journal*, 28(4), 656–715. doi:10.1002/j.1538-7305.1949.tb00928.x

Shyu, S. J. (2014, December). Threshold Visual Cryptographic Scheme with Meaningful Shares. *IEEE Signal Processing Letters, 21*(12), 1521–1525. doi:10.1109/LSP.2014.2344093

Siddharth, Anjali, & Jaya. (2012). A Keyless Approach to Image Encryption. *International Conference on Communication Systems and Network Technologies.* IEEE.

Sinha, A., & Singh, K. (n.d.). *Image encryption using fractional Fourier transform and 3D Jigsaw transform.* Retrieved from http://pdfworld.net/pdf-2013/Image-encryption-using-fractionalFourier-transform-and-3D-Jigsaw-transform-pdf.pdf

Srivastava, A. (2012, June). A survey report on Different Techniques of Image Encryption. *International Journal of Emerging Technology and Advanced Engineering, 2*(6), 163–167.

Steffi, M. A. A., & Sharma, D. (2011). Comparative Study of Partial Encryption of Images and Video. *International Journal of Modern Engineering Research, 1*(1), 179–185.

Sun, Y., Chen, L., Xu, R., & Kong, R. (2014, January). Yuanyuan Sun1*, Lina Chen2, Rudan Xu1, Ruiqing Kong1, "An Image Encryption Algorithm Utilizing Julia Sets and Hilbert Curves. *PLoS ONE, 9*(1), e84655. doi:10.1371/journal.pone.0084655 PMID:24404181

Taneja, N., Raman, B., & Gupta, I. (2011, March). Combinational domain encryption for still visual data. *Multimedia Tools and Applications, 59*(3), 775–793. doi:10.1007/s11042-011-0775-4

Wang, Q., Guo, Q., Lei, L., & Zhou, J. (2013). Multiple-image encryption based on interference principle and phase-only mask multiplexing in Fresnel transform domain. *Applied Optics, 52*(28), 6849–6857. doi:10.1364/AO.52.006849 PMID:24085198

Wei, W., Fen-lin, L., Xinl, G., & Yebin, Y. (2010). Color image encryption algorithm based on hyper chaos. *2nd IEEE International Conference on Information Management and Engineering*, 271–274. doi:10.1109/ICIME.2010.5477430

Wong, A., & Bishop, W. (2007). Backwards Compatible, MultiLevel Region-of-Interest (ROI) Image Encryption Architecture with Biometric Authentication. *International Conference on Signal Processing and Multimedia Applications*, 324–329.

Yadav, R. S., Beg, M. H. D. R., & Tripathi, M. M. (2013). Image Encryption Techniques: A Critical Comparison. *International Journal of Computer Science Engineering and Information Technology Research, 3*(1), 67–74.

Yekkala, A. K., Udupa, N., Bussa, N., & Madhavan, C. E. V. (2007). Lightweight Encryption for Images. *International Conference on Consumer Electronics*, 3, 1–2.

Younis, H. A., Abdalla, T. Y., & Abdalla, A. Y. (2009). Vector Quantization Techniques For Partial Encryption of Waveletbased Compressed Digital Images. *Iraqi Journal of Electrical and Electronic Engineering*, 5(1), 74–89.

Yu, Z., Zhe, Z., Haibing, Y., Wenjie, P., & Yunpeng, Z. (2010). A chaos-based image encryption algorithm using wavelet transform. *2nd International Conference on Advanced Computer Control*, 2(4), 217–222.

Zamani, Javanmard, Jafarzadeh, & Zamani. (2014). *A Novel Image Encryption Scheme Based on Hyper Chaotic Systems and Fuzzy Cellular Automata*. IEEE.

Zhou, N., Wang, Y., Gong, L., Chen, X., & Yang, Y. (2012, October). Novel color image encryption algorithm based on the reality preserving fractional Mellin transform. *Optics & Laser Technology*, 44(7), 2270–2281. doi:10.1016/j.optlastec.2012.02.027

Zhou, N., Zhang, A., Zhen, F., & Gong, L. (2014). Novel image compression–encryption hybrid algorithm based on key-controlled measurement matrix in compressive sensing. *Optics & Laser Technology*, 62, 152–160. doi:10.1016/j.optlastec.2014.02.015

Related References

To continue our tradition of advancing information science and technology research, we have compiled a list of recommended IGI Global readings. These references will provide additional information and guidance to further enrich your knowledge and assist you with your own research and future publications.

Achahbar, O., & Abid, M. R. (2015). The Impact of Virtualization on High Performance Computing Clustering in the Cloud. *International Journal of Distributed Systems and Technologies*, 6(4), 65–81. doi:10.4018/IJDST.2015100104

Addya, S. K., Sahoo, B., & Turuk, A. K. (2015). Virtual Machine Placement Strategy for Cloud Data Center. In N. Rao (Ed.), *Enterprise Management Strategies in the Era of Cloud Computing* (pp. 261–287). Hershey, PA: IGI Global. doi:10.4018/978-1-4666-8339-6.ch012

Afghah, F., & Razi, A. (2014). Game Theoretic Study of Cooperative Spectrum Leasing in Cognitive Radio Networks. *International Journal of Handheld Computing Research*, 5(2), 61–74. doi:10.4018/ijhcr.2014040104

Ahmad, A., & Ahmad, S. (2014). Radio Resource Management in Cognitive Radio Sensor Networks. In M. Rehmani & Y. Faheem (Eds.), *Cognitive Radio Sensor Networks: Applications, Architectures, and Challenges* (pp. 27–47). Hershey, PA: IGI Global. doi:10.4018/978-1-4666-6212-4.ch002

Akherfi, K., Harroud, H., & Gerndt, M. (2016). A Mobile Cloud Middleware to Support Mobility and Cloud Interoperability. *International Journal of Adaptive, Resilient and Autonomic Systems*, *7*(1), 41–58. doi:10.4018/IJARAS.2016010103

Akyuz, G. A., & Rehan, M. (2016). A Generic, Multi-Period and Multi-Partner Cost Optimizing Model for Cloud-Based Supply Chain. *International Journal of Cloud Applications and Computing*, *6*(2), 55–63. doi:10.4018/IJCAC.2016040106

Al-Mutairi, M. S. (2016). Fuzzy Optimal Approaches to 2-P Cooperative Games. *International Journal of Applied Industrial Engineering*, *3*(2), 22–35. doi:10.4018/IJAIE.2016070102

Al-nsour, S., Alryalat, H., & Alhawari, S. (2014). Integration between Cloud Computing Benefits and Customer Relationship Management (CRM) Processes to Improve Organizations Performance. *International Journal of Cloud Applications and Computing*, *4*(1), 1–14. doi:10.4018/ijcac.2014010101

Al-Somali, S., & Baghabra, H. (2016). Investigating the Determinants of IT Professionals Intention to Use Cloud-Based Applications and Solutions: An Extension of the Technology Acceptance. *International Journal of Cloud Applications and Computing*, *6*(3), 45–62. doi:10.4018/IJCAC.2016070104

Alavi, S. M., & Zhou, C. (2016). Auction-Based Resource Management in Multi-Cell OFDMA Networks. In C. Yang & J. Li (Eds.), *Game Theory Framework Applied to Wireless Communication Networks* (pp. 273–295). Hershey, PA: IGI Global. doi:10.4018/978-1-4666-8642-7.ch011

Alcarria, R., Martín, D., Robles, T., & Sánchez-Picot, Á. (2016). Enabling Efficient Service Distribution using Process Model Transformations. *International Journal of Data Warehousing and Mining*, *12*(1), 1–19. doi:10.4018/IJDWM.2016010101

Aljawarneh, S. A., & Yassein, M. O. (2016). A Conceptual Security Framework for Cloud Computing Issues. *International Journal of Intelligent Information Technologies*, *12*(2), 12–24. doi:10.4018/IJIIT.2016040102

Alkadi, I. (2016). Assessing Security with Regard to Cloud Applications in STEM Education. In L. Chao (Ed.), *Handbook of Research on Cloud-Based STEM Education for Improved Learning Outcomes* (pp. 260–276). Hershey, PA: IGI Global. doi:10.4018/978-1-4666-9924-3.ch017

AlZain, M. A., Li, A. S., Soh, B., & Pardede, E. (2015). Multi-Cloud Data Management using Shamirs Secret Sharing and Quantum Byzantine Agreement Schemes. *International Journal of Cloud Applications and Computing*, *5*(3), 35–52. doi:10.4018/IJCAC.2015070103

Amone, W. (2016). Game Theory. In B. Christiansen & E. Lechman (Eds.), *Neuroeconomics and the Decision-Making Process* (pp. 262–286). Hershey, PA: IGI Global. doi:10.4018/978-1-4666-9989-2.ch014

Aniyikaiye, J., & Udoh, E. (2016). Web Services Gateway: Taking Advantage of the Cloud. *International Journal of Grid and High Performance Computing*, *8*(1), 85–92. doi:10.4018/IJGHPC.2016010108

Arinze, B., Sylla, C., & Amobi, O. (2016). Cloud Computing for Teaching and Learning: Design Strategies. In L. Chao (Ed.), *Handbook of Research on Cloud-Based STEM Education for Improved Learning Outcomes* (pp. 159–171). Hershey, PA: IGI Global. doi:10.4018/978-1-4666-9924-3.ch011

Asadi, M., Agah, A., & Zimmerman, C. (2014). Applying Game Theory in Securing Wireless Sensor Networks by Minimizing Battery Usage. In A. Amine, O. Mohamed, & B. Benatallah (Eds.), *Network Security Technologies: Design and Applications* (pp. 58–73). Hershey, PA: IGI Global. doi:10.4018/978-1-4666-4789-3.ch004

Bathory, D. S. (2015). Proof for Evolution and Coming Out of Prison with Relational Dynamics. *International Journal of Applied Behavioral Economics*, *4*(1), 58–69. doi:10.4018/ijabe.2015010104

Beloudane, A., & Belalem, G. (2015). Towards an Efficient Management of Mobile Cloud Computing Services based on Multi Agent Systems. *Journal of Information Technology Research*, *8*(3), 59–72. doi:10.4018/JITR.2015070104

Ben Ayed, H. K., & Hamed, A. (2014). Toward Proactive Mobile Tracking Management. *International Journal of Information Security and Privacy*, *8*(4), 26–43. doi:10.4018/IJISP.2014100102

Benatia, I., Laouar, M. R., Bendjenna, H., & Eom, S. B. (2016). Implementing a Cloud-Based Decision Support System in a Private Cloud: The Infrastructure and the Deployment Process. *International Journal of Decision Support System Technology*, *8*(1), 25–42. doi:10.4018/IJDSST.2016010102

Benmerzoug, D. (2015). Towards AiP as a Service: An Agent Based Approach for Outsourcing Business Processes to Cloud Computing Services. *International Journal of Information Systems in the Service Sector*, 7(2), 1–17. doi:10.4018/ijisss.2015040101

Bibi, S., Katsaros, D., & Bozanis, P. (2015). Cloud Computing Economics. In V. Díaz, J. Lovelle, & B. García-Bustelo (Eds.), *Handbook of Research on Innovations in Systems and Software Engineering* (pp. 125–149). Hershey, PA: IGI Global. doi:10.4018/978-1-4666-6359-6.ch005

Boehmer, W. (2015). Do We Need Security Management Systems for Data Privacy? In M. Gupta (Ed.), *Handbook of Research on Emerging Developments in Data Privacy* (pp. 263–299). Hershey, PA: IGI Global. doi:10.4018/978-1-4666-7381-6.ch013

Bouamama, S., & Belalem, G. (2015). The New Economic Environment to Manage Resources in Cloud Computing. *Journal of Information Technology Research*, 8(2), 34–49. doi:10.4018/jitr.2015040103

Bousia, A., Kartsakli, E., Antonopoulos, A., Alonso, L., & Verikoukis, C. (2016). Game Theoretic Infrastructure Sharing in Wireless Cellular Networks. In C. Yang & J. Li (Eds.), *Game Theory Framework Applied to Wireless Communication Networks* (pp. 368–398). Hershey, PA: IGI Global. doi:10.4018/978-1-4666-8642-7.ch014

Cesur-Kiliçaslan, S., & Işik, T. (2015). A General View of Poverty in Turkey as an Issue for Social Work in the Light of Behavioral Finance and Game Theory. In Z. Copur (Ed.), *Handbook of Research on Behavioral Finance and Investment Strategies: Decision Making in the Financial Industry* (pp. 25–37). Hershey, PA: IGI Global. doi:10.4018/978-1-4666-7484-4.ch002

Chahal, R. K., & Singh, S. (2015). Trust Calculation Using Fuzzy Logic in Cloud Computing. In K. Munir, M. Al-Mutairi, & L. Mohammed (Eds.), *Handbook of Research on Security Considerations in Cloud Computing* (pp. 127–172). Hershey, PA: IGI Global. doi:10.4018/978-1-4666-8387-7.ch007

Chaka, C. (2015). Personal Mobile Cloud Computing Affordances for Higher Education: One Example in South Africa. In N. Rao (Ed.), *Enterprise Management Strategies in the Era of Cloud Computing* (pp. 79–103). Hershey, PA: IGI Global. doi:10.4018/978-1-4666-8339-6.ch004

Chang, J., & Johnston, M. (2015). Approaches to Cloud Computing in the Public Sector: Case Studies in UK Local Government. In S. Aljawarneh (Ed.), *Advanced Research on Cloud Computing Design and Applications* (pp. 51–72). Hershey, PA: IGI Global. doi:10.4018/978-1-4666-8676-2.ch005

Chen, W., Wan, Y., Peng, B., & Amos, C. I. (2015). Genome Sequencing in the Cloud. In V. Chang, R. Walters, & G. Wills (Eds.), *Delivery and Adoption of Cloud Computing Services in Contemporary Organizations* (pp. 318–339). Hershey, PA: IGI Global. doi:10.4018/978-1-4666-8210-8.ch013

Choudhary, P. K., Mital, M., Sharma, R., & Pani, A. K. (2015). Cloud Computing and IT Infrastructure Outsourcing: A Comparative Study. *International Journal of Organizational and Collective Intelligence*, *5*(4), 20–34. doi:10.4018/IJOCI.2015100103

Clanché, P., Jančařík, A., & Novotná, J. (2015). Off-Line Communication in Mathematics Using Mobile Devices. In M. Meletiou-Mavrotheris, K. Mavrou, & E. Paparistodemou (Eds.), *Integrating Touch-Enabled and Mobile Devices into Contemporary Mathematics Education* (pp. 147–176). Hershey, PA: IGI Global. doi:10.4018/978-1-4666-8714-1.ch007

Costan, A. A., Iancu, B., Rasa, P. C., Radu, A., Pcculea, A., & Dadarlat, V. T. (2017). Intercloud: Delivering Innovative Cloud Services. In I. Hosu & I. Iancu (Eds.), *Digital Entrepreneurship and Global Innovation* (pp. 59–78). Hershey, PA: IGI Global. doi:10.4018/978-1-5225-0953-0.ch004

Das, R. (2014). A Game Theoretic Approach to Corporate Lending by the Banks in India. In B. Christiansen & M. Basilgan (Eds.), *Economic Behavior, Game Theory, and Technology in Emerging Markets* (pp. 271–288). Hershey, PA: IGI Global. doi:10.4018/978-1-4666-4745-9.ch015

Dawson, M. (2017). Exploring Secure Computing for the Internet of Things, Internet of Everything, Web of Things, and Hyperconnectivity. In M. Dawson, M. Eltayeb, & M. Omar (Eds.), *Security Solutions for Hyperconnectivity and the Internet of Things* (pp. 1–12). Hershey, PA: IGI Global. doi:10.4018/978-1-5225-0741-3.ch001

Dermentzi, E., Tambouris, E., & Tarabanis, K. (2016). Cloud Computing in eGovernment: Proposing a Conceptual Stage Model. *International Journal of Electronic Government Research*, *12*(1), 50–68. doi:10.4018/IJEGR.2016010103

Diviacco, P., & Leadbetter, A. (2017). Balancing Formalization and Representation in Cross-Domain Data Management for Sustainable Development. In P. Diviacco, A. Leadbetter, & H. Glaves (Eds.), *Oceanographic and Marine Cross-Domain Data Management for Sustainable Development* (pp. 23–46). Hershey, PA: IGI Global. doi:10.4018/978-1-5225-0700-0.ch002

Dreher, P., Scullin, W., & Vouk, M. (2015). Toward a Proof of Concept Implementation of a Cloud Infrastructure on the Blue Gene/Q. *International Journal of Grid and High Performance Computing*, 7(1), 32–41. doi:10.4018/ijghpc.2015010103

Elkabbany, G. F., & Rasslan, M. (2017). Security Issues in Distributed Computing System Models. In M. Dawson, M. Eltayeb, & M. Omar (Eds.), *Security Solutions for Hyperconnectivity and the Internet of Things* (pp. 211–259). Hershey, PA: IGI Global. doi:10.4018/978-1-5225-0741-3.ch009

Elkhodr, M., Shahrestani, S., & Cheung, H. (2017). Internet of Things Research Challenges. In M. Dawson, M. Eltayeb, & M. Omar (Eds.), *Security Solutions for Hyperconnectivity and the Internet of Things* (pp. 13–36). Hershey, PA: IGI Global. doi:10.4018/978-1-5225-0741-3.ch002

Faheem, M., Kechadi, T., & Le-Khac, N. A. (2015). The State of the Art Forensic Techniques in Mobile Cloud Environment: A Survey, Challenges and Current Trends. *International Journal of Digital Crime and Forensics*, 7(2), 1–19. doi:10.4018/ijdcf.2015040101

Foti, M., & Vavalis, M. (2015). Intelligent Bidding in Smart Electricity Markets. *International Journal of Monitoring and Surveillance Technologies Research*, 3(3), 68–90. doi:10.4018/IJMSTR.2015070104

Gangwar, H., & Date, H. (2015). Exploring Information Security Governance in Cloud Computing Organisation. *International Journal of Applied Management Sciences and Engineering*, 2(1), 44–61. doi:10.4018/ijamse.2015010104

Garita, M. (2014). The Rationality of Dumping: The Case of Guatemala. In B. Christiansen & M. Basilgan (Eds.), *Economic Behavior, Game Theory, and Technology in Emerging Markets* (pp. 359–367). Hershey, PA: IGI Global. doi:10.4018/978-1-4666-4745-9.ch019

Georgalos, K. (2014). Playing with Ambiguity: An Agent Based Model of Vague Beliefs in Games. In D. Adamatti, G. Dimuro, & H. Coelho (Eds.), *Interdisciplinary Applications of Agent-Based Social Simulation and Modeling* (pp. 125–142). Hershey, PA: IGI Global. doi:10.4018/978-1-4666-5954-4.ch008

Ghafoor, K. Z., Mohammed, M. A., Abu Bakar, K., Sadiq, A. S., & Lloret, J. (2014). Vehicular Cloud Computing: Trends and Challenges. In J. Rodrigues, K. Lin, & J. Lloret (Eds.), *Mobile Networks and Cloud Computing Convergence for Progressive Services and Applications* (pp. 262–274). Hershey, PA: IGI Global. doi:10.4018/978-1-4666-4781-7.ch014

Grandinetti, L., Pisacane, O., & Sheikhalishahi, M. (2014). Cloud in Enterprises and Manufacturing. In *Pervasive Cloud Computing Technologies: Future Outlooks and Interdisciplinary Perspectives* (pp. 150–164). Hershey, PA: IGI Global. doi:10.4018/978-1-4666-4683-4.ch008

Grandinetti, L., Pisacane, O., & Sheikhalishahi, M. (2014). Cloud Computing and Operations Research. In *Pervasive Cloud Computing Technologies: Future Outlooks and Interdisciplinary Perspectives* (pp. 192–224). Hershey, PA: IGI Global. doi:10.4018/978-1-4666-4683-4.ch010

Hallappanavar, V. L., & Birje, M. N. (2017). Trust Management in Cloud Computing. In M. Dawson, M. Eltayeb, & M. Omar (Eds.), *Security Solutions for Hyperconnectivity and the Internet of Things* (pp. 151–183). Hershey, PA: IGI Global. doi:10.4018/978-1-5225-0741-3.ch007

Hashemi, S., Monfaredi, K., & Hashemi, S. Y. (2015). Cloud Computing for Secure Services in E-Government Architecture. *Journal of Information Technology Research*, 8(1), 43–61. doi:10.4018/JITR.2015010104

Hassan, B. M., Fouad, K. M., & Hassan, M. F. (2015). Keystroke Dynamics Authentication in Cloud Computing: A Survey. *International Journal of Enterprise Information Systems*, 11(4), 99–120. doi:10.4018/IJEIS.2015100105

He, B., Tran, T. T., & Xie, B. (2014). Authentication and Identity Management for Secure Cloud Businesses and Services. In S. Srinivasan (Ed.), *Security, Trust, and Regulatory Aspects of Cloud Computing in Business Environments* (pp. 180–201). Hershey, PA: IGI Global. doi:10.4018/978-1-4666-5788-5.ch011

He, W., & Wang, F. (2015). A Hybrid Cloud Model for Cloud Adoption by Multinational Enterprises. *Journal of Global Information Management*, *23*(1), 1–23. doi:10.4018/jgim.2015010101

Huang, K., Li, M., Zhong, Z., & Zhao, H. (2016). Applications of Game Theory for Physical Layer Security. In C. Yang & J. Li (Eds.), *Game Theory Framework Applied to Wireless Communication Networks* (pp. 297–332). Hershey, PA: IGI Global. doi:10.4018/978-1-4666-8642-7.ch012

Hulsey, N. (2016). Between Games and Simulation: Gamification and Convergence in Creative Computing. In A. Connor & S. Marks (Eds.), *Creative Technologies for Multidisciplinary Applications* (pp. 130–148). Hershey, PA: IGI Global. doi:10.4018/978-1-5225-0016-2.ch006

Isaias, P., Issa, T., Chang, V., & Issa, T. (2015). Outlining the Issues of Cloud Computing and Sustainability Opportunities and Risks in European Organizations: A SEM Study. *Journal of Electronic Commerce in Organizations*, *13*(4), 1–25. doi:10.4018/JECO.2015100101

Islam, S., Fenz, S., Weippl, E., & Kalloniatis, C. (2016). Migration Goals and Risk Management in Cloud Computing: A Review of State of the Art and Survey Results on Practitioners. *International Journal of Secure Software Engineering*, *7*(3), 44–73. doi:10.4018/IJSSE.2016070103

Jasim, O. K., Abbas, S., El-Horbaty, E. M., & Salem, A. M. (2014). Cryptographic Cloud Computing Environment as a More Trusted Communication Environment. *International Journal of Grid and High Performance Computing*, *6*(2), 38–51. doi:10.4018/ijghpc.2014040103

Jasmine, K. S., & Sudha, M. (2015). Business Transformation though Cloud Computing in Sustainable Business. In F. Soliman (Ed.), *Business Transformation and Sustainability through Cloud System Implementation* (pp. 44–57). Hershey, PA: IGI Global. doi:10.4018/978-1-4666-6445-6.ch004

Ji, W., Chen, B., Chen, Y., Kang, S., & Zhang, S. (2016). Game Theoretic Analysis for Cooperative Video Transmission over Heterogeneous Devices: Mobile Communication Networks and Wireless Local Area Networks as a Case Study. In C. Yang & J. Li (Eds.), *Game Theory Framework Applied to Wireless Communication Networks* (pp. 427–456). Hershey, PA: IGI Global. doi:10.4018/978-1-4666-8642-7.ch016

Related References

Jouini, M., & Rabai, L. B. (2014). A Security Risk Management Metric for Cloud Computing Systems. *International Journal of Organizational and Collective Intelligence, 4*(3), 1–21. doi:10.4018/ijoci.2014070101

Jouini, M., & Rabai, L. B. (2016). A Security Framework for Secure Cloud Computing Environments. *International Journal of Cloud Applications and Computing, 6*(3), 32–44. doi:10.4018/IJCAC.2016070103

Kandil, A., El-Tantawy, O. A., El-Sheikh, S. A., & El-latif, A. M. (2016). Operation and Some Types of Soft Sets and Soft Continuity of (Supra) Soft Topological Spaces. In S. John (Ed.), *Handbook of Research on Generalized and Hybrid Set Structures and Applications for Soft Computing* (pp. 127–171). Hershey, PA: IGI Global. doi:10.4018/978-1-4666-9798-0.ch008

Kang, Y., & Yang, K. C. (2016). Analyzing Multi-Modal Digital Discourses during MMORPG Gameplay through an Experiential Rhetorical Approach. In B. Baggio (Ed.), *Analyzing Digital Discourse and Human Behavior in Modern Virtual Environments* (pp. 220–243). Hershey, PA: IGI Global. doi:10.4018/978-1-4666-9899-4.ch012

Kasemsap, K. (2015). Adopting Cloud Computing in Global Supply Chain: A Literature Review. *International Journal of Social and Organizational Dynamics in IT, 4*(2), 49–62. doi:10.4018/IJSODIT.2015070105

Kasemsap, K. (2015). The Role of Cloud Computing Adoption in Global Business. In V. Chang, R. Walters, & G. Wills (Eds.), *Delivery and Adoption of Cloud Computing Services in Contemporary Organizations* (pp. 26–55). Hershey, PA: IGI Global. doi:10.4018/978-1-4666-8210-8.ch002

Kasemsap, K. (2016). The Fundamentals of Neuroeconomics. In B. Christiansen & E. Lechman (Eds.), *Neuroeconomics and the Decision-Making Process* (pp. 1–32). Hershey, PA: IGI Global. doi:10.4018/978-1-4666-9989-2.ch001

Katzis, K. (2015). Mobile Cloud Resource Management. In G. Mastorakis, C. Mavromoustakis, & E. Pallis (Eds.), *Resource Management of Mobile Cloud Computing Networks and Environments* (pp. 69–96). Hershey, PA: IGI Global. doi:10.4018/978-1-4666-8225-2.ch004

Khan, N., & Al-Yasiri, A. (2016). Cloud Security Threats and Techniques to Strengthen Cloud Computing Adoption Framework. *International Journal of Information Technology and Web Engineering, 11*(3), 50–64. doi:10.4018/IJITWE.2016070104

Kim, S. (2014). Bandwidth Management Algorithms by Using Game Models. In *Game Theory Applications in Network Design* (pp. 311–351). Hershey, PA: IGI Global. doi:10.4018/978-1-4666-6050-2.ch012

Kim, S. (2014). Game Models in Various Applications. In *Game Theory Applications in Network Design* (pp. 44–128). Hershey, PA: IGI Global. doi:10.4018/978-1-4666-6050-2.ch003

Kim, S. (2014). Game Theory for Network Security. In *Game Theory Applications in Network Design* (pp. 158–171). Hershey, PA: IGI Global. doi:10.4018/978-1-4666-6050-2.ch006

Kuada, E. (2017). Security and Trust in Cloud Computing. In M. Dawson, M. Eltayeb, & M. Omar (Eds.), *Security Solutions for Hyperconnectivity and the Internet of Things* (pp. 184–210). Hershey, PA: IGI Global. doi:10.4018/978-1-5225-0741-3.ch008

Kumar, D., Sahoo, B., & Mandal, T. (2015). Heuristic Task Consolidation Techniques for Energy Efficient Cloud Computing. In N. Rao (Ed.), *Enterprise Management Strategies in the Era of Cloud Computing* (pp. 238–260). Hershey, PA: IGI Global. doi:10.4018/978-1-4666-8339-6.ch011

Kumar, S. A. (2014). Organizational Control Related to Cloud. In S. Srinivasan (Ed.), *Security, Trust, and Regulatory Aspects of Cloud Computing in Business Environments* (pp. 234–246). Hershey, PA: IGI Global. doi:10.4018/978-1-4666-5788-5.ch014

Lai, W., Chang, T., & Lee, T. (2016). Distributed Dynamic Resource Allocation for OFDMA-Based Cognitive Small Cell Networks Using a Regret-Matching Game Approach. In C. Yang & J. Li (Eds.), *Game Theory Framework Applied to Wireless Communication Networks* (pp. 230–253). Hershey, PA: IGI Global. doi:10.4018/978-1-4666-8642-7.ch009

Li, W. H., Zhu, K., & Fu, H. (2017). Exploring the Design Space of Bezel-Initiated Gestures for Mobile Interaction. *International Journal of Mobile Human Computer Interaction*, *9*(1), 16–29. doi:10.4018/IJMHCI.2017010102

Likavec, S., Osborne, F., & Cena, F. (2015). Property-based Semantic Similarity and Relatedness for Improving Recommendation Accuracy and Diversity. *International Journal on Semantic Web and Information Systems*, *11*(4), 1–40. doi:10.4018/IJSWIS.2015100101

Limam, S., & Belalem, G. (2014). A Migration Approach for Fault Tolerance in Cloud Computing. *International Journal of Grid and High Performance Computing, 6*(2), 24–37. doi:10.4018/ijghpc.2014040102

Lin, W., Yang, C., Zhu, C., Wang, J. Z., & Peng, Z. (2014). Energy Efficiency Oriented Scheduling for Heterogeneous Cloud Systems. *International Journal of Grid and High Performance Computing, 6*(4), 1–14. doi:10.4018/IJGHPC.2014100101

Liu, C., Huang, K., Lee, Y., & Lai, K. (2015). Efficient Resource Allocation Mechanism for Federated Clouds. *International Journal of Grid and High Performance Computing, 7*(4), 74–87. doi:10.4018/IJGHPC.2015100106

Martins, R. A., Kumar, K., Mukherjee, A., Nabin, M. H., & Bhattacharya, S. (2014). Decision-Making in Economics: Critical Lessons from Neurobiology. In B. Christiansen & M. Basilgan (Eds.), *Economic Behavior, Game Theory, and Technology in Emerging Markets* (pp. 46–56). Hershey, PA: IGI Global. doi:10.4018/978-1-4666-4745-9.ch004

Mayer, I., Bekebrede, G., Warmelink, H., & Zhou, Q. (2014). A Brief Methodology for Researching and Evaluating Serious Games and Game-Based Learning. In T. Connolly, T. Hainey, E. Boyle, G. Baxter, & P. Moreno-Ger (Eds.), *Psychology, Pedagogy, and Assessment in Serious Games* (pp. 357–393). Hershey, PA: IGI Global. doi:10.4018/978-1-4666-4773-2.ch017

Mezghani, K., & Ayadi, F. (2016). Factors Explaining IS Managers Attitudes toward Cloud Computing Adoption. *International Journal of Technology and Human Interaction, 12*(1), 1–20. doi:10.4018/IJTHI.2016010101

Mihaljević, M. J., & Imai, H. (2014). Security Issues of Cloud Computing and an Encryption Approach. In M. Despotović-Zrakić, V. Milutinović, & A. Belić (Eds.), *Handbook of Research on High Performance and Cloud Computing in Scientific Research and Education* (pp. 388–408). Hershey, PA: IGI Global. doi:10.4018/978-1-4666-5784-7.ch016

Militano, L., Iera, A., Scarcello, F., Molinaro, A., & Araniti, G. (2016). Game Theoretic Approaches for Wireless Cooperative Content-Sharing. In C. Yang & J. Li (Eds.), *Game Theory Framework Applied to Wireless Communication Networks* (pp. 399–426). Hershey, PA: IGI Global. doi:10.4018/978-1-4666-8642-7.ch015

Mohammed, F., & Ibrahim, O. B. (2015). Drivers of Cloud Computing Adoption for E-Government Services Implementation. *International Journal of Distributed Systems and Technologies, 6*(1), 1–14. doi:10.4018/ijdst.2015010101

Moura, J. A., Marinheiro, R. N., & Silva, J. C. (2014). Game Theory for Collaboration in Future Networks. In R. Trestian & G. Muntean (Eds.), *Convergence of Broadband, Broadcast, and Cellular Network Technologies* (pp. 94–123). Hershey, PA: IGI Global. doi:10.4018/978-1-4666-5978-0.ch005

Nagar, N., & Suman, U. (2014). Two Factor Authentication using M-pin Server for Secure Cloud Computing Environment. *International Journal of Cloud Applications and Computing, 4*(4), 42–54. doi:10.4018/ijcac.2014100104

Nezarat, A., & Dastghaibifard, G. (2016). A Game Theoretic Method for Resource Allocation in Scientific Cloud. *International Journal of Cloud Applications and Computing, 6*(1), 15–41. doi:10.4018/IJCAC.2016010102

Ng, A., Watters, P., & Chen, S. (2014). A Technology and Process Analysis for Contemporary Identity Management Frameworks. In M. Khosrow-Pour (Ed.), *Inventive Approaches for Technology Integration and Information Resources Management* (pp. 1–52). Hershey, PA: IGI Global. doi:10.4018/978-1-4666-6256-8.ch001

Orike, S., & Brown, D. (2016). Big Data Management: An Investigation into Wireless and Cloud Computing. *International Journal of Interdisciplinary Telecommunications and Networking, 8*(4), 34–50. doi:10.4018/IJITN.2016100104

Ouf, S., & Nasr, M. (2015). Cloud Computing: The Future of Big Data Management. *International Journal of Cloud Applications and Computing, 5*(2), 53–61. doi:10.4018/IJCAC.2015040104

Outanoute, M., Baslam, M., & Bouikhalene, B. (2015). Genetic Algorithm Learning of Nash Equilibrium: Application on Price-QoS Competition in Telecommunications Market. *Journal of Electronic Commerce in Organizations, 13*(3), 1–14. doi:10.4018/JECO.2015070101

Patra, P. K., Singh, H., Singh, R., Das, S., Dey, N., & Victoria, A. D. (2016). Replication and Resubmission Based Adaptive Decision for Fault Tolerance in Real Time Cloud Computing: A New Approach. *International Journal of Service Science, Management, Engineering, and Technology, 7*(2), 46–60. doi:10.4018/IJSSMET.2016040104

Related References

Peng, M., Sun, Y., Sun, C., & Ahmed, M. (2016). Game Theory-Based Radio Resource Optimization in Heterogeneous Small Cell Networks (HSCNs). In C. Yang & J. Li (Eds.), *Game Theory Framework Applied to Wireless Communication Networks* (pp. 137–183). Hershey, PA: IGI Global. doi:10.4018/978-1-4666-8642-7.ch006

Pereira, J. P. (2014). Simulation of Competition in NGNs with a Game Theory Model. In R. Trestian & G. Muntean (Eds.), *Convergence of Broadband, Broadcast, and Cellular Network Technologies* (pp. 216–243). Hershey, PA: IGI Global. doi:10.4018/978-1-4666-5978-0.ch010

Phelps, M., & Jennex, M. E. (2015). Ownership of Collaborative Works in the Cloud. *International Journal of Knowledge Management, 11*(4), 35–51. doi:10.4018/IJKM.2015100103

Ramakrishna, V., & Dey, K. (2017). Mobile Application and User Analytics. In S. Mukherjea (Ed.), *Mobile Application Development, Usability, and Security* (pp. 231–259). Hershey, PA: IGI Global. doi:10.4018/978-1-5225-0945-5.ch011

Rao, N. R. (2015). Cloud Computing: An Enabler in Managing Natural Resources in a Country. In N. Rao (Ed.), *Enterprise Management Strategies in the Era of Cloud Computing* (pp. 155–169). Hershey, PA: IGI Global. doi:10.4018/978-1-4666-8339-6.ch007

Ratten, V. (2015). An Entrepreneurial Approach to Cloud Computing Design and Application: Technological Innovation and Information System Usage. In S. Aljawarneh (Ed.), *Advanced Research on Cloud Computing Design and Applications* (pp. 1–14). Hershey, PA: IGI Global. doi:10.4018/978-1-4666-8676-2.ch001

Ratten, V. (2015). Cloud Computing Technology Innovation Advances: A Set of Research Propositions. *International Journal of Cloud Applications and Computing, 5*(1), 69–76. doi:10.4018/ijcac.2015010106

Rawat, A., & Gambhir, S. (2015). Biometric: Authentication and Service to Cloud. In G. Deka & S. Bakshi (Eds.), *Handbook of Research on Securing Cloud-Based Databases with Biometric Applications* (pp. 251–268). Hershey, PA: IGI Global. doi:10.4018/978-1-4666-6559-0.ch012

Rawat, D. B., & Shetty, S. (2016). Game Theoretic Cloud-Assisted Opportunistic Spectrum Access in Cognitive Radio Networks. *International Journal of Grid and High Performance Computing, 8*(2), 94–110. doi:10.4018/IJGHPC.2016040106

Rindos, A., Vouk, M., & Jararweh, Y. (2014). The Virtual Computing Lab (VCL): An Open Source Cloud Computing Solution Designed Specifically for Education and Research. *International Journal of Service Science, Management, Engineering, and Technology, 5*(2), 51–63. doi:10.4018/ijssmet.2014040104

Ritzhaupt, A. D., Poling, N., Frey, C., Kang, Y., & Johnson, M. (2016). A Phenomenological Study of Games, Simulations, and Virtual Environments Courses: What Are We Teaching and How? *International Journal of Gaming and Computer-Mediated Simulations, 8*(3), 59–73. doi:10.4018/IJGCMS.2016070104

Romm-Livermore, C., Raisinghani, M. S., & Rippa, P. (2016). The Politics of E-Learning: A Game Theory Analysis. *International Journal of Online Pedagogy and Course Design, 6*(2), 1–14. doi:10.4018/IJOPCD.2016040101

Rusko, R. (2016). The Role of the Mixed Strategies and Selective Inflexibility in the Repeated Games of Business: Multiple Case Study Analysis. In B. Christiansen & E. Lechman (Eds.), *Neuroeconomics and the Decision-Making Process* (pp. 132–146). Hershey, PA: IGI Global. doi:10.4018/978-1-4666-9989-2.ch008

Salama, M., Zeid, A., Shawish, A., & Jiang, X. (2014). A Novel QoS-Based Framework for Cloud Computing Service Provider Selection. *International Journal of Cloud Applications and Computing, 4*(2), 48–72. doi:10.4018/ijcac.2014040104

Santos, J. L. (2015). An Agent-Based Model of Insurance and Protection Decisions on IT Systems. *International Journal of Agent Technologies and Systems, 7*(3), 1–17. doi:10.4018/IJATS.2015070101

Seçilmiş, İ. E. (2014). A Survey of Game Theory Applications in Turkey. In B. Christiansen & M. Basilgan (Eds.), *Economic Behavior, Game Theory, and Technology in Emerging Markets* (pp. 155–168). Hershey, PA: IGI Global. doi:10.4018/978-1-4666-4745-9.ch009

Shen, Y., Li, Y., Wu, L., Liu, S., & Wen, Q. (2014). Cloud Computing Overview. In Y. Shen, Y. Li, L. Wu, S. Liu, & Q. Wen (Eds.), *Enabling the New Era of Cloud Computing: Data Security, Transfer, and Management* (pp. 1–24). Hershey, PA: IGI Global. doi:10.4018/978-1-4666-4801-2.ch001

Shi, Z., & Beard, C. (2014). QoS in the Mobile Cloud Computing Environment. In J. Rodrigues, K. Lin, & J. Lloret (Eds.), *Mobile Networks and Cloud Computing Convergence for Progressive Services and Applications* (pp. 200–217). Hershey, PA: IGI Global. doi:10.4018/978-1-4666-4781-7.ch011

Singh, A., Dutta, K., & Singh, A. (2014). Resource Allocation in Cloud Computing Environment using AHP Technique. *International Journal of Cloud Applications and Computing*, 4(1), 33–44. doi:10.4018/ijcac.2014010103

Singh, J., & Kumar, V. (2014). Multi-Disciplinary Research Issues in Cloud Computing. *Journal of Information Technology Research*, 7(3), 32–53. doi:10.4018/jitr.2014070103

Sivagurunathan, S., & Swasthimathi, L. S. (2016). Cloud Computing Applications in Education through E-Governance: An Indian Perspective. In Z. Mahmood (Ed.), *Cloud Computing Technologies for Connected Government* (pp. 247–268). Hershey, PA: IGI Global. doi:10.4018/978-1-4666-8629-8.ch010

Stennikov, V., Penkovskii, A., & Khamisov, O. (2016). Problems of Modeling and Optimization of Heat Supply Systems: Bi-Level Optimization of the Competitive Heat Energy Market. In P. Vasant & N. Voropai (Eds.), *Sustaining Power Resources through Energy Optimization and Engineering* (pp. 54–75). Hershey, PA: IGI Global. doi:10.4018/978-1-4666-9755-3.ch003

Stranacher, K., Tauber, A., Zefferer, T., & Zwattendorfer, B. (2014). The Austrian Identity Ecosystem: An E-Government Experience. In A. Ruiz-Martinez, R. Marin-Lopez, & F. Pereniguez-Garcia (Eds.), *Architectures and Protocols for Secure Information Technology Infrastructures* (pp. 288–309). Hershey, PA: IGI Global. doi:10.4018/978-1-4666-4514-1.ch011

Subramanian, T., & Savarimuthu, N. (2016). Cloud Service Evaluation and Selection Using Fuzzy Hybrid MCDM Approach in Marketplace. *International Journal of Fuzzy System Applications*, 5(2), 118–153. doi:10.4018/IJFSA.2016040108

Suthakar, K. I., & Devi, M. K. (2016). Resource Scheduling for Big Data on Cloud: Scheduling Resources. In R. Kannan, R. Rasool, H. Jin, & S. Balasundaram (Eds.), *Managing and Processing Big Data in Cloud Computing* (pp. 185–205). Hershey, PA: IGI Global. doi:10.4018/978-1-4666-9767-6.ch013

Suwais, K. (2014). Assessing the Utilization of Automata in Representing Players Behaviors in Game Theory. *International Journal of Ambient Computing and Intelligence*, 6(2), 1–14. doi:10.4018/IJACI.2014070101

Takabi, H., Zargar, S. T., & Joshi, J. B. (2014). Mobile Cloud Computing and Its Security and Privacy Challenges. In D. Rawat, B. Bista, & G. Yan (Eds.), *Security, Privacy, Trust, and Resource Management in Mobile and Wireless Communications* (pp. 384–407). Hershey, PA: IGI Global. doi:10.4018/978-1-4666-4691-9.ch016

Thomas, M. V., & Chandrasekaran, K. (2016). Identity and Access Management in the Cloud Computing Environments. In G. Kecskemeti, A. Kertesz, & Z. Nemeth (Eds.), *Developing Interoperable and Federated Cloud Architecture* (pp. 61–90). Hershey, PA: IGI Global. doi:10.4018/978-1-5225-0153-4.ch003

Tomaiuolo, M. (2014). Trust Management and Delegation for the Administration of Web Services. In I. Portela & F. Almeida (Eds.), *Organizational, Legal, and Technological Dimensions of Information System Administration* (pp. 18–37). Hershey, PA: IGI Global. doi:10.4018/978-1-4666-4526-4.ch002

Truong, D. (2015). Efficiency and Risk Management Models for Cloud-Based Solutions in Supply Chain Management. *International Journal of Business Analytics*, 2(2), 14–30. doi:10.4018/IJBAN.2015040102

Tuncalp, D. (2015). Management of Privacy and Security in Cloud Computing: Contractual Controls in Service Agreements. In V. Chang, R. Walters, & G. Wills (Eds.), *Delivery and Adoption of Cloud Computing Services in Contemporary Organizations* (pp. 409–434). Hershey, PA: IGI Global. doi:10.4018/978-1-4666-8210-8.ch017

Udoh, E., Patterson, B., & Cordle, S. (2016). Using the Balanced Scorecard Approach to Appraise the Performance of Cloud Computing. *International Journal of Grid and High Performance Computing*, 8(1), 50–57. doi:10.4018/IJGHPC.2016010104

Umar, R., & Mesbah, W. (2015). Throughput-Efficient Spectrum Access in Cognitive Radio Networks: A Coalitional Game Theoretic Approach. In N. Kaabouch & W. Hu (Eds.), *Handbook of Research on Software-Defined and Cognitive Radio Technologies for Dynamic Spectrum Management* (pp. 454–477). Hershey, PA: IGI Global. doi:10.4018/978-1-4666-6571-2.ch017

Voderhobli, K. (2015). The Need for Traffic Based Virtualisation Management for Sustainable Clouds. *International Journal of Organizational and Collective Intelligence*, 5(4), 8–19. doi:10.4018/IJOCI.2015100102

Vujin, V., Simić, K., & Kovačević, B. (2014). Digital Identity Management in Cloud. In M. Despotović-Zrakić, V. Milutinović, & A. Belić (Eds.), *Handbook of Research on High Performance and Cloud Computing in Scientific Research and Education* (pp. 56–81). Hershey, PA: IGI Global. doi:10.4018/978-1-4666-5784-7.ch003

Wang, C., Wei, H., Bennis, M., & Vasilakos, A. V. (2016). Game-Theoretic Approaches in Heterogeneous Networks. In C. Yang & J. Li (Eds.), *Game Theory Framework Applied to Wireless Communication Networks* (pp. 88–102). Hershey, PA: IGI Global. doi:10.4018/978-1-4666-8642-7.ch004

Wenge, O., Schuller, D., Rensing, C., & Steinmetz, R. (2014). On Developing Fair and Orderly Cloud Markets: QoS- and Security-Aware Optimization of Cloud Collaboration. *International Journal of Organizational and Collective Intelligence*, 4(3), 22–43. doi:10.4018/ijoci.2014070102

Windsor, D. (2014). Business Ethics in Emerging Economies: Identifying Game-Theoretic Insights for Key Issues. In B. Christiansen & M. Basilgan (Eds.), *Economic Behavior, Game Theory, and Technology in Emerging Markets* (pp. 30–45). Hershey, PA: IGI Global. doi:10.4018/978-1-4666-4745-9.ch003

Windsor, D. (2015). Game-Theoretic Insights Concerning Key Business Ethics Issues Occurring in Emerging Economies. In D. Palmer (Ed.), *Handbook of Research on Business Ethics and Corporate Responsibilities* (pp. 34–55). Hershey, PA: IGI Global. doi:10.4018/978-1-4666-7476-9.ch003

Wu, D., & Cai, Y. (2016). Coalition Formation Game for Wireless Communications. In C. Yang & J. Li (Eds.), *Game Theory Framework Applied to Wireless Communication Networks* (pp. 28–62). Hershey, PA: IGI Global. doi:10.4018/978-1-4666-8642-7.ch002

Wu, J., Ding, F., Xu, M., Mo, Z., & Jin, A. (2016). Investigating the Determinants of Decision-Making on Adoption of Public Cloud Computing in E-government. *Journal of Global Information Management, 24*(3), 71–89. doi:10.4018/JGIM.2016070104

Xu, S., & Xia, C. (2016). Resource Allocation for Device-to-Device Communications in LTE-A Network: A Stackelberg Game Theory Approach. In C. Yang & J. Li (Eds.), *Game Theory Framework Applied to Wireless Communication Networks* (pp. 212–229). Hershey, PA: IGI Global. doi:10.4018/978-1-4666-8642-7.ch008

Xu, X., Gao, R., Li, M., & Wang, Y. (2016). Interference Mitigation with Power Control and Allocation in the Heterogeneous Small Cell Networks. In C. Yang & J. Li (Eds.), *Game Theory Framework Applied to Wireless Communication Networks* (pp. 103–136). Hershey, PA: IGI Global. doi:10.4018/978-1-4666-8642-7.ch005

Xu, Y., Wang, J., & Wu, Q. (2016). Distributed Learning of Equilibria with Incomplete, Dynamic, and Uncertain Information in Wireless Communication Networks. In C. Yang & J. Li (Eds.), *Game Theory Framework Applied to Wireless Communication Networks* (pp. 63–86). Hershey, PA: IGI Global. doi:10.4018/978-1-4666-8642-7.ch003

Yaacoub, E., Ghazzai, H., & Alouini, M. (2016). A Game Theoretic Framework for Green HetNets Using D2D Traffic Offload and Renewable Energy Powered Base Stations. In C. Yang & J. Li (Eds.), *Game Theory Framework Applied to Wireless Communication Networks* (pp. 333–367). Hershey, PA: IGI Global. doi:10.4018/978-1-4666-8642-7.ch013

Yahaya, M. O. (2017). On the Role of Game Theory in Modelling Incentives and Interactions in Mobile Distributed Systems. In K. Munir (Ed.), *Security Management in Mobile Cloud Computing* (pp. 92–120). Hershey, PA: IGI Global. doi:10.4018/978-1-5225-0602-7.ch005

Yao, Y. (2015). Cloud Computing: A Practical Overview Between Year 2009 and Year 2015. *International Journal of Organizational and Collective Intelligence, 5*(3), 32–43. doi:10.4018/ijoci.2015070103

Yao, Y. (2016). Emerging Cloud Computing Services: A Brief Opinion Article. *International Journal of Organizational and Collective Intelligence, 6*(4), 98–102. doi:10.4018/IJOCI.2016100105

Related References

Yarlikas, S., & Bilgen, S. (2014). Measures for Cloud Computing Effectiveness Assessment. *International Journal of Cloud Applications and Computing*, *4*(3), 20–43. doi:10.4018/ijcac.2014070102

Zardari, M. A., & Jung, L. T. (2016). Classification of File Data Based on Confidentiality in Cloud Computing using K-NN Classifier. *International Journal of Business Analytics*, *3*(2), 61–78. doi:10.4018/IJBAN.2016040104

Zhong, W., Wang, J., & Tao, M. (2016). Potential Games and Its Applications to Wireless Networks. In C. Yang & J. Li (Eds.), *Game Theory Framework Applied to Wireless Communication Networks* (pp. 1–27). Hershey, PA: IGI Global. doi:10.4018/978-1-4666-8642-7.ch001

Compilation of References

[OWASP. (2016). *OWASP Internet of Things Project - OWASP*. Retrieved from https://www.owasp.org/index.php/OWASP_Internet_of_Things_Top_Ten_Project#tab=OWASP_Internet_of_Things_Top_10_for_2014

Abd El-Latif, A., Niu, X., & Amin, M. (2012, October). A new image cipher in time and frequency domains. *Optics Communications, 285*(21–22), 4241–4251. doi:10.1016/j.optcom.2012.06.041

Abdmeziem, M. R., Tandjaoui, D., & Romdhani, I. (2015, October). A Decentralized Batch-based Group Key Management Protocol for Mobile Internet of Things (DBGK).*Proceedings of the 14th IEEE International Conference on Ubiquitous Computing and Communications (IUCC-2015)*. doi:10.1109/CIT/IUCC/DASC/PICOM.2015.166

Abugharsa, A. B., & Almangush, H. (2011). A New Image Encryption Approach using Block-Based on Shifted Algorithm. *International Journal of Computer Science and Network Security, 11*(12), 123–130.

Abuturab, M. R. (2012, May). Securing color information using Arnold transform in gyrator transform domain. *Optics and Lasers in Engineering, 50*(5), 772–779. doi:10.1016/j.optlaseng.2011.12.006

Accettura, N., & Piro, G. (2014). Optimal and secure protocols in the IETF 6TiSCH communication stack. *Industrial Electronics (ISIE), 2014 IEEE 23rd International Symposium on*. IEEE.

Ahmad, A. A. A., & Baicher, G. S. (2012). Wireless sensor network architecture. *IPCSIT, 35*, 11-15.

Ahmad, M., & Alam, M. (2009). A New Algorithm of Encryption and Decryption of Images Using Chaotic Mapping. *International Journal on Computer Science and Engineering, 2*(1), 46–50.

Ahmed & Ahmed. (2012). Efficency Analysis and Security Evaluation Parameters of Image Encryption schemes. *International Journal of Video & Image Processing And Network Security, 12.*

Ahn, L. V., Blum, M., & Langford, J. (2004). Telling humans and computers apart automatically. *Communications of the ACM, 47*(2), 56–60. doi:10.1145/966389.966390

Akkaya, K., & Younis, M. (2005). A survey on routing protocols for wireless sensor networks. *Ad Hoc Networks, 3*(3), 325–349. doi:10.1016/j.adhoc.2003.09.010

Akyildiz, I. F., Su, W., Sankarasubramaniam, Y., & Cayirci, E. (2002). Wireless sensor networks: A survey. *Computer Networks, 38*(4), 393–422. doi:10.1016/S1389-1286(01)00302-4

Akyildiz, I. F., Weilian Su, , Sankarasubramaniam, Y., & Cayirci, E. (2002, August). A Survey on Sensor Setworks. *IEEE Communications Magazine, 40*(8), 102–114. doi:10.1109/MCOM.2002.1024422

Alam, S., & Mohammad, M. R. (2011). Chowdhury, and Josef Noll. "Interoperability of security-enabled internet of things. *Wireless Personal Communications, 61*(3), 567–586. doi:10.1007/s11277-011-0384-6

Alcaraz, C., Roman, R., Najera, P., & Lopez, J. (2013). Security of industrial sensor network-based remote substations in the context of the Internet of Things. *Ad Hoc Networks, 11*(3), 1091–1104. doi:10.1016/j.adhoc.2012.12.001

Al-Hamami & G. Waleed al-Saadoon (Eds.), *Handbook of research on threat detection and countermeasures in network security* (pp. 80–94). Hershey, PA: IGI Global.

Al-Khanjari, Z. A., & Nayyef, A. A. (2015). Real time internal intrusion detection: A case study of embedded sensors and detectors in e-government websites. In A. Al-Hamami & G. Waleed al-Saadoon (Eds.), *Handbook of research on threat detection and countermeasures in network security* (pp. 48–65). Hershey, PA: IGI Global. doi:10.4018/978-1-4666-6583-5.ch004

Alohali, B. (2016). Security in Cloud of Things (CoT). In Z. Ma (Ed.), *Managing big data in cloud computing environments* (pp. 46–70). Hershey, PA: IGI Global. doi:10.4018/978-1-4666-9834-5.ch003

Alsaadi, E. (2015). Internet of Things: Features, Challenges, and Vulnerabilities. *International Journal of Advanced Computer Science and Information Technology*, 4(1), 1–13. Retrieved May 10, 2016

Al-Saadoon, G. M. (2015). Automatic intrusion detection and secret multi agent preservation using authentication measurement network threat. In A. Al-Hamami & G. Waleed al-Saadoon (Eds.), *Handbook of research on threat detection and countermeasures in network security* (pp. 33–47). Hershey, PA: IGI Global. doi:10.4018/978-1-4666-6583-5.ch003

Alshaikhli, I. F., & AlAhmad, M. A. (2015). Cryptographic hash function: A high level view. In A. doi:10.4018/978-1-4666-6583-5.ch006

Alvarez & Li. (2006). Some Basic Cryptographic requirement for Chaos-Based Cryptosystems. *International Journal of Bifurcation and Chaos, 16*.

Amazon. (n.d.). *Amazon Prime Air*. Retrieved from: https://www.amazon.com/b?node=8037720011

Amendola, S., Lodato, R., Manzari, S., Occhiuzzi, C., & Marrocco, G. (2014). RFID technology for IoT-based personal healthcare in smart spaces. *IEEE Internet of Things Journal, 1*(2), 144-152.

Andre, P.S. (2011). Extensible Messaging and Presence Protocol (XMPP): Core. *Request for Comments*, 6120.

Anthony & Uber. (2016). *Uber rolls out Self Driving cars in Pittsburgh*. Retrieved from: https://newsroom.uber.com/pittsburgh-self-driving-uber/

Ashraf, Q. M., & Habaebi, M. H. (2015). Autonomic schemes for threat mitigation in Internet of Things. *Journal of Network and Computer Applications, 49*, 112–127. doi:10.1016/j.jnca.2014.11.011

Atanasov, I., Nikolov, A., Pencheva, E., Dimova, R., & Ivanov, M. (2015). An approach to data annotation for Internet of Things. *International Journal of Information Technology and Web Engineering, 10*(4), 1–19. doi:10.4018/IJITWE.2015100101

Atzori, L., Iera, A., & Morabito, G. (2010). The internet of things: A survey. *Computer Networks, 54*(15), 2787–2805. doi:10.1016/j.comnet.2010.05.010

Atzori, L., Iera, A., Morabito, G., Esposito, C., Khan, R., Khan, S. U. S., & Ny, O. B. et al. (2016). The Internet of Things the Internet of Things. *Computer Networks, 3*(257521), 678–683. doi:10.5480/1536-5026-34.1.63

Atzori, L., Iera, A., Morabito, G., & Nitti, M. (2012). The Social Internet of Things (SIoT) – When social networks meet the Internet of Things: Concept, architecture and network characterization. *Computer Networks, 56*(16), 3594–3608. doi:10.1016/j.comnet.2012.07.010

Babar, S., Stango, A., Prasad, N., Sen, J., & Prasad, R. (2011). *Proposed embedded security framework for Internet of Things (IoT).* Paper presented at the 2nd International Conference on Wireless Communication, Vehicular Technology, Information Theory and Aerospace & Electronic Systems Technology (Wireless VITAE 2011), Chennai, India.

Babar, S. (2010). *Proposed security model and threat taxonomy for the internet of things (IoT). In Recent Trends in Network Security and Applications* (pp. 420–429). Springer Berlin Heidelberg.

Background on traffic sign detection and recognition. (n.d.). Retrieved from: http://www.springer.com/cda/content/document/cda_downloaddocument/9781447122449-c2.pdf?SGWID=0-0-45-1246851-p174192870

Barcena, M. B., & Wueest, C. (2015, March). *Insecurity in the Internet of Things.* Symantec Corporation. Retrieved from https://www.symantec.com/content/dam/symantec/docs/white-papers/insecurity-in-the-internet-of-things-en.pdf

Barnaghi, P., Wang, W., Henson, C., & Taylor, K. (2012). Semantics for the Internet of Things: Early progress and back to the future. *International Journal on Semantic Web and Information Systems, 8*(1), 1–21. doi:10.4018/jswis.2012010101

Batina, L., Mentens, N., Sakiyama, K., Preneel, B., & Verbauwhede, I. (2006, September). Low-Cost Elliptic Curve Cryptography for Wireless Sensor Networks. *Proceedings of the Third European Workshop ESAS*, 6-17.

Bazzani, M., Conzon, D., Scalera, A., Spirito, M., & Trainito, C. (2012). *Enabling the IoT paradigm in e-health solutions through the VIRTUS middleware*. Paper presented at the 2012 11th IEEE International Conference on Trust, Security and Privacy in Computing and Communications (TrustCom 2012), Liverpool, United Kingdom. doi:10.1109/TrustCom.2012.144

Bd, P., Sunjiv Soyjaudah, K., & Devi, K. A, S. (2013). Secure Transmission of an Image using Partial Encryption based Algorithm. *International Journal of Computers and Applications*, *63*(16), 33–36. doi:10.5120/10553-5746

Ben Othmane, L., & Weffers, H. (n.d.). *A survey of security and privacy in connected vehicles*. Retrieved from: https://www.informatik.tu-darmstadt.de/fileadmin/user_upload/Group_CASED/Publikationen/2010/TUD-CS-2015-1208.pdf

Ben Saied, Y., & Olivereau, A. (2012, June). D-HIP: A Distributed Kkey Exchange Scheme for HIP-Based Internet of Things.*Proceedings of the IEEE International Symposium on World of Wireless Mobile and Multimedia Networks (WoWMoM)*, 1-7. doi:10.1109/WoWMoM.2012.6263785

Ben-Saied, Y., Olivereau, A., Zeghlache, D., & Laurent, M. (2014). Lightweight collaborative key establishment scheme for the Internet of Things. *Computer Networks*, *64*, 273–295. doi:10.1016/j.comnet.2014.02.001

Berson, A. (1996). *Client/Server architecture*. New York, NY: McGraw–Hill.

Bertoncello, M., & Wee, D. (2015). *10 ways autonomous driving could redefine the automotive world*. Retrieved from: http://www.mckinsey.com/industries/automotive-and-assembly/our-insights/ten-ways-autonomous-driving-could-redefine-the-automotive-world

Bischoff, U., & Kortuem, G. (2007). *Life cycle support for sensor network applications*. Paper presented at the 2nd International Workshop on Middleware for Sensor Networks (MidSens 2007), Newport Beach, CA. doi:10.1145/1376860.1376861

Bonetto, R., Bui, N., Lakkundi, V., & Olivereau, A. (2012, June). Secure communication for smart IoT objects: Protocol stacks, use cases and practical examples. *Proceedings of the World of Wireless, Mobile and Multimedia Networks (WoWMoM)IEEE International Symposium*, 1-7.

Borgia, E. (2014). The Internet of Things vision: Key features, applications and open issues. *Computer Communications*, *54*, 1–31. doi:10.1016/j.comcom.2014.09.008

Bormann, Carsten, Ersue, & Keranen. (2014). Terminology for Constrained-Node Networks. No. RFC 7228.

Boubeta-Puig, J., Ortiz, G., & Medina-Bulo, I. (2014). Approaching the Internet of Things through integrating SOA and complex event processing. In Z. Sun & J. Yearwood (Eds.), *Handbook of research on demand-driven web services: Theory, technologies, and applications* (pp. 304–323). Hershey, PA: IGI Global. doi:10.4018/978-1-4666-5884-4.ch014

Boudriga, N. (2010). *Security of mobile communications*. Boca Raton, FL: CRC Press.

Bradley, D., Russell, D., Ferguson, I., Isaacs, J., MacLeod, A., & White, R. (2015). The Internet of Things: The future or the end of mechatronics. *Mechatronics*, *27*, 57–74. doi:10.1016/j.mechatronics.2015.02.005

Brahimi, Bessalah, Tarabet, & Kholladi. (2008). A new selective encryption technique of JPEG2000 code stream for medical images transmission. *5th International Multi-Conference on Systems, Signals and Devices*, 1–4.

Broggi, A., Buzzoni, M., Debattisti, S., Grisleri, P., Laghi, M. C., Medici, P., & Versari, P. (2013). Extensive tests of autonomous driving technologies. *IEEE Transactions on Intelligent Transportation Systems*, *14*(3), 1403–1415. doi:10.1109/TITS.2013.2262331

Burmester, M., & De Medeiros, B. (2007). RFID security: attacks, countermeasures and challenges. *The 5th RFID Academic Convocation, The RFID Journal Conference*.

Business, F. (2016). *How self-driving cars will change the economy*. Retrieved from: http://www.foxbusiness.com/features/2016/01/20/how-self-driving-cars-will-change-economy.html

Casado, L., & Tsigas, P. (2009). *Contikisec: A secure network layer for wireless sensor networks under the contiki operating system. In Identity and Privacy in the Internet Age* (pp. 133–147). Springer Berlin Heidelberg.

Castellani, A. P., Bui, N., Casari, P., Rossi, M., Shelby, Z., & Zorzi, M. (2010). Architecture and protocols for the internet of things: A case study. *2010 8th IEEE International Conference on Pervasive Computing and Communications Workshops, PERCOM Workshops 2010*, (pp. 678–683). http://doi.org/doi:10.1109/PERCOMW.2010.5470520

Castellani, A., Bui, N., Casari, P., Rossi, M., Shelby, Z., & Zorzi, M. (2010, March). Architecture and protocols for the internet of things: A case study. In *Pervasive Computing and Communications Workshops (PERCOM Workshops), 2010 8th IEEE International Conference on* (pp. 678-683). IEEE. doi:10.1109/PERCOMW.2010.5470520

Chaqfeh, M. A., & Mohamed, N. (2012). *Challenges in middleware solutions for the Internet of Things*. Paper presented at the 2012 International Conference on Collaboration Technologies and Systems (CTS 2012), Denver, CO. doi:10.1109/CTS.2012.6261022

Chen, D., Chang, G., Jin, L., Ren, X., Li, J., & Li, F. (2011). *A novel secure architecture for the Internet of Things*. Paper presented at the 5th International Conference on Genetic and Evolutionary Computing (ICGEC 2011), Xiamen, China. doi:10.1109/ICGEC.2011.77

Chen, M.-C., & Chang, T.-W. (2010). *Introduction of vehicular network architectures*. Retrieved from: http://www.igi-global.com/chapter/introduction-vehicular-network-architectures/39516

Chen, Y. (2012). *Challenges and opportunities of Internet of Things*. Paper presented at the 17th Asia and South Pacific Design Automation Conference (ASP-DAC 2012), Sydney, Australia. doi:10.1109/ASPDAC.2012.6164978

Chen, H., Du, X., Liu, Z., & Yang, C. (2013, June). Color image encryption based on the affine transform and gyrator transform. *Optics and Lasers in Engineering*, *51*(6), 768–775. doi:10.1016/j.optlaseng.2013.01.016

Cisco. (2008). *Strategies to protect against Distributed Denial of Service Attacks*. Document ID:13634. Cisco.

Clark, B. (2015). *How self-driving cars work*. Retrieved from: http://www.makeuseof.com/tag/how-self-driving-cars-work-the-nuts-and-bolts-behind-googles-autonomous-car-program/

Coetzee, L., & Eksteen, J. (2011, May). The Internet of Things-promise for the future? An introduction. In *IST-Africa Conference Proceedings, 2011* (pp. 1-9). IEEE.

Colistra, G., Pilloni, V., & Atzori, L. (2014). The problem of task allocation in the Internet of Things and the consensus-based approach. *Computer Networks, 73*, 98–111. doi:10.1016/j.comnet.2014.07.011

Collotta, M., Bello, L. L., & Mirabella, O. (2010). *An innovative frequency hopping management mechanism for Bluetooth-based industrial networks.* Paper presented at the 5th International Symposium on Industrial Embedded Systems (SIES 2010), Trento, Italy. doi:10.1109/SIES.2010.5551385

Collotta, M., Messineo, A., Nicolosi, G., & Pau, G. (2014). A self-powered Bluetooth network for intelligent traffic light junction management. *WSEAS Transactions on Information Science and Applications, 11*, 12–23.

Collotta, M., & Pau, G. (2015). Bluetooth for Internet of Things: A fuzzy approach to improve power management in smart homes. *Computers & Electrical Engineering, 44*, 137–152. doi:10.1016/j.compeleceng.2015.01.005

Copie, A. Manaţe, B., Munteanu, V. I., & Fortiş, T. (2015). An Internet of Things governance architecture with applications in healthcare. In F. Xhafa, P. Moore, & G. Tadros (Eds.), Advanced technological solutions for e-health and dementia patient monitoring (pp. 322–344). Hershey, PA: IGI Global.

Corpuz, E. (2016). *The Tesla Model 3 will incorporate Tesla's solar roof technology.* Retrieved from: http://futurism.com/elon-musk-the-model-3-will-incorporate-teslas-solar-roof-technology/

Cowan, J. (2015). *Article.* Retrieved May 1, 2016, from http://www.iot-now.com/2015/03/26/31426-securing-the-identity-of-things-idot-for-the-internet-of-things/

Crank, I. T. (2015). *Vehicle to vehicle communication.* Retrieved from: https://crankit.in/vehicle-to-vehicle-v2v-communication/

Crosby & Wallach. (2003). Denial of service via algorithmic complexity attacks. *Proceedings of USENIX Security 2003.*

Dan Munro. (2015). *Defenders Unite Against Cyber Threats In Healthcare*. Retrieved May 2015, from http://www.forbes.com/sites/danmunro/2015/05/10/

DDoS Attack Types and Mitigation. (n.d.). Retrieved from https://www.incapsula.com/ddos/ddos-attacks

Dean, D., Franklin, M., & Stubblefield, A. (2001). An algebraic approach to IP traceback.*Proceedings of Network and Distributed Systems Security Symposium (NDSS)*, 3–12.

Defending Against Denial of Web Services Using Sessions. (2006). NEC Europe Ltd.

Deng, N. (2012). RFID Technology and Network Construction in the Internet of Things. *Computer Science & Service System (CSSS), 2012 International Conference on*. IEEE.

DHL. (n.d.). *Self-driving cars*. Retrieved from: http://www.dhl.com/en/about_us/logistics_insights/dhl_trend_research/self_driving_vehicles.html

Dierks, T., & Allen, C. (1999). The TLS protocol. *Request for Comments*, 2246.

Dohr, A., Modre-Osprian, R., Drobics, M., Hayn, D., & Schreier, G. (2010). The Internet of Things for Ambient Assisted Living. *ITNG, 10*, 804–809.

Douceur. (2002). The sybil attack. *IPTPS*, 251–260.

Douceur, J. R. (2002). *The sybil attack. In Peer-to-peer Systems* (pp. 251–260). Springer Berlin Heidelberg. doi:10.1007/3-540-45748-8_24

Efremov, S., Pilipenko, N., & Voskov, L. (2015). An integrated approach to common problems in the Internet of Things. *Procedia Engineering, 100*, 1215–1223. doi:10.1016/j.proeng.2015.01.486

Energetics Incorporated Columbia, Maryland, Foundations for Innovation in Cyber-Physical Systems, Workshop Report, NIST. (2013). Retrieved from http://www.nist.gov/el/upload/CPS-WorkshopReport-1-30-13-Final.pdf

Ervin. (2014). *Building a Trusted Foundation for the Internet of Things - Guidebook*. Recovered from http://www.safenet-inc.com/resources/

Eugster, P., Felber, P., Guerraoui, R., & Kermarrec, A. (2003). The many faces of publish/subscribe. *ACM Computing Surveys, 35*(2), 114–131. doi:10.1145/857076.857078

Evans, D., & Eyers, D. (2012). *Efficient data tagging for managing privacy in the Internet of Things.* Paper presented at the 2012 IEEE International Conference on Green Computing and Communications (GreenCom 2012), Besançon, France. doi:10.1109/GreenCom.2012.45

Ferenstein, G. (2015). *How much will the self-driving version of your car save on insurance.* Retrieved from: https://medium.com/the-ferenstein-wire/how-much-the-self-driving-version-of-your-car-will-save-on-insurance-in-1-graph-16ebcc27f26e#.sp2n267c3

Flayh, Parveen, & Ahson. (2009). Wavelet based partial image encryption. *International Multimedia, Signal Processing and Communication Technologies (IMSPCT)*, 32–35.

Fleisch, E. (2010). *What is the Internet of things? An Economic Perspective.* Auto-ID Labs White Paper WP-BIZAPP-053. Retrieved from http://www.autoidlabs. org/uploads/media/AUTOIDLABS-WP-BIZAPP-53.pdf

Fleisch, E. (2010). What is the internet of things? An economic perspective. Economics. *Management and Financial Markets*, 5(2), 125.

Forouzan. (2011). *Cryptography and Network Security.* McGraw Hill Education Private Limited.

Fotouhi, H., Moreira, D., & Alves, M. (2015). mRPL: Boosting mobility in the Internet of Things. *Ad Hoc Networks*, 26, 17–35. doi:10.1016/j.adhoc.2014.10.009

Frankel, S., Kishnan, S. (2011). IP Security (IPsec) and Internet Key Exchange (IKE) document roadmap. *Request for Comments*, 6071.

Frohlich, M. T., & Westbrook, R. (2001). Arcs of integration: An international study of supply chain strategies. *Journal of Operations Management*, 19(2), 185–200. doi:10.1016/S0272-6963(00)00055-3

Ganesan, Govindan, Shenker, & Estrin. (2001). Highly-resilient, energy-efficient multipath routing in wireless sensor networks. *Mobile Computing and Communications Review, 4*(5).

Garcia-Morchon, O., Keoh, S., Kumar, S., Hummnen, R., & Struik, R. (2012). Security Considerations in the IP-based Internet of Things. *draft-garcia-core-security-04.*

Garcia-Morchon. (2013). *Security Considerations in the IP-based Internet of Things*. Academic Press.

Garcia-Morchon, O., Kuptsov, D., Gurtov, A., & Wehrle, K. (2013). Cooperative security in distributed networks. *Computer Communications, 36*(12), 1284–1297. doi:10.1016/j.comcom.2013.04.007

Gartner. (2015). *Gartner Survey on IoT*. Retrieved from http://www.gartner.com/newsroom/id/3165317

Geng, W., Talwar, S., Johnsson, K., Himayat, N., & Johnson, K. D. (2011). M2M: From mobile to embedded internet. *IEEE Communications Magazine, 49*(4), 36–43. doi:10.1109/MCOM.2011.5741144

Giannikos, M., Kokoli, K., Fotiou, N., Marias, G. F., & Polyzos, G. C. (2013). *Towards secure and context-aware information lookup for the Internet of Things*. Paper presented at the International Conference on Computing, Networking and Communications (ICNC 2013), San Diego, CA. doi:10.1109/ICCNC.2013.6504160

Gligor, Blaze, & Ioannidis. (2000). Denial of service - panel discussion. *Security Protocols Workshop*.

Gnimpieba, D. R., Nait-Sidi-Moh, A., Durand, D., & Fortin, J. (2015). Using Internet of Things technologies for a collaborative supply chain: Application to tracking of pallets and containers. *Procedia Computer Science, 56*, 550–557. doi:10.1016/j.procs.2015.07.251

Godsmark, P. (2016). *Autonomous vehicles- the compelling business cases*. Retrieved from: https://avimpacts.com/2016/08/11/autonomous-vehicles-compelling-business-cases/

Grover, K., & Lim, A. (2015). A survey of broadcast authentication schemes for wireless sensor networks. *Ad Hoc Networks, 24*, 288–316. doi:10.1016/j.adhoc.2014.06.008

Gubbi, J., Buyya, R., Marusic, S., & Palaniswami, M. (2013). Internet of Things (IoT): A vision, architectural elements, and future directions. *Future Generation Computer Systems, 29*(7), 1645–1660. doi:10.1016/j.future.2013.01.010

Gummadi, V. (2015). *Driverless cars – What's their future in India?* Retrieved from: https://www.linkedin.com/pulse/driverless-cars-boon-bane-india-its-future-vijay-gummadi

Hawrylak, P. J., Reed, S., Butler, M., & Hale, J. (2014). The access of things: Spatial access control for the Internet of Things. In M. Matin (Ed.), *Handbook of research on progressive trends in wireless communications and networking* (pp. 189–207). Hershey, PA: IGI Global. doi:10.4018/978-1-4666-5170-8. ch007

He, Cao, & Lu. (2012). Color image encryption based on orthogonal composite grating and double random phase encoding technique. *Optik - International Journal for Light and Electron Optics, 123*(17), 1592–1596.

Hechri, A., & Mtibaa, A. (2011). Lanes and Road signs recognition. *International Journal of Computer Science Issues, 8*(6). Retrieved from: http://www.ijcsi.org/papers/IJCSI-8-6-1-402-408.pdf

Heer, T., Garcia-Morchon, O., Hummen, R., Keoh, S. L., Kumar, S. S., & Wehrle, K. (2011). Security Challenges in the IP-based Internet of Things. *Wireless Personal Communications, 61*(3), 527–542. doi:10.1007/s11277-011-0385-5

Hegarty, R. (n.d.). Digital Evidence Challenges in the Internet of Things. *WDFIA Papers,* 163-172.

Hossain & Hyder. (2015). Traffic road sign detection and recognition for automotive vehicles. *International Journal of Computer Applications, 120*(24). Retrieved from: http://research.ijcaonline.org/volume120/number24/pxc3904265.pdf

Houle, K.J., & Weaver, G.M. (2001). *Trends in Denial of Service Attack Technology.* CERT Coordination Center.

How Lidar Works. (n.d.). Retrieved from: http://www.lidar-uk.com/how-lidar-works/

Howard, B. (2013). *What is adaptive cruise control and how does it work?* Retrieved from: http://www.extremetech.com/extreme/157172-what-is-adaptive-cruise-control-and-how-does-it-work

Howard, B. (2013). *What is lane departure warning, and how does it work?* Retrieved from: https://www.extremetech.com/g00/extreme/165320-what-is-lane-departure-warning-and-how-does-it-work

Hu, Perrig, & Johnson. (2003). Packet leashes: a defense against wormhole attacks in wireless networks. *INFOCOM 2003. Twenty-Second Annual Joint Conference of the IEEE Computer and Communications. IEEE Societies* (Vol. 3). IEEE. doi:10.1109/ICACT.2006.206151

Hummen, R., Hiller, J., Henze, M., & Wehrle, K. (2013, October). Slimfit – A HIP DEX Compression Layer for the IP-based Internet of Things. *Proceedings of the IEEE WiMob 2013 Workshop IoT*, 259-266. doi:10.1109/WiMOB.2013.6673370

Hummen, R., Hiller, J., Wirtz, H., Henze, M., Shafagh, H., & Wehrle, K. (2013, June). 6LoWPAN fragmentation attacks and mitigation mechanisms. *Proceedings of the sixth ACM conference on Security and privacy in wireless and mobile networks*, 55-66. doi:10.1145/2462096.2462107

Hu, Y.-C., Perrig, A., & Johnson, D. B. (2003, April). Packet Leashes: A Defense Against Wormhole Attacks in Wireless Networks. *Proceedings - IEEE INFOCOM*.

IANS. (2015). *Traffic violations to attract steeper fines*. Retrieved from: http://www.indiatvnews.com/news/india/traffic-violations-to-attract-steeper-fines-half-baked-49591.html

Jain, D., Krishna, P. V., & Saritha, V. (2012). *A Study on Internet of Things based Applications*. arXiv preprint arXiv:1206.3891.

Jawad, & Sulong. (2013). A Review of Color Image Encryption Techniques. *International Journal of Computer Science Issues, 10*(6).

Jiang, T., Iyer, U., Tolani, A., & Hussain, S. (2015). *Self-driving cars: disruptive or incremental?* Retrieved from: http://cet.berkeley.edu/wp-content/uploads/Self-Driving-Cars.pdf

Jiang, Shyuand. (2013, May). General constructions for threshold multiple-secret visual cryptographic schemes. *IEEE Trans. Inf. Forensics Security, 8*(5), 733–743. doi:10.1109/TIFS.2013.2250432

Kaleem & Ahmed. (n.d.). Implementation of RC% block cipher algorithm for image cryptosystem. *International Journal of Information Technology, 3*.

Kamali, M. R. (2010). A New Modified Version of Advanced Encryption Standard Based Algorithm for Image Encryption. *International Conference on Electronics and Information Engineering (ICEIE), 1*, 141–145.

Karagiannis, V., Chatzimisios, P., Vazquez-Gallego, F., & Alonso-Zarate, J. (2015). A Survey on Application Layer Protocols for the Internet of Things. *Transaction on IoT and Cloud Computing*, *3*(1), 11–17. doi:10.5281/ZE-NODO.51613

Karakostas, B. (2013). A DNS architecture for the Internet of Things: A case study in transport logistics. *Procedia Computer Science*, *19*, 594–601. doi:10.1016/j.procs.2013.06.079

Karlof, C., & Wagner, D. (2003). Secure Routing in Wireless Sensor Networks: Attacks and Countermeasures. *Proc. First IEEE Int'l. Wksp. Sensor Network Protocols and Applications*, 113–27. doi:10.1109/SNPA.2003.1203362

Karlof, C., & Wagner, D. (2003). Secure routing in wireless sensor networks: Attacks and countermeasures. *Ad Hoc Networks*, *1*(2), 293–315. doi:10.1016/S1570-8705(03)00008-8

Kasemsap, K. (2016). Mastering big data in the digital age. In M. Singh & D. G. (Eds.), Effective big data management and opportunities for implementation (pp. 104–129). Hershey, PA: IGI Global. doi:10.4018/978-1-5225-0182-4.ch008

Kasemsap, K. (2017b). The role of radio frequency identification in modern libraries. In I. Management Association (Ed.), Identity theft: Breakthroughs in research and practice (pp. 174–200). Hershey, PA: IGI Global. doi:10.4018/978-1-5225-0808-3.ch009

Kasemsap, K. (2015a). The role of cloud computing adoption in global business. In V. Chang, R. Walters, & G. Wills (Eds.), *Delivery and adoption of cloud computing services in contemporary organizations* (pp. 26–55). Hershey, PA: IGI Global. doi:10.4018/978-1-4666-8210-8.ch002

Kasemsap, K. (2015b). Adopting cloud computing in global supply chain: A literature review. *International Journal of Social and Organizational Dynamics in IT*, *4*(2), 49–62. doi:10.4018/IJSODIT.2015070105

Kasemsap, K. (2016b). Mastering digital libraries in the digital age. In E. de Smet & S. Dhamdhere (Eds.), *E-discovery tools and applications in modern libraries* (pp. 275–305). Hershey, PA: IGI Global. doi:10.4018/978-1-5225-0474-0.ch015

Kasemsap, K. (2016c). Multifaceted applications of data mining, business intelligence, and knowledge management. *International Journal of Social and Organizational Dynamics in IT, 5*(1), 57–69. doi:10.4018/IJSODIT.2016010104

Kasemsap, K. (2016d). The roles of business process modeling and business process reengineering in e-government. In J. Martins & A. Molnar (Eds.), *Handbook of research on innovations in information retrieval, analysis, and management* (pp. 401–430). Hershey, PA: IGI Global. doi:10.4018/978-1-4666-8833-9.ch015

Kasemsap, K. (2016e). The fundamentals of business intelligence. *International Journal of Organizational and Collective Intelligence, 6*(2), 12–25. doi:10.4018/IJOCI.2016040102

Kasemsap, K. (2017a). Software as a service, Semantic Web, and big data: Theories and applications. In A. Turuk, B. Sahoo, & S. Addya (Eds.), *Resource management and efficiency in cloud computing environments* (pp. 264–285). Hershey, PA: IGI Global. doi:10.4018/978-1-5225-1721-4.ch011

Kasemsap, K. (2017c). Analyzing the role of health information technology in global health care. In N. Wickramasinghe (Ed.), *Handbook of research on healthcare administration and management* (pp. 287–307). Hershey, PA: IGI Global. doi:10.4018/978-1-5225-0920-2.ch017

Kasemsap, K. (2017d). Mastering web mining and information retrieval in the digital age. In A. Kumar (Ed.), *Web usage mining techniques and applications across industries* (pp. 1–28). Hershey, PA: IGI Global. doi:10.4018/978-1-5225-0613-3.ch001

Kasinathan, P., Pastrone, C., Spirito, M. A., & Vinkovits, M. (2013, October). Denial-of-Service detection in 6LoWPAN based Internet of Things. *Proceedings of IEEE 9th International Conference on Wireless and Mobile Computing, Networking and Communications (WiMob)*, 600-607.

Kaur, R., & Singh, E. K. (2013). Image Encryption Techniques : A Selected Review. *Journal of Computer Engineering, 9*(6), 80–83.

Kekre, Thepade, & Maloo. (2010). Query by Image Content using Color-Texture Features Extracted from Haar Wavelet Pyramid. *IJCA*, 52-60.

Kekre, Thepade, Athawale, Shah, Verlekar, & Shirke. (2010). Energy Compaction and Image Splitting for Image Retrieval using Kekre Transform over Row and Column Feature Vectors. *International Journal of Computer Science and Network Security, 10*(1).

Kekre, H. B. (2014). Image Scrambling Using Non Sinusoidal Transform And Key Based Scrambling Technique. *International Journal of Computers & Technology, 12*(8), 3809–3822.

Kekre, H. B., & Kavita, B. (2008). Walsh Transform over color distribution of Rows and Columns of Images for CBIR. *International Conference on Content Based Image Retrieval (ICCBIR).*PES Institute of Technology.

Kelly, Tebje, Suryadevara, & Mukhopadhyay. (2013). Towards the implementation of IoT for environmental condition monitoring in homes. *IEEE Sensors Journal, 13*(10), 3846–3853.

Keoh, S. (2014). Securing the Internet of Things. *Internet of Things Journal, 1*(3), 265-275. Retrieved May 10, 2016, from http://ieeexplore.ieee.org/xpl/articleDetails.jsp?reload=true&arnumber=6817545&punumber=6488907

Khambre, P. D., Simbhare, S. S., & Chavan, P. S. (2012). Secure Data in Wireless Sensor Network via AES (Advanced Encryption Standard). *International Journal of Computer Science and Information Technologies, 3*(2), 3588–3592.

Khan, M., & Shah, T. (n.d.). *A Literature Review on Image Encryption Techniques*. Springer. DOI .10.1007/s13319-014-0029-0

Khanna, S., Venkatesh, S. S., Fatemieh, O., Khan, F., & Gunter, C. A. (2012). Adaptive Selective Verification: An Efficient Adaptive Countermeasure to Thwart DoS Attacks. *IEEE/ACM Transactions on Networking, 20*(3), 715–728. doi:10.1109/TNET.2011.2171057

Khoo, B. (2011). RFID as an enabler of the internet of things: issues of security and privacy. *Internet of Things (iThings/CPSCom), 2011 International Conference on and 4th International Conference on Cyber, Physical and Social Computing.* IEEE. doi:10.1109/ICT4M.2013.6518912

KnowIndia. (n.d.). *Indian auto industry*. Retrieved from: http://www.know-india.net/auto.html

Kong, D., & Shen, X. (2014). Multiple-image encryption based on optical wavelet transform and multichannel fractional Fourier transform. *Optics & Laser Technology, 57*, 343–349. doi:10.1016/j.optlastec.2013.08.013

Korosec, K. (2016). Google self-driving cars have learnt how to interpret cyclists' hand signals. *Fortune 500*. Retrieved from: http://fortune.com/2016/07/06/google-self-driving-cars-cyclist/

Kothmayr, T., Hu, W., Schmitt, C., Brunig, M., & Carle, G. (2011, November). Poster: Securing the Internet of Things with DTLS.*Proceedings of the 9th ACM Conference on Embedded Networked Sensor Systems*, 345-346.

Kothmayr, T., Schmitt, C., Hu, W., Brünig, M., & Carle, G. (2013). DTLS based security and two-way authentication for the Internet of Things. *Ad Hoc Networks, 11*(8), 2710–2723. doi:10.1016/j.adhoc.2013.05.003

Kotis, K., & Katasonov, A. (2013). Semantic interoperability on the Internet of Things: The semantic smart gateway framework. *International Journal of Distributed Systems and Technologies, 4*(3), 47–69. doi:10.4018/jdst.2013070104

Kozlov, D., Veijalainen, J., & Ali, Y. (2012). Security and privacy threats in IoT architectures. *Proceedings of the 7th International Conference on Body Area Networks*. ICST (Institute for Computer Sciences, Social-Informatics and Telecommunications Engineering).

Krambeck, D. (2016). *Tesla vs Google. Do Lidar sensors belong in AVs?* Retrieved from: http://www.allaboutcircuits.com/news/tesla-vs-google-do-lidar-sensors-belong-in-autonomous-vehicles/

Krishnamoorthi, R., & Malarchelvi, P. D. S. K. (2008). Selective Combinational Encryption of Gray Scale Images using Orthogonal Polynomials based Transformation. *International Journal of Computer Science and Network Security, 8*(5), 195–204.

Kröner, A., Haupert, J., & Barthel, R. (2015). Digital object memory. In M. Khosrow-Pour (Ed.), *Encyclopedia of information science and technology* (3rd ed.; pp. 7605–7613). Hershey, PA: IGI Global. doi:10.4018/978-1-4666-5888-2.ch749

Kulkarni, N. S., Raman, B., & Gupta, I. (2008). Selective encryption of multimedia images. *32th National Systems Conference*, 467–470.

Kumar, M., Aggarwal, A., & Garg, A. (2014). A Review on Various Digital Image Encryption Techniques and Security Criteria. *International Journal of Computer Applications, 96*(13).

Kumar, J. S., & Patel, D. R. (2014). A survey on internet of things: Security and privacy issues. *International Journal of Computers and Applications, 90*(11).

Kumar, M., Mishra, D. C., & Sharma, R. K. (2014). A first approach on an RGB image encryption. *Optics and Lasers in Engineering, 52*, 27–34. doi:10.1016/j.optlaseng.2013.07.015

Kumar, P. (2012). RC4 Enrichment Algorithm Approach for Selective Image Encryption. *International Journal of Computer Science & Communication Networks, 2*(2), 181–189.

Kumar, V. (2015). Ontology Based Public Healthcare System in Internet of Things (IoT). *Procedia Computer Science, 50*, 99–102. doi:10.1016/j.procs.2015.04.067

Kuppusamy, K., & Thamodaran, K. (2012). Optimized partial image encryption scheme using PSO. *International Conference on Pattern Recognition, Informatics and Medical Engineering*, 236–241. doi:10.1109/ICPRIME.2012.6208350

Laranjo, I., Macedo, J., & Santos, A. (2013). Internet of Things for medication control: E-health architecture and service implementation. *International Journal of Reliable and Quality E-Healthcare, 2*(3), 1–15. doi:10.4018/ijrqeh.2013070101

Le, A., Loo, J., Lasebae, A., Aiash, M., & Luo, Y. (2012). 6LoWPAN: A study on QoS security threats and countermeasures using intrusion detection system approach. *International Journal of Communication Systems, 25*(9), 1189–1212. doi:10.1002/dac.2356

Lee, I. (2016). A conceptual framework of the Internet of Things (IoT) for smart supply chain management. In I. Lee (Ed.), *Encyclopedia of e-commerce development, implementation, and management* (pp. 1177–1189). Hershey, PA: IGI Global. doi:10.4018/978-1-4666-9787-4.ch084

Lee, J., Oh, S., & Jang, J. W. (2015). A work in progress: Context based encryption scheme for Internet of Things. *Procedia Computer Science, 56,* 271–275. doi:10.1016/j.procs.2015.07.208

Li, K., Zhou, W., Li, P., Hai, J., & Liu, J. (2009). Distinguishing DDoS Attacks from Flash Crowds Using Probability Metrics. In *Proceedings of 3rd Intl Conference on Network and System Security* (NSS 09). IEEE.

Liang, W., Li, Z., Zhang, H., Wang, S., & Bie, R. (2014). *Vehicular Ad Hoc Networks.* Retrieved from: http://dsn.sagepub.com/content/11/8/745303.full

Lian, S. (2008). *Multimedia content encryption: techniques and applications.* CRC Press.

Litman, T. (2016). *Autonomous Vehicle Implementation predictions.* Retrieved from: http://www.vtpi.org/avip.pdf

Lize, G., Jingpei, W., & Bin, S. (2014). Trust management mechanism for Internet of Things. *Communications, China, 11*(2), 148–156. doi:10.1109/CC.2014.6821746

Logan, A. (2015). *How does adaptive cruise control work?* Retrieved from: http://www.proctorcars.com/how-does-adaptive-cruise-control-work/

Loke, S.W. (2015). The internet of flying-things: opportunities and challenges with airborne fog computing and mobile cloud in the clouds. *IEEE Internet of Things Journal,* 1-5.

Luo, Z., Lai, M., Cheung, M., Han, S., Zhang, T., Luo, Z., & Tipoe, G. et al. (2010). Developing local association network based IoT solutions for body parts tagging and tracking. *International Journal of Systems and Service-Oriented Engineering, 1*(4), 42–64. doi:10.4018/jssoe.2010100104

Maia, P., Batista, T., Cavalcante, E., Baffa, A., Delicato, F. C., Pires, P. F., & Zomaya, A. (2014). A web platform for interconnecting body sensors and improving health care. *Procedia Computer Science, 40,* 135–142. doi:10.1016/j.procs.2014.10.041

Manaţe, B., Fortiş, F., & Moore, P. (2015). An architecture to implement the Internet-of-Things using the Prometheus methodology. *International Journal of Distributed Systems and Technologies, 6*(4), 1–20.

Martins, D., & Guyennet, H. (2010, September). Wireless sensor network attacks and security mechanisms: A short survey. In *Network-Based Information Systems (NBiS), 2010 13th International Conference on* (pp. 313-320). IEEE.

Mastan, J. M. K., Sathishkumar, G. A., & Bagan, K. B. (2011). A Color Image Encryption Technique Based on a Substitution Permutation Network. *Advances in Computing and Communications, 4,* 524–533. doi:10.1007/978-3-642-22726-4_54

Mattern, F., & Floerkemeier, C. (2010). From the Internet of Computers to the Internet of Things. In *From active data management to event-based systems and more* (pp. 242–259). Springer Berlin Heidelberg. doi:10.1007/978-3-642-17226-7_15

Matthew, R. (1989). On the derivation of a chaotic encryption algorithm. *Cryptologia, 8*(1), 29–42. doi:10.1080/0161-118991863745

Mayzaud, A. (2014). *A study of rpl dodag version attacks. In Monitoring and Securing Virtualized Networks and Services* (pp. 92–104). Springer Berlin Heidelberg.

McCue, T. J. (2015). *Billion market for internet of things in healthcare by 2020.* Retrieved April 22, 2015, from www.forbes.com/sites/tjmccue/2015/04/22/117

McGoogan, C. (2016). *Google self-driving car involved in serious crash.* Retrieved from: http://www.telegraph.co.uk/technology/2016/09/26/googles-self-driving-car-involved-in-serious-crash-after-van-jum/

Medaglia, C. M., & Serbanati, A. (2010). *An overview of privacy and security issues in the internet of things. In The Internet of Things* (pp. 389–395). Springer New York.

Meena & Jadon. (2014). Distributed Denial of Service Attacks and Their Suggested Defense Remedial Approaches. *International Journal of Advance Research in Computer Science and Management Studies, 2*(4).

Menezes, A. J., Oorschot, P. C. V., & Vanstone, S. A. (1997). *Handbook of applied cryptography.* Boca Raton, FL: CRC Press.

Mcnczcs, A., van Oorschot, P., & Vanstone, S. (1996). *Applied cryptography.* Boca Raton, FL: CRC. doi:10.1201/9781439821916

Mhlaba, A., & Masinde, M. (2015). Implementation of middleware for Internet of Things in asset tracking applications: In-lining approach. *Industrial Informatics (INDIN), 2015 IEEE 13th International Conference on*. IEEE. doi:10.1109/EMTC.2014.6996650

Michell, V. A. (2016). The Internet of Things and opportunities for pervasive safety monitored health environments. In *E-health and telemedicine: Concepts, methodologies, tools, and applications* (pp. 1568–1605). Hershey, PA: IGI Global. doi:10.4018/978-1-4666-8756-1.ch079

Micrium. (2014). *IoT for Embedded Systems: The New Industrial Revolution*. Retrieved from https://www.micrium.com/iot/overview/

Miessler, D. (2015). Securing the Internet of Things: Mapping Attack Surface Areas Using the OWASP IoT Top 10.*RSA Conference*.

Miorandi, D., Sicari, S., Pellegrini, F. D., & Chlamtac, I. (2012). Internet of Things: Vision, applications and research challenges. *Ad Hoc Networks*, *10*(7), 1497–1516. doi:10.1016/j.adhoc.2012.02.016

Mirkovic, J., Prier, G., & Reiher, P. (2002). Attacking DDoS at the Source. *Proceedings of the ICNP 2002*.

Mirkovic, J., & Reiher, P. (2002). A Taxonomy of DDoS Attack and DDoS Defense mechanisms. *Proceedings of the 2nd ACM SIGCOMM Internet Measurement Workshop*.

Miyata, S., Yanou, A., Nakamura, H., & Takehara, S. (2009). Feature extraction and recognition of road signs using dynamic image processing. *Image Processing*. Retrieved from: http://www.intechopen.com/books/image-processing/feature-extraction-and-recognition-of-road-sign-using-dynamic-image-processing

Mobahat, H. (2010). *Authentication and lightweight cryptography in low cost RFID*. Paper presented at the 2nd International Conference on Software Technology and Engineering (ICSTE 2010), San Juan, Puerto Rico. doi:10.1109/ICSTE.2010.5608776

Mohamed, Zaibi, & Kachouri. (2011). Implementation of RC5 and RC6 block ciphers on digital images. *8th International Multi-Conference*. IEEE.

Montenegro, G., Kushalnagar, N., Hui, J., & Culler, D. (2007). Transmission of IPv6 packets over IEEE 802.15.4 networks. *Request for Comments*, 4944.

Moskowitz, R. (2016). HIP Diet EXchange (DEX). *draftmoskowitz-hip-rg-dex-05*.

Moskowitz, R., Heer, T., Jokela, P., & Henderson, T. (2015). Host Identity Protocol Version 2 (HIPv2). *Request for Comments*, 7401.

Munir. (2014). *A Block-based Image Encryption Algorithm in Frequency Domain using Chaotic Permutation*. IEEE.

Munir, R. (2012). Robustness Analysis of Selective Image Encryption Algorithm Based on Arnold Cat Map Permutation. *Proceedings of 3rd Makassar International Conference on Electrical Engineering and Informatics*, 1–5.

Nam, C., & Kim, D. H. (2014). A study of open middleware for wireless sensor networks. Proceedings of Advanced Science and Technology Letters, 60, 105-109. doi:10.14257/astl.2014.60.26

Naor, M., & Shamir, A. (1995). Visual cryptography. *Proc. EUROCRYPT'94*, 50, 1–12.

Naor, M., & Shamir, A. (1995). Visual cryptography. *Advances in Cryptography: Eurocrypt'94*.

National tyres and autocare. (n.d.). *10 astonishing technologies that power Google self-driving cars*. Retrieved from: https://www.national.co.uk/tech-powers-google-car/

Newcomb, D. (2016). *Can self-driving cars kill traffic lights?* Retrieved from: http://in.pcmag.com/cars/102032/opinion/can-self-driving-cars-kill-traffic-lights

Newsome, J. (2004). The sybil attack in sensor networks: analysis & defenses. *Proceedings of the 3rd international symposium on Information processing in sensor networks*. ACM. doi:10.1145/984622.984660

Ngai, Liu, & Lyu. (2006). On the intruder detection for sinkhole attack in wireless sensor networks. *Communications, 2006. ICC'06. IEEE International Conference on* (Vol. 8). IEEE.

Nguyen, K. T., Laurent, M., & Oualha, N. (2015). Survey on secure communication protocols for the Internet of Things. *Ad Hoc Networks*, *32*, 17–31. doi:10.1016/j.adhoc.2015.01.006

Nien, H. H., Huang, W. T., Hung, C. M., Chen, S. C., Wu, S. Y., Huang, C. K., & Hsu, Y. H. (2009). Hybrid image encryption using multi-chaos-system. *7th International Conference on Information, Communications and Signal Processing (ICICS)*, 1–5.

Ning, H., Liu, H., & Yang, L. T. (2013). Cyber-entity security in the Internet of Things. *Computer*, *46*(4), 46–53. doi:10.1109/MC.2013.74

Noaman & Alla. (2008). Encryption Quality Analysis of the RCBC Block Cipher Compared with RC6 and RC5 Algorithms. *International Journal of Imaging, 10*.

Oasis-Standard. (2014). Retrieved May 1, 2016, from http://docs.oasis-open.org/mqtt/mqtt/v3.1.1/os/mqtt-v3.1.1-os.html

Oh, Yang, & Chon. (2010). A Selective Encryption Algorithm Based on AES for Medical Information. *Healthcare Informatics Research, 16*(1), 22–9.

Olivier, F., Carlos, G., & Florent, N. (2015). New Security Architecture for IoT Network. *Procedia Computer Science*, *52*, 1028–1033. doi:10.1016/j.procs.2015.05.099

ONeill, M. (2014). The Internet of Things: Do more devices mean more risks? *Computer Fraud & Security*, *2014*(1), 16–17. doi:10.1016/S1361-3723(14)70008-9

Oriwoh, E., & Williams, G. (2015). Internet of Things: The argument for smart forensics. In M. Cruz-Cunha & I. Portela (Eds.), *Handbook of research on digital crime, cyberspace security, and information assurance* (pp. 407–423). Hershey, PA: IGI Global. doi:10.4018/978-1-4666-6324-4.ch026

Ou, Y., Sur, C., & Rhee, K. H. (2007). Region-Based Selective Encryption for Medical Imaging. *1st Annual International Workshop*, 4427(4613), 62–73.

Ovidiu, V., & Peter, F. (2013). *Internet of Things: Converging Technologies for Smart Environments and Integrated Ecosystems*. Aalborg, Denmark: The River Publishers Series in Communications.

Compilation of References

Owasp. (2013). OWASP Top 10 - 2013. *OWASP Top 10*, 22.

Padmavathi, G., & Shanmugapriya, D. (2009). *A survey of attacks, security mechanisms and challenges in wireless sensor networks.* arXiv preprint arXiv: 0909.0576

Paganini, P. (2014). Retrieved May 1, 2016, from http://securityaffairs.co/wordpress/21397/cyber-crime/iot-cyberattack-large-scale.html

Palattella, M. R. (2014). *6TiSCH Wireless Industrial Networks: Determinism Meets IPv6. In Internet of Things* (pp. 111–141). Springer International Publishing.

Palattella, M., Accettura, N., Vilajosana, X., Watteyne, T., Grieco, L., Boggia, G., & Dohler, M. (2013). Standardized protocol stack for the Internet of (important) Things. *IEEE Communications Surveys and Tutorials, 15*(3), 1389–1406. doi:10.1109/SURV.2012.111412.00158

Pan, J., Paul, S., & Jain, R. (2011). A survey of the research on future Internet architectures. *IEEE Communications Magazine, 49*(7), 26–36. doi:10.1109/MCOM.2011.5936152

Parameshachari, B. D., & Soyjaudah, K. M. S. (2012). Analysis and Comparison of Fully Layered Image Encryption Techniques and Partial Image Encryption Techniques. *Communications in Computer and Information Science, 292*, 599–604. doi:10.1007/978-3-642-31686-9_70

Pareek, Narendra, & Patidar. (2011). A Symmetric Encryption Scheme for Colour BMP Images. *International Journal of Computer Applications in Special Issue on Network Security and Cryptography*, 42– 46.

Pareek, N. K., Patidar, V., & Sud, K. K. (2006). Image encryption using chaotic logistic map. *Image and Vision Computing, 24*(9), 926–934. doi:10.1016/j.imavis.2006.02.021

Park, J., Shin, S., & Kang, N. (2013). Mutual Authentication and Key Agreement Scheme between Lightweight Devices in Internet of Things. *The Journal of Korean Institute of Communications and Information Sciences, 38*(9), 707–714. doi:10.7840/kics.2013.38B.9.707

Patel, P., & Cassou, D. (2015). Enabling high-level application development for the Internet of Things. *Journal of Systems and Software*, *103*, 62–84. doi:10.1016/j.jss.2015.01.027

Pathan, A.-S. K., Lee, H.-W., & Hong, C. S. (2006). Security in wireless sensor networks: issues and challenges. *ICACT 2006. The 8th International Conference* (Vol. 2). IEEE.

Pathan. (2010). Denial of Service in Wireless Sensor Networks: Issues and Challenges. In A. V. Stavros (Ed.), *Advances in Communications and Media Research* (Vol. 6). Nova Science Publishers, Inc.

Paxson, V., & Weaver, N. (2003). *DDoS protection strategies*. Stanford.

Perrig, A., Szewczyk, R., Tygar, J. D., Wen, V., & Culler, D. E. (2002, September). SPINS: Security Protocols for Sensor Networks. *Wireless Networks*, *8*(5), 521–534. doi:10.1023/A:1016598314198

Petit, J., Feiri, M., Kargl, F., & Stottelaar, B. (n.d.). *Remote attacks on automated vehicle sensors*. Retrieved from: https://www.blackhat.com/docs/eu-15/materials/eu-15-Petit-Self-Driving-And-Connected-Cars-Fooling-Sensors-And-Tracking-Drivers-wp1.pdf

Petrov, V., Edelev, S., Komar, M., & Koucheryavy, Y. (2014). *Towards the era of wireless keys: How the IoT can change authentication paradigm*. Paper presented at the 2014 1st IEEE World Forum on Internet of Things (WF-IoT 2014), Seoul, South Korea. doi:10.1109/WF-IoT.2014.6803116

Piro, G., Boggia, G., & Grieco, L. A. (2014). A standard compliant security framework for ieee 802.15.4 networks. *Internet of Things (WF-IoT), 2014 IEEE World Forum on*. IEEE.

Pirzada, U. (2015). *The Tesla autopilot*. Retrieved from: http://wccftech.com/tesla-autopilot-story-in-depth-technology/2/

Plumer, B. (2016). *Five big challenges that self-driving cars still have to overcome*. Retrieved from: http://www.vox.com/2016/4/21/11447838/self-driving-cars-challenges-obstacles

Pongle, P., & Chavan, G. (2015). A survey: Attacks on RPL and 6LoWPAN in IoT. *Pervasive Computing (ICPC), 2015 International Conference on*. IEEE. doi:10.1109/PERVASIVE.2015.7087034

Ponnusamy, V., Tay, Y. P., Lee, L. H., Low, T. J., & Zhao, C. W. (2016). Energy harvesting methods for Internet of Things. In V. Ponnusamy, N. Zaman, T. Low, & A. Amin (Eds.), *Biologically-inspired energy harvesting through wireless sensor technologies* (pp. 51–70). Hershey, PA: IGI Global. doi:10.4018/978-1-4666-9792-8.ch003

Porambage, P., Braeken, A., Schmitt, C., Gurtov, C., Ylianttila, M., & Stiller, B. (2015). Group Key Establishment for Enabling Secure Multicast Communication in Wireless Sensor Networks Deployed for IoT Applications. *IEEE Access*, *3*, 1503–1511. doi:10.1109/ACCESS.2015.2474705

Pratt, Chen, & Welch. (1974). Slant Transform Image Coding. *IEEE Trans. Comm., 22*.

Preiss, T. (2014). Implementing dynamic address changes in contikios. *Information Society (i-Society), 2014 International Conference on.* IEEE.

Pulakkat, H. (2016). *Why Indian roads will take decades*. Retrieved from: http://economictimes.indiatimes.com/industry/auto/news/why-indian-roads-will-take-decades-to-be-ready-for-self-driving-cars/articleshow/52018034.cms

Qin, Y., & Gong, Q. (2013). Interference-based multiple-image encryption with silhouette removal by position multiplexing. *Applied Optics*, *52*(17), 3987–3992. doi:10.1364/AO.52.003987 PMID:23759846

Qin, Y., Jiang, H., & Gong, Q. (2014). Interference-based multiple-image encryption by phase-only mask multiplexing with high quality retrieved images. *Optics and Lasers in Engineering*, *62*, 95–102. doi:10.1016/j.optlaseng.2014.05.010

Rahmani, R., & Kanter, T. (2015). Layering the internet-of-things with multicasting in flowsensors for internet-of-services. *International Journal of Multimedia and Ubiquitous Engineering*, *10*(12), 37–52. doi:10.14257/ijmue.2015.10.12.05

Rajagopalan, H., & Rahmat-Samii, Y. (2010, July). On-body RFID tag design for human monitoring applications. In *2010 IEEE Antennas and Propagation Society International Symposium* (pp. 1-4). IEEE.

Rakhunde, S. M., & Nikose, A. A. (2014). New Approach for Reversible Data Hiding Using Visual Cryptography.*Sixth International Conference on Computational Intelligence and Communication Networks.* doi:10.1109/CICN.2014.180

Ramahrishnan, S., Elakkiya, B., Geetha, R., Vasuki, P., & Mahalingam, S. (2014). Image encryption using chaotic maps in hybrid domain. *International Journal of Communication and Computer Technologies*, 2(5), 44–48.

Rao, V. (2012). *Which industries will be disrupted by AVs*. Retrieved from: https://www.quora.com/Which-industries-and-jobs-will-self-driving-cars-and-trucks-disrupt-or-destroy/

Rao, Y. V. S., Mitra, A., & Prasanna, S. R. M. (2006). A Partial Image Encryption Method with Pseudo Random Sequences. Lecture Notes in Computer Science: vol. 4332. International Commission on Intervention and State Sovereignty (ICISS), (pp. 315–325). Berlin: Springer.

Ray, A. (2012). *Bangalore sees 16,000 traffic violations daily*. Retrieved from:http://timesofindia.indiatimes.com/city/bengaluru/Bangalore-sees-16000-traffic-violations-daily/articleshow/15332697.cms

Ray, B. R., Abawajy, J., & Chowdhury, M. (2014). Scalable RFID security framework and protocol supporting Internet of Things. *Computer Networks*, 67, 89–103. doi:10.1016/j.comnet.2014.03.023

Raza, S., Voigt, T., & Roedig, U. (2011). 6LoWPAN Extension for IPsec. *Proceedings of the Interconnecting Smart Objects with the Internet Workshop*, 1-3.

Raza, S., Seitz, L., Sitenkov, D., & Selander, G. (2016). S3K: Scalable security with symmetric keys—DTLS key establishment for the Internet of Things. *IEEE Transactions on Automation Science and Engineering*, 13(3), 1270–1280. doi:10.1109/TASE.2015.2511301

Raza, S., Trabalza, D., & Voigt, T. (2012, May). 6LoWPAN compressed DTLS for CoAP.*Proceedings of the 8th IEEE International Conference on Distributed Computing in Sensor Systems*, 287 – 289.

Reaidy, P. J., Gunasekaran, A., & Spalanzani, A. (2015). Bottom-up approach based on Internet of Things for order fulfillment in a collaborative warehousing environment. *International Journal of Production Economics*, 159, 29–40. doi:10.1016/j.ijpe.2014.02.017

Rescorla, E., & Modadugu, N. (2006). Datagram Transport Layer Security. *Request for Comments*, 4347.

Rghioui, A., L'aarje, A., Elouaai, F., & Bouhorma, M. (2014, October). The internet of things for healthcare monitoring: security review and proposed solution. In *2014 Third IEEE International Colloquium in Information Science and Technology (CIST)* (pp. 384-389). IEEE.

Rghioui, A., Bouhorma, M., & Benslimane, A. (2013). Analytical study of security aspects in 6LoWPAN networks. *Information and Communication Technology for the Muslim World (ICT4M),* 20135th *International Conference on.* IEEE.

Rhouma, Arroyo, & Belghith. (2009). A new color image cryptosystem based on a piecewise linear chaotic map. *6th International Multi-Conference on Systems, Signals and Devices,* 1–6.

Rodrigues, J. M., Puech, W., & Bors, A. G. (2006). A Selective Encryption for Heterogeneous Color JPEG Images Based on VLC and AES Stream Cipher. *3rd European Conference on Colour in Graphics, Imaging and Vision (CGIV'06),* 1, 34–39.

Rodriguez-Sahagun, M. T., Mercado-Sanchez, J. B., Lopez-Mancilla, D., Jaimes-Reategui, R., & Garcia-Lopez, J. H. (2010). Image Encryption Based on Logistic Chaotic Map for Secure Communications. *IEEE Electronics,Robotics and Automotive Mechanics Conference,* 319–324. doi:10.1109/CERMA.2010.44

Roman, R., Alcaraz, C., Lopez, J., & Sklavos, N. (2011). Key management systems for sensor networks in the context of the Internet of Things. *Computers & Electrical Engineering, 37*(2), 147–159. doi:10.1016/j.compeleceng.2011.01.009

Roman, R., Zhou, J., & Lopez, J. (2013). On the features and challenges of security and privacy in distributed Internet of Things. *Computer Networks, 57*(10), 2266–2279. doi:10.1016/j.comnet.2012.12.018

Rong, K., Hu, G., Lin, Y., Shi, Y., & Guo, L. (2015). Understanding business ecosystem using a 6C framework in Internet-of-Things-based sectors. *International Journal of Production Economics, 159,* 41–55. doi:10.1016/j.ijpe.2014.09.003

Rose, K., Eldridge, S., & Lyman, C. (2015, October). The internet of things: an overview. *Internet Society*, 53. http://doi.org/10.1017/CBO9781107415324.004

Ruisong, Ye. (2011). *An Image Encryption Scheme with Efficient Permutation and Diffusion Processes*. SpringerVerlag Berlin Heidelberg.

Sadeghi, A. R., Wachsmann, C., & Waidner, M. (2015, June). Security and privacy challenges in industrial internet of things. In *Proceedings of the 52nd Annual Design Automation Conference* (p. 54). ACM. doi:10.1145/2744769.2747942

Sahraoui, S., & Bilami, A. (2014, May). Compressed and distributed host identity protocol for end-to-end security in the IoT.*Proceedings of the Fifth International Conference on Next Generation Networks and Services (NGNS)*, 295 – 301. doi:10.1109/NGNS.2014.6990267

Sahraoui, S., & Bilami, A. (2015). Efficient HIP-based approach to ensure lightweight end-to-end security in the internet of things. *Computer Networks*, *91*, 26–45. doi:10.1016/j.comnet.2015.08.002

Sahraoui, S., & Bilami, A. (2016, May). Asymmetric End-to-End Security for Human-to-Thing Communications in the Internet of Things.*Proceedings of the 4th International Symposium on Modeling and Implementation of Complex Systems (MISC 2016)*, 249-260. doi:10.1007/978-3-319-33410-3_18

Sajjad, S. M., & Yousaf, M. (2014). Security analysis of IEEE 802.15. 4 MAC in the context of Internet of Things (IoT). *Information Assurance and Cyber Security (CIACS)*, 2014*Conference on*. IEEE.

Sanchez, D. (2015). Collective technologies- autonomous vehicles. *Securing Australia's Future (SAF) Project 05*. Retrieved from: http://www.acola.org.au/PDF/SAF05/2Collective%20technologies.pdf

Santo, D. (2016). *Autonomous cars' pick: camera, Lidar, radar?* Retrieved from: http://www.eetimes.com/author.asp?section_id=36&doc_id=1330069

Santos, A., Macedo, J., Costa, A., & Nicolau, M. J. (2014). Internet of things and smart objects for M-health monitoring and control. *Procedia Technology*, *16*, 1351–1360. doi:10.1016/j.protcy.2014.10.152

Santos, D. F. S., Almeida, H. O., & Perkusich, A. (2015). A personal connected health system for the Internet of Things based on the constrained application protocol. *Computers & Electrical Engineering, 44*, 122–136. doi:10.1016/j.compeleceng.2015.02.020

Sarikaya, B., Ohba, Y., Moskowitz, R., Cao, Z., & Cragie, R. (2012). Security Bootstrapping Solution for Resource-Constrained Devices. *Technical report IETF Internet Draft draft-sarikaya-coresbootstrapping-05.*

Sasidharan, S., & Philip, D. S. (2011). A Fast Partial Encryption Scheme with Wavelet Transform and RC4. *International Journal of Advances in Engineering & Technology, 1*(4), 322–331.

SaveTheDemocracy. (n.d.). *Reality of one of the RTOs in India.* Retrieved from: http://www.savethedemocracy.org/reality-check/reality-of-one-of-the-rtos-of-india/

Savola, R. M., Abie, H., & Sihvonen, M. (2012). Towards metrics-driven adaptive security management in e-health IoT applications. *Proceedings of the 7th International Conference on Body Area Networks.* ICST (Institute for Computer Sciences, Social-Informatics and Telecommunications Engineering). doi:10.4108/icst.bodynets.2012.250241

Saxena, M. (2007). *Security in Wireless Sensor Networks-A Layer based classification.* Technical Report. Centre for Education and Research in Information Assurance & Security-CERIAS, Purdue University. Retrieved from pages.cs.wisc.edu/~msaxena/papers/2007-04-cerias.pdf

Schaffer, G. P. (2006). Worms and viruses and botnets, oh my!: Rational responses to emerging internet threats. *IEEE Security and Privacy, 4*(3), 52–58. doi:10.1109/MSP.2006.83

Schneider, S. (2013). Retrieved May 1, 2016, from http://electronicdesign.com/iot/understanding-protocols-behind-internet-things

Schneier, B. (1996). *Applied cryptography: protocols algorithms and source code in C.* New York: Wiley.

Schweber, B. (n.d.). *The Autonomous Car: A Diverse Array of Sensors Drives Navigation, Driving, and Performance.* Retrieved from: http://www.mouser.in/applications/autonomous-car-sensors-drive-performance/

Sciancalepore, S. (2014). On securing IEEE 802.15. 4 networks through a standard compliant framework.*Euro Med Telco Conference (EMTC)*. IEEE.

Securing the Internet of Things. A Proposed Framework. (n.d.). Retrieved January 2, 2015, from http://www.cisco.com/web/about/security/intelligence/iot_framework.html#1

Sehgal, A., Perelman, V., Kuryla, S., & Schonwalder, J. (2012). Management of resource constrained devices in the Internet of Things. *IEEE Communications Magazine*, *50*(12), 144–149. doi:10.1109/MCOM.2012.6384464

Seltzer. (2014, June). Brute and protocol attacks. *Zero Day*.

Sen. (2009). A Survey on Wireless Sensor Network Security. *International Journal of Communications Network and Information Security*, *1*(2), 59-82.

Shaev, Y. (2014). From the sociology of things to the Internet of Things. *Procedia: Social and Behavioral Sciences*, *149*, 874–878. doi:10.1016/j.sbspro.2014.08.266

Shang, X., Zhang, R., & Chen, Y. (2012). Internet of Things (IoT) service architecture and its application in e-commerce. *Journal of Electronic Commerce in Organizations*, *10*(3), 44–55. doi:10.4018/jeco.2012070104

Shannon, C. E. (1948). The mathematical theory of communication. *The Bell System Technical Journal*, *27*(3), 379–423. doi:10.1002/j.1538-7305.1948.tb01338.x

Shannon, C. E. (1949). Communication theory of secrecy systems. *The Bell System Technical Journal*, *28*(4), 656–715. doi:10.1002/j.1538-7305.1949.tb00928.x

Sharma, K., & Ghose, M. K. (2010). Wireless sensor networks: An overview on its security threats. *IJCA*, 42-45.

Shelby, Z., Kartke, K., Bormann, C., & Frank, B. (2012). Constrained application protocol (CoAP). *draft-ietf-core-coap-12*.

Shelby, Z., & Bormann, C. (2011). *6LoWPAN: The wireless embedded Internet*. Hoboken, NJ: John Wiley & Sons.

Shi, E., & Perrig, A. (2004, December). Designing Secure Sensor Networks. *Wireless Commun. Mag.*, *11*(6), 38–43. doi:10.1109/MWC.2004.1368895

Shin, D. (2014). A socio-technical framework for Internet-of-Things design: A human-centered design for the Internet of Things. *Telematics and Informatics*, *31*(4), 519–531. doi:10.1016/j.tele.2014.02.003

Shyu, S. J. (2014, December). Threshold Visual Cryptographic Scheme with Meaningful Shares. *IEEE Signal Processing Letters*, *21*(12), 1521–1525. doi:10.1109/LSP.2014.2344093

Sicari, S., Rizzardi, A., Grieco, L. A., & Coen-Porisini, A. (2015). Security, privacy and trust in Internet of Things: The road ahead. *Computer Networks*, *76*, 146–164. doi:10.1016/j.comnet.2014.11.008

Siddharth, Anjali, & Jaya. (2012). A Keyless Approach to Image Encryption. *International Conference on Communication Systems and Network Technologies*. IEEE.

Singla, A., & Sachdeva, R. (2013). Review on Security Issues and Attacks in Wireless Sensor Networks. *International Journal of Advanced Research in Computer Science and Software Engineering, 3*(4). Retrieved from www.ijarcsse.com

Sinha, A., & Singh, K. (n.d.). *Image encryption using fractional Fourier transform and 3D Jigsaw transform.* Retrieved from http://pdfworld.net/pdf-2013/Image-encryption-using-fractionalFourier-transform-and-3D-Jigsaw-transform-pdf.pdf

Smirnov, A., Kashevnik, A., Shilov, N., & Teslya, N. (2013, June). Context-based access control model for smart space. *Proceedings of the 5th International Conference on Cyber Conflict*, 1-15.

Song, S., & Mitchell, C. J. (2011). Scalable RFID security protocols supporting tag ownership transfer. *Computer Communications*, *34*(4), 556–566. doi:10.1016/j.comcom.2010.02.027

Souza, A. M. C., & Amazonas, J. R. A. (2015). An outlier detect algorithm using big data processing and Internet of Things architecture. *Procedia: Computer Science*, *52*, 1010–1015.

Srivastava, A. (2012, June). A survey report on Different Techniques of Image Encryption. *International Journal of Emerging Technology and Advanced Engineering*, *2*(6), 163–167.

Standard, P. (2015). *The many impacts of AVs*. Retrieved from: https://psmag.com/the-many-impacts-of-autonomous-vehicles-9149b31c4f7d#.g7dx0ulns

Steffi, M. A. A., & Sharma, D. (2011). Comparative Study of Partial Encryption of Images and Video. *International Journal of Modern Engineering Research*, *1*(1), 179–185.

Stewart, J. (2016). *Tesla's self-driving car plan seems insane but it might just work*. Retrieved from: https://www.wired.com/2016/10/teslas-self-driving-car-plan-seems-insane-just-might-work/

Sun, Y., Chen, L., Xu, R., & Kong, R. (2014, January). Yuanyuan Sun1*, Lina Chen2, Rudan Xu1, Ruiqing Kong1, "An Image Encryption Algorithm Utilizing Julia Sets and Hilbert Curves. *PLoS ONE*, *9*(1), e84655. doi:10.1371/journal.pone.0084655 PMID:24404181

Taneja, N., Raman, B., & Gupta, I. (2011, March). Combinational domain encryption for still visual data. *Multimedia Tools and Applications*, *59*(3), 775–793. doi:10.1007/s11042-011-0775-4

Thatte, G., Mitra, U., & Heidemann, J. (2011). Parametric Methods for Anomaly Detection in Aggregate Traffic. *IEEE/ACM Transactions on Networking*, *19*(2), 512–525. doi:10.1109/TNET.2010.2070845

The Economist. (2012). *Self-driving cars in the military*. Retrieved from: http://www.businessinsider.com/the-military-is-getting-into-self-driving-vehicles-too-2012-12?IR=T

The Guardian. (2016). *Tesla driver dies in first fatal crash*. Retrieved from: https://www.theguardian.com/technology/2016/jun/30/tesla-autopilot-death-self-driving-car-elon-musk

Tian, H., Bi, J., & Jiang, X. (2012). An adaptive probabilistic marking scheme for fast and secure traceback. *Networking Science*. DOI: 10.1007/s13119-012-0007-x

TNN. (2003). *Caught red-handed. Cops taking bribes*. Retrieved from: http://timesofindia.indiatimes.com/delhi-times/Caught-red-handed-Cops-taking-bribes/articleshow/63371.cms

Tomizuka, M. (2002). Mechatronics: From the 20th to 21st century. *Control Engineering Practice*, *10*(8), 877–886. doi:10.1016/S0967-0661(02)00016-3

Toms, L. (2016). 5 Common Cyber Attacks in the IoT - Threat Alert on a Grand Scale. *GlobalSign Blog*. Retrieved from https://www.globalsign.com/en/blog/five-common-cyber-attacks-in-the-iot/

Tovey, A. (2016). *The end of the cabbie?* Retrieved from: http://www.telegraph.co.uk/business/2016/05/19/the-end-of-the-cabbie-uber-tests-driverless-taxis/

Trabalza, D., Raza, S., & Voigt, T. (2013, April). INDIGO: Secure CoAP for Smartphones Enabling E2E Secure Communication in the 6IoT. *Proceedings of the International Conference on Wireless Sensor Networks for Developing Countries (WSN4DC 2013)*.

Trujillo-Rasua, R., & Solanas, A. (2011). Efficient probabilistic communication protocol for the private identification of RFID tags by means of collaborative readers. *Computer Networks*, *55*(15), 3211–3223. doi:10.1016/j.comnet.2011.05.013

Turcu, C. E., & Turcu, C. O. (2013). Internet of Things as key enabler for sustainable healthcare delivery. *Procedia: Social and Behavioral Sciences*, *73*, 251–256. doi:10.1016/j.sbspro.2013.02.049

Turkanovic, M., Brumen, O., & Holbl, M. (2014). A novel user authentication and key agreement scheme for heterogeneous ad hoc wireless sensor networks, based on the Internet of Things notion. *Ad Hoc Networks*, *20*, 96–112. doi:10.1016/j.adhoc.2014.03.009

Ukil, A., Bandyopadhyay, S., & Pal, A. (2014). *IoT-privacy: To be private or not to be private*. Paper presented at the 2014 33rd IEEE International Conference on Computer Communications (INFOCOM 2014), Toronto, Canada. doi:10.1109/INFCOMW.2014.6849186

Ukil, A., Sen, J., & Koilakonda, S. (2011). Embedded security for Internet of Things. Emerging Trends and Applications in Computer Science (NCETACS), 2011 2nd National Conference on. IEEE.

USDOT. (2016). *Federal Automated Vehicles Policy*. Retrieved from: https://www.transportation.gov/AV

Valera, A. J. J., Zamora, M. A., & Skarmeta, A. F. (2010, January). An architecture based on internet of things to support mobility and security in medical environments. In *2010 7th IEEE Consumer Communications and Networking Conference* (pp. 1-5). IEEE.

Veltri, L., Cirani, S., Busanelli, S., & Ferrari, G. (2013). A novel batch-based group key management protocol applied to the Internet of Things. *Ad Hoc Networks, 11*(8), 2724–2737. doi:10.1016/j.adhoc.2013.05.009

Viret, J., Bindel, A., Conway, P., Justham, L., Lugo, H., & West, A. (2011, September). Embedded RFID TAG inside PCB board to improve supply chain management. In *Microelectronics and Packaging Conference (EMPC), 2011 18th European* (pp. 1-5). IEEE.

Wallgren, L., Raza, S., & Voigt, T. (2013). Routing Attacks and Counter-measures in the RPL-based Internet of Things. *International Journal of Distributed Sensor Networks*.

Wang, L., Wang, W., Zhu, L., & Yu, F. (2013). CoAP option extensions: profile and sec-flag. *Internet draft*.

Wang, Y., Attebury, G., & Ramamurthy, B. (2006). A survey of security issues in wireless sensor networks. IEEE Commun. Surv. Tutorials, 8.

Wang, C., Sohraby, K., Li, B., Daneshmand, M., & Hu, Y. (2006). A survey of transport protocols for wireless sensor networks. *IEEE Network, 20*(3), 34–40. doi:10.1109/MNET.2006.1637930

Wang, Q., Guo, Q., Lei, L., & Zhou, J. (2013). Multiple-image encryption based on interference principle and phase-only mask multiplexing in Fresnel transform domain. *Applied Optics, 52*(28), 6849–6857. doi:10.1364/AO.52.006849 PMID:24085198

Weber, R. H. (2010). Internet of Things: New security and privacy challenges. *Computer Law & Security Report, 26*(1), 23–30. doi:10.1016/j.clsr.2009.11.008

Wei, L., Zhu, H., Cao, Z., Dong, X., Jia, W., Chen, Y., & Vasilakos, A. V. (2014). Security and privacy for storage and computation in cloud computing. *Information Sciences, 258*, 371–386. doi:10.1016/j.ins.2013.04.028

Wei, W., Fen-lin, L., Xinl, G., & Yebin, Y. (2010). Color image encryption algorithm based on hyper chaos. *2nd IEEE International Conference on Information Management and Engineering*, 271–274. doi:10.1109/ICIME.2010.5477430

Wikipedia. (n.d.). *Autonomous cruise control system.* Retrieved from: https://en.wikipedia.org/wiki/Autonomous_cruise_control_system#Timeline

Wikipedia. (n.d.). *Demographics of India.* Retrieved from: https://en.wikipedia.org/wiki/Demographics_of_India

Wikipedia. (n.d.). *Google Self-Driving Car.* Retrieved from: https://en.wikipedia.org/wiki/Google_self-driving_car

Wikipedia. (n.d.). *Lane Departure Warning System.* Retrieved from: https://en.wikipedia.org/wiki/Lane_departure_warning_system

Wikipedia. (n.d.). *Lidar.* Retrieved from: https://en.wikipedia.org/wiki/Lidar#Design

Wikipedia. (n.d.). *Personal Area Network.* Retrieved from: https://en.wikipedia.org/wiki/Personal_area_network#Wireless_personal_area_network

Wikipedia. (n.d.). *Sonar.* Retrieved from: https://en.wikipedia.org/wiki/Sonar

Wikipedia. (n.d.). *Vehicular Ad Hoc Network.* Retrieved from: https://en.wikipedia.org/wiki/Vehicular_ad_hoc_network

William, A. (2015). *Internet of Things and Security of Things.* Retrieved May 19, 2015, from http://www.healthcareitnews.com/author/william-tanenbaum

Winter, T., Thubert, P., Brandt, A., Hui, J., Kelseky, R., Levis, P., Pister, K., Struik, R., Vasseur J.P., & Alexander, R. (2012). RPL: IPv6 routing protocol for low-power and lossy networks. *Request for Comments, 6550.*

Wong, A., & Bishop, W. (2007). Backwards Compatible, MultiLevel Region-of-Interest (ROI) Image Encryption Architecture with Biometric Authentication. *International Conference on Signal Processing and Multimedia Applications*, 324 – 329.

Wrightson, T. (2012). *Wireless network security: A beginner's guide.* New York, NY: McGraw–Hill.

Wu, Z. Q., Zhou, Y. W., & Ma, J. F. (2011). A security transmission model for Internet of Things. *Jisuanji Xuebao/Chinese Journal of Computers, 34*(8), 1351–1364.

Xiao, Gibbons, & Lebrun. (2009). RFID Technology, Security Vulnerabilities, and Countermeasures. In *Supply Chain the Way to Flat Organization*. Intech.

Xiao, Y. (2006). Security and privacy in RFID and applications in telemedicine. *Communications Magazine, IEEE, 44*(4), 64–72. doi:10.1109/MCOM.2006.1632651

Xie, Y., & Yu, S. Z. (2009). Monitoring the Application-Layer DDoS Attacks for Popular Websites. *IEEE/ACM Transactions on Networking, 17*(1), 15–25. doi:10.1109/TNET.2008.925628

Xing, K., Srinivasan, S. S. R., Jose, M., Li, J., & Cheng, X. (2010). Attacks and countermeasures in sensor networks: A survey. *Network Security*, 251–272.

Yadav, R. S., Beg, M. H. D. R., & Tripathi, M. M. (2013). Image Encryption Techniques: A Critical Comparison. *International Journal of Computer Science Engineering and Information Technology Research, 3*(1), 67–74.

Yang, J., & Fang, B. (2011). Security model and key technologies for the Internet of Things. *Journal of China Universities of Posts and Telecommunications, 8*(2), 109–112. doi:10.1016/S1005-8885(10)60159-8

Yegin, A., & Shelby, Z. (2011). CoAP Security Options. *draft-yegin-coap-security-options-00*.

Yekkala, A. K., Udupa, N., Bussa, N., & Madhavan, C. E. V. (2007). Lightweight Encryption for Images. *International Conference on Consumer Electronics, 3*, 1–2.

Yogita, P., Nancy, S., & Yaduvi, S. (2016). Internet of Things (IoT): Challenges and Future Directions. *International Journal of Advanced Research in Computer and Communication Engineering., 5*(3), 960–964.

Younis, H. A., Abdalla, T. Y., & Abdalla, A. Y. (2009). Vector Quantization Techniques For Partial Encryption of Waveletbased Compressed Digital Images. *Iraqi Journal of Electrical and Electronic Engineering, 5*(1), 74–89.

Yu, B., & Xiao, B. (2006). Detecting selective forwarding attacks in wireless sensor networks. *Parallel and Distributed Processing Symposium, 2006. IPDPS 2006. 20th International*. IEEE.

Yu, J., Wang, N., Wang, G., & Yu, D. (2013). Connected dominating sets in wireless ad hoc and sensor networks: A comprehensive survey. *Computer Communications*, *36*(2), 121–134. doi:10.1016/j.comcom.2012.10.005

Yu, Z., Zhe, Z., Haibing, Y., Wenjie, P., & Yunpeng, Z. (2010). A chaos-based image encryption algorithm using wavelet transform. *2nd International Conference on Advanced Computer Control*, *2*(4), 217–222.

Zainab, H., Hesham, A., & Mahmoud, M. (2015). Internet of Things (IoT): Definitions, Challenges and Recent Research Directions. *International Journal of Computers and Applications*, *128*(1), 37–47. doi:10.5120/ijca2015906430

Zamani, Javanmard, Jafarzadeh, & Zamani. (2014). *A Novel Image Encryption Scheme Based on Hyper Chaotic Systems and Fuzzy Cellular Automata*. IEEE.

Zargar, S. T., Joshi, J., & Tipper, D. (2013). A survey of defense mechanisms against distributed denial of service (DDoS) flooding attacks. *IEEE Communications Surveys and Tutorials*, *15*(4), 2046–2069. doi:10.1109/SURV.2013.031413.00127

Zawoad, S. (n.d.). FAIoT: Towards Building a Forensics Aware Eco System for the Internet of Things. *University of Alabama at Birmingham*.

Zhang, D., Yang, L. T., & Huang, H. (2011). *Searching in Internet of Things: Vision and challenges*. Paper presented at the 9th International Symposium on Parallel and Distributed Processing with Applications (ISPA 2011), Busan, South Korea. doi:10.1109/ISPA.2011.53

Zhang, X. M., & Zhang, N. (2011, May). An open, secure and flexible platform based on internet of things and cloud computing for ambient aiding living and telemedicine. In *Computer and Management (CAMAN), 2011 International Conference on* (pp. 1-4). IEEE.

Zhang, K., & Lu, R. (2014). Sybil attacks and their defenses in the internet of things. *IEEE Internet of ThingsJournal*, *1*(5), 372–383. doi:10.1109/JIOT.2014.2344013

Zhao, K., & Ge, L. (2013). *A survey on the Internet of Things security*. Paper presented at the 9th International Conference on Computational Intelligence and Security (CIS 2013), Chengdu, China. doi:10.1109/CIS.2013.145

Zhao, Y. (2013). *Research on data security technology in Internet of Things*. Paper presented at the 2nd International Conference on Mechatronics and Control Engineering (ICMCE 2013), Dalian, China. doi:10.4028/www.scientific.net/AMM.433-435.1752

Zhao, F., Sun, Z., & Jin, H. (2015). Topic-centric and semantic-aware retrieval system for Internet of Things. *Information Fusion*, *23*, 33–42. doi:10.1016/j.inffus.2014.01.001

Zhao, S., Cheng, B., Yu, L., Hou, S., Zhang, Y., & Chen, J. (2016). Internet of Things service provisioning platform for cross-application cooperation. *International Journal of Web Services Research*, *13*(1), 1–22. doi:10.4018/IJWSR.2016010101

Zheng, J., Simplot-Ryl, D., Bisdikian, C., & Mouftah, H. T. (2011). The Internet of Things. *IEEE Communications Magazine*, *49*(11), 30–31. doi:10.1109/MCOM.2011.6069706

Zhou, N., Wang, Y., Gong, L., Chen, X., & Yang, Y. (2012, October). Novel color image encryption algorithm based on the reality preserving fractional Mellin transform. *Optics & Laser Technology*, *44*(7), 2270–2281. doi:10.1016/j.optlastec.2012.02.027

Zhou, N., Zhang, A., Zhen, F., & Gong, L. (2014). Novel image compression–encryption hybrid algorithm based on key-controlled measurement matrix in compressive sensing. *Optics & Laser Technology*, *62*, 152–160. doi:10.1016/j.optlastec.2014.02.015

About the Contributors

Bashar Alohali is a PhD research student in Network Security at Liverpool John Moores University. His fields of interest are smart grid and cyber security, computer forensics, computer networks and security, sensor-based applications for smart cities, critical infrastructure protection and cloud computing. He obtained his master's degree in computer systems security from the University of Glamorgan in 2011.

Balamurugan Balusamy had completed his B.E (computer science) from Bharathidasan University and M.E. (computer Science) from Anna University. He completed his Ph.D. in cloud security domain specifically on access control techniques. He has published papers and chapters in several renowned journals and conferences.

Azeddine Bilami received the Ph.D. degree in 2005. He is currently serving as a Full Professor at the Computer Science Department, and the Head of LaSTIC laboratory at University of Batna. Prof. A. Bilami has published papers in many international conferences and prominent journals including IEEE Communications Letters, IJCA (Actapress), IJSNet (INDERSCIENCE), IGI Global, Springer Verlag, and Elsevier publications. He also served as a member of editor boards, a member of steering committees and a member of Technical committees in many international conferences and journals (COMCOM [Elsevier], HINDAWI journals, IAJIT, NGNS …). His area of expertise include high-performance interconnects for parallel architectures and multiprocessors, System-on-Chip architectures, TCP/IP and Internet, Security, Mobility, QoE and QoS in wireless and mobile networks. His current research interests are mainly focused on Security and Routing Protocols in Wireless Networks, WSNs and the Internet of Things (IoT).

Dyutimoy Biswas is currently a student in School of Electrical Engineering in VIT University, Vellore, India.

Paul Joseph D is currently a research scholar in VIT University, Vellore, India. He finished his masters degree in computer science and joined PhD. His areas of interests are Information Security, Cyber Security and Digital Forensics. Currently with deep passion towards forensics and hands on experience on ethical hacking, he started his research in Digital forensics in the light of Cyber security.

Kijpokin Kasemsap received his BEng degree in Mechanical Engineering from King Mongkut's University of Technology, Thonburi, his MBA degree from Ramkhamhaeng University, and his DBA degree in Human Resource Management from Suan Sunandha Rajabhat University. Dr. Kasemsap is a Special Lecturer in the Faculty of Management Sciences, Suan Sunandha Rajabhat University, based in Bangkok, Thailand. Dr. Kasemsap is a Member of the International Association of Engineers (IAENG), the International Association of Engineers and Scientists (IAEST), the International Economics Development and Research Center (IEDRC), the International Association of Computer Science and Information Technology (IACSIT), the International Foundation for Research and Development (IFRD), and the International Innovative Scientific and Research Organization (IISRO). Dr. Kasemsap also serves on the International Advisory Committee (IAC) for the International Association of Academicians and Researchers (INAAR). Dr. Kasemsap is the sole author of over 250 peer-reviewed international publications and book chapters on business, education, and information technology.

Jayanta Mondal is a PhD student in Kallinga Institute of Indutrial Technology (KIIT) University, Bhubaneswar, Odisha, India. His research interest include Cryptography, Data Mining, Cloud Computing and Information Security. He obtained his M.Tech. degree in Computer Science from Berhampur University, Odisha, India in 2013 and B.Tech. in IT from West Bengal University of Technology in 2011.

Jasmine Norman, an Associate Professor of VIT University, completed her PhD in Computer Science and Master's degree in Computer Science with special interest on Information Security having an experience of 20 years. Her areas of interests include Information Security, Network Security, narrowed down to public key crypto systems, lattice based cryptography and authentication schemes and other research areas include cyber security. Currently she is guiding five PhD students in her research areas in VIT university.

Somasundaram Ragupathy is a Research scholar in the School of Computer Science and Engineering at VIT University, Vellore, India. He received his Master's in Computer Science and Engineering from Arulmigu Meenakshi Amman College of Engineering, Anna University Chennai. Currently working as an Assistant Professor in the Department of Computer Science and Engineering at Arulmigu Meenakshi Amman College of Engineering, Anna University. He has teaching experience of around Three years. His area of specialization is Network Security. He had presented three papers in national and international conferences.

Somia Sahraoui is a Ph.D. student in the Computer Science Department, University of Batna 2. She received the Master degree in Networks Engineering and Communication, in 2012. Her research interests are focused on communication security in Wireless Sensor Networks and the Internet of Things.

H. Parveen Sultana received the MCA from Madras University, Chennai, India, and M.Phil in Computer Applications from Manonmaniam Sundaranar University, Tirunelveli, India. She is currently with the School of Computer Science and Engineering, VIT University, Vellore, India. She received her Ph.D from the School of Computer Science and Engineering, VIT University, Vellore, India. Her research interests include Cyber physical systems, mobile and wireless systems and data structures. She has authored a few research papers in various reputed journals and conferences. She also authored a book on Cyber Physical Systems.

Debabala Swain is presently working as an Assistant Professor in the Kalinga Institute of Industrial Technology (KIIT) University, Bhubaneswar, Odisha, India. She has received her Bachelor's in Engineering from Biju Pattanayak University of Technology, Odisha, India, M.Tech in Computer Science from the Berhampur University, Odisha, India. Then obtained her PhD in Computer Science in 2013 from the Utkal University, Odisha, India. Her research interests include Computer Architecture, Information Security And Wireless Networking.

Mythili Thirugnanam is an Associate Professor in the School of Computer Science and Engineering at VIT University, Vellore, India. She received a Master's in Software Engineering from VIT University. She has been awarded doctorate in Computer Science and Engineering at VIT University in 2014. She has teaching experience of around 9 years. She has a research experience of 3 years in handling sponsored projects funded by Govt. of India. Her area of specialization includes Image Processing, Software Engineering and Knowledge Engineering. She has published more than 20 papers in international journals and presented around seven papers in various national and international conferences.

Index

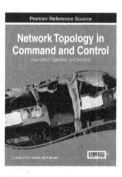

Information Resources Management Association

Become an IRMA Member

Members of the **Information Resources Management Association (IRMA)** understand the importance of community within their field of study. The Information Resources Management Association is an ideal venue through which professionals, students, and academicians can convene and share the latest industry innovations and scholarly research that is changing the field of information science and technology. Become a member today and enjoy the benefits of membership as well as the opportunity to collaborate and network with fellow experts in the field.

IRMA Membership Benefits:

- **One FREE Journal Subscription**
- **30% Off Additional Journal Subscriptions**
- **20% Off Book Purchases**
- Updates on the latest events and research on Information Resources Management through the IRMA-L listserv.
- Updates on new open access and downloadable content added to Research IRM.
- A copy of the Information Technology Management Newsletter twice a year.
- A certificate of membership.

IRMA Membership $195

Scan code or visit **irma-international.org** and begin by selecting your free journal subscription.

Membership is good for one full year.

Printed in the United States
By Bookmasters